One Path for All

ONE PATH FOR ALL

*Gregory of Nyssa on the Christian Life
and Human Destiny*

Rowan A. Greer

ASSISTED BY
J. Warren Smith

CASCADE *Books* · Eugene, Oregon

ONE PATH FOR ALL
Gregory of Nyssa on the Christian Life and Human Destiny

Cascade Books
An Imprint of Wipf and Stock Publishers
199 W. 8th Ave., Suite 3
Eugene, OR 97401

www.wipfandstock.com

ISBN 13: 978-1-62564-633-0

Cataloguing-in-Publication Data

Greer, Rowan A.

One path for all : Gregory of Nyssa on the christian life and human destiny / Rowan A. Greer with J. Warren Smith.

viii + 250 p. ; 23 cm. Includes bibliographical references and indexes.

ISBN 13: 978-1-62564-633-0

1. Gregory, of Nyssa, Saint, approximately 335–approximately 394—Contributions in Christian doctrine of man. 2. Theological anthropology—Christianity—History of doctrines—Early church, approximately 30–600. 3. I. Smith, J. Warren, 1964–. II. Title.

BT701.2 .G69 2015

Manufactured in the U.S.A.   02/25/2015

CONTENTS

ABBREVIATIONS

PRIMARY WORKS

Athanasius

C. Ar.	*Apologia contra Arianos*
C. Gent.	*Oratio contra gentes*
De inc.	*De incarnatione*

Eusebius

Hist. eccl.	*Historia ecclesiastica*

Gregory of Nyssa

C. Eun.	*Contra Eunomium*
De an. et res.	*De anima et resurrectione*
De beat.	*De beatitudinibus*
De hom. op.	*De hominis opificio*
De inst.	*De instituto Christiano*
De paup. amand.	*De pauperibus amandis*
De virg.	*De virginitate*
FM.	*In XL Martyres*
Ep.	*Epistles*
Graec. aff. cur.	*Ad Graecos*
In cant.	*In Canticum canticorum*
In diem lum.	*In diem luminum*
In Flac.	*Oratio funebris in Flacillam inperatricem*
In inscr. ps.	*In inscriptiones Psalmorum*
In Mel.	*Oratio funebris in Meletium episcopum*

In Pulch.	*Oratio consolatoria in Pulcheriam*
In. sanct. Pasch.	*In sanctum et salutare Pascha*
Mort.	*De mortuis oratio*
Or. cat.	*Oratio catechetica*
Perf.	*De prefectione*
Prof.	*De professione Christiana*
St. 1	*In sanctum Stephanum I*
St. 2	*In sanctum Stephanum II*
Th.	*De sancto Theodoro*
Vit. Mos.	*De vita Moysis*
Vit. s. Macr.	*Vita sanctae Macrinae*

Lucian

Pisc.	*Piscator*

Origen

Comm. Jn.	*Commentarium in Johanne*
De. princ.	*De principiis*

Tertullian

Apol.	*Apologeticus*

SECONDARY WORKS

ANF	*The Ante-Nicene Fathers* (Eerdmans)
CWS	Classics of Western Spirituality (Paulist)
FC	The Fathers of the Church (Catholic University of America)
GCS	Die griechischen christlichen Schriftsteller der ersten (drei) Jahrhunderte
GNO	*Gregorii Nysseni Opera* (Works of Gregory Nyssen; Brill)
LCC	Library of Christian Classics (Westminster)
LCL	Loeb Classical Library (Harvard)
LXX	Septuagint
NPNF	*The Nicene and Post-Nicene Fathers* (Eerdmans)
SC	Sources chrétiennes (Cerf)

INTRODUCTION

The task of describing a writer's thought, as well as that of interpreting past events, belongs to a disciplined imagination. The discipline, of course, involves assembling and assessing what can be regarded as evidence no matter whether we are thinking of texts or of surviving material artifacts of various kinds. The imagination seeks to put in order what discipline has assembled into a framework for interpretation. Needless to say, the same or nearly the same body of evidence can result in widely differing interpretations, sometimes complementary but sometimes contradictory. It is somewhat like joining the pieces of a jigsaw puzzle so as to complete the picture found on the puzzle box. Yet the analogy breaks down because there is no picture to guide the process of assembling the pieces, as well as because the pieces can be arranged in several different ways. It might also be argued that in much modern historical writing the problem is that there are too many pieces of evidence, some of which must be either ignored or discarded. But in the study of late antiquity the problem is that so very many of the pieces have been lost, and only imagination can supply the contexts in which those that survive may be placed.

With respect to Gregory of Nyssa the difficulty is first of all that only educated guesses can establish the broad outline of his life and work, as well as a reasonable chronological order in which to place his writings. While there appears to be broad agreement at a general level, coming to terms with matters of detail engenders ongoing scholarly debate. For example, Pierre Maraval's 1971 edition of the *Life of Macrina* (SC 178) provides a careful and persuasive treatment of the chronology of Gregory's life surrounding the time of his sister's death; but in his 1990 edition of Gregory's letters (SC 363) further reflection has led him to quite significant revisions. Neither my competence nor my purpose allow me the possibility of entering the debates regarding the reconstruction of Gregory's life and the dating of his writings. My interest is to examine his thought and to supply one perspective by which it can be interpreted. Yet even here there are perplexities. Gregory is not a systematic thinker, and he is well aware that what he has to say about God and about the destiny of humanity and this world must remain speculative and must recognize the limitations imposed upon our capacity for knowledge not only by our fallen condition but also by the fact that we are creatures.

It is my conviction that the framework binding together Gregory's rather kaleidoscopic thought is not so much his use of Greek philosophy or even his commitment to the dogmatic development represented primarily by the Trinitarian conclusions of the Council of Constantinople in 381, as by a Christian piety focused upon God's saving work in Christ as articulated in scripture. With this is mind, I should suggest that this framework for his thought may be located in the liturgy. This is the setting not only for prayer and rite, but also for the reading of scripture and its interpretation in preaching. The lectionary use of scripture meant that Christians encountered it not merely by reading it, as we should, but by hearing it in the sometimes strange and perplexing ways different passages were juxtaposed in the liturgy. Moreover, the architectural and iconographic setting for worship, so far as they can be recovered, supply another dimension of this basic liturgical framework. Even though there is no direct relationship between Gregory's piety and the iconographic program of, say, San Vitale in Ravenna, the apse mosaic in that sixth-century basilica has long seemed to me to encapsulate Gregory's thought. A youthful Christ, clad in purple, is seated on the blue globe of the universe, beneath which the four rivers of paradise flow forth. He is flanked by two angels, who present to him St. Vitalis on his right and Bishop Ecclesius on his left. Christ offers the crown of martyrdom to Vitalis, while in his left hand he holds the scroll with seven seals described in Revelation. All this can be associated with Gregory's visionary hope of the new creation, which though initiated by the incarnate Christ, is yet to come in its fullness as the destiny not only of humanity but of the whole of creation.

The apse mosaic just described is, moreover, the focal point of the two mosaic programs on either side of the nave of San Vitale. Both depict processions; in one we find the emperor Justinian and in the other the empress Theodosia. But the male and female processions in which the imperial figures are placed include other figures, and it is also possible to correlate the entire program with a moment in the liturgy, possibly the Great Entrance.[1]

1. See Mathews, *Clash of Gods*, 171: "Yet for all the attention that art historians have given the emperor and empress, it must be pointed out that royalty are doubly out-ranked by clergy in the mosaic program at Saint Vitalis. . . . In Justinian's panel the Gospel, the Word of God, accompanied by incense, occupies first place. In second place

In any case, one way of interpreting the iconography is to see the processions as a movement toward Christ as the agent of the new creation. The convention of converging processions has a long life in early Christian art, and the point I am making could be illustrated by many other examples.[2] That point revolves around the centrality of the incarnate Christ and the idea that the entire plenitude of humanity is to be located on a processional path leading to Christ and to its destiny in him. It is possible to argue that Gregory's insistence upon the humanity of Christ and upon the metaphor of a journey forward rather than an ascent is more evident in what appear to be his later works and following his ordination as a bishop.[3] Though I prefer to suppose that what Gregory emphasizes in his mature works is already implicit in the earlier writings, my concern will be to argue that he ends by insisting upon the fact that all Christians are walking on the same path leading to the new creation, however much their progress may differ. It is this thesis that will dominate the interpretive essays following the texts translated in the first part of what follows.

Two points can elaborate the basic perspective from which I have chosen to interpret Gregory's thought. First, I take as granted that Gregory treats with utter seriousness Paul's conviction in Gal 3:28 that in Christ "there is no longer Jew or Greek, there is no longer slave or free, there is no longer male and female; for all of you are one in Christ Jesus." In particular, Gregory and the other Cappadocians, despite residual attitudes that can be regarded as springing from a culture labeled misogynist, see no inequality between the sexes in terms of a common Christian vocation.[4] In his seventh homily on Song of Songs, Gregory identifies the "mother" who crowns the bridegroom, Christ (Song 3:11), with the Father on the grounds that, if in Christ there is neither male nor female at a human level, we must certainly

---

it is Bishop Maximianus, carrying his cross, for in church the bishop always preceded the emperor. Then comes Justinian."

2. Ibid., 150: "The target of convergence, the omega point that is Christ, can be expressed in a wide variety of ways. Christ can appear in any number of his chameleon guises. He can assume the moments of glory of his historical life—his Baptism, Transfiguration, or Ascension . . . —or he can fast-forward history to its end. . . . Moreover, the processions themselves potentially include the whole world of the saved, the hierarchically ordered communion of saints. Male and female saints are represented, the Apostles and martyrs, the clergy and members of the imperial court, and, under the symbol of a file of sheep, the common herd of the faithful."

3. See Mosshammer, "Gregory's Intellectual Development," 359–87, esp. 360: "In the interim between these two works the Bishop of Nyssa seems to have discovered—or at least learned how to articulate—what it means to affirm that the church is the living Body of Christ."

4. See Harrison, "Male and Female in Cappadocian Theology," 441–71.

exclude that distinction from any account of the divine.[5] He honors this conviction by treating his sister, Macrina, as his teacher; and the point can easily be made more broadly. My concern, however, is not so much with human distinctions that often prove divisive, as with the question whether Gregory wishes to distinguish a Christian elite from simple believers. My conclusion will be that, while Gregory clearly recognizes differences with respect to the progress different people have made in the Christian life, he rejects the idea that these differences represent any division within the body of Christ. All Christians are on the single path; and at least once this path goes beyond the confines of this life, all humans will journey on it.

The second point is merely a disclaimer that the perspective I propose is one completely novel or one that is meant to call into question other perspectives from which to examine Gregory's thought. Cardinal Daniélou's book, *Platonisme et théologie mystique*, by its title points to what first preoccupied the study of Gregory's writings. The debt of his thought to Platonism and to the Christian Platonist Origen, his contribution to the development of erudite theology, and his mystical ideas—all are, of course, important. More recent study has approached Gregory as one of the architects of the dogma of the Trinity established at the Council of Constantinople in 382, as well as examining the way he assesses the person and work of Christ. Attention has also been directed toward aspects of his thought that seem to echo our own concerns whether positively or negatively. These differing facets clearly have the possibility of informing one another.[6]

There is another preliminary observation that occurs to me. I suppose it unlikely that any historians or critics are finally able to discard their own concerns and presuppositions in attempting to interpret past events and writings. My own preoccupation, or better, my own question, concerns the meaning of "community." People always seem to speak at greater length and to worry more with what they find missing in their own experience. In our time there is considerable reflection regarding what "community" might mean at both a local and a global level. We seem to have lost any real sense that communities are more than associations of the like-minded. If it is only individuals that in this sense constitute a community, the path to what could be termed a collective solipsism lies open. Thus, whenever like-mindedness is compromised, the community breaks apart. What I am suggesting is that

---

5. *GNO* 6:212–13.

6. Moreover, let me call attention to Reinhard Jacob Kees, *Die Lehre von der Oikonomia Gottes in der Oratio Catechetica Gregors von Nyssa.* His careful study of the *Catechetical Oration* treats it as a summary of the whole of Gregory's mature thought, however much the themes involved have been adapted to the purpose of the work, that is, to advise catechists and to prepare them for their teaching.

a viable community must take precedence over individuals, not by disabling their flourishing, but by enabling it. For that to happen the community—within limits—must embrace and foster diverse ways in which individuals can bring honor to their society. In other words, the ideal community will be one that seeks to establish a diversified unity, a unity in diversity. The ideal may finally be paradoxical, but it can be thought an attempt to find a middle ground between imposing a sameness upon all the constituencies of a community and leaving open the possibility that individual differences may become so divisive as to destroy community.

My thought, then, is that we can find this paradoxical middle way in Paul's accounts of the body of Christ in Rom 12 and 1 Cor 12. In these passages he is arguing for diversity, but for a diversity that will not compromise unity provided the differing gifts granted to individual Christians are employed to contribute their part to building up in love the body of Christ. Gregory, I think, honors this view. He clearly recognizes the diverse ways in which the Christian life appears, and he knows that this can often lead to conflict and division. In one sense he realizes that the ideal he embraces can never be fully realized in this life, but instead must await its completion in the world to come and at the final end, the *apokatastasis*. But he can also discern the ideal at work in this world. In this sense his thought is eschatological; his vision of human destiny, based largely upon what he finds in scripture, constantly informs what he says about our present life. At least these are the conclusions for which I wish to argue in the essays following the select translations of part one. Gregory refuses to allow his ideal to shatter in the face of the realities of Christian controversy and of the failure of Christians to embody that ideal.

GREGORY'S LIFE AND WORK: THE TENSION BETWEEN THE IDEAL AND THE ACTUAL

Gregory is well aware of the gap between the ideal of the new creation in the body of Christ not only as it is reflected in the life of the church, but also as he finds it in his own failures to embody that ideal in his own life. Yet this sensibility by no means hinders him in his articulation of the marvelous harmony of all things in Christ. For him and for all Christians the path that leads from baptism and the confession of faith made at that time involves a procession and a journey, but it must also be seen as a struggle and a battle. The details of Gregory's life, like those of most ancient figures, are obscure; and what we can know is difficult to locate precisely in time both because of scant and sometimes conflicting evidence and the necessity of drawing inferences from it. We do not even know when Gregory was baptized. Nor do we have anything like Augustine's *Confessions* that would assist us in trying to imagine his personality. Nevertheless, in his second homily in praise of the Forty Martyrs of Sebaste, Gregory does recount a dream that he presents as decisive for his own commitment to the Christian path (*FM.* 2 167–68). In the dream the forty soldiers threaten him, preventing his entrance into the service being conducted for the deposition of their relics; and Gregory understands this as a rebuke for his reluctance to accept his mother's invitation to the feast at Annisa on the family estate in Pontus. Since Emmelia, Gregory's mother, probably died in 370, the experience he describes must have been before that time. Born probably about 335, we can be reasonably sure that as a young man he was his brother's pupil, when Basil returned from Athens in 355 in order to teach rhetoric at Caesarea in Cappadocia. Gregory apparently began a career as a teacher of rhetoric, married, and possibly fathered a child. Nothing else is known as certain, though Gregory does refer to his marriage in his earliest work, *On Virginity*, written perhaps as early as 370.[7]

It is, however, likely enough that we can date Gregory's decision to follow the Christian path to some time in the 360s, when he was, say, about thirty years old. In any case we have several glimpses of the struggles and difficulties he encountered from the time of Basil's ordination as the metropolitan bishop of Caesarea in 369 or 370, a year or two before Gregory became the bishop of Nyssa as part of his brother's campaign to secure the boundaries of his diocese despite civil changes that threatened them. The earliest setback for Gregory occurred as a result of Basil's election as bishop. Those who had contested his candidacy included another Gregory, who was a bishop and the uncle of Basil and of our Gregory, who took it upon himself to bring about a reconciliation between Basil and their uncle Gregory. Our Gregory tried to do this by forging conciliatory letters from

7. See Pierre Maraval's two reconstructions of the events in Gregory's life immediately following the death of his brother Basil. In his edition of the *Life of Macrina* (SC 178) Maraval dates Basil's death 1 January, 379. He places Gregory at a council in Antioch in the fall or early winter of that year, arguing that the council sent Gregory to Jerusalem in 380. From there Gregory returned to Cappadocia and in a short time went to Annisa to visit Macrina, who died 19 July, 380. Following her death Gregory went to Nyssa, then to Ibora, spent October and November in Sebaste. The first day of 381 he preached his encomium of Basil in Caesarea. In his later edition of Gregory's letters (SC 363) Maraval dates Basil's death in 377, probably in August and after Gregory's return to Nyssa from exile. The council of Antioch is dated in the spring of 378, after which Gregory returned to Cappadocia. By July of that year, learning that Macrina was dying, he was present for her death and funeral. His trips to Ibora and Sebaste follow Macrina's death, but his embassy to Jerusalem was commissioned by the Council of Constantinople in 381.

the uncle to Basil, presumably assuming that medicinal lies in a good cause were permissible. Needless to say, Basil discovered from his uncle that at least the first letter had been forged by Gregory.[8] Basil's letter 58 delivers a strong rebuke to his younger brother: "Would that I could upbraid your utter simplicity as it deserves!"[9] Basil concludes his letter by saying that he is willing to meet with the recalcitrant bishops at a time and place of their own choosing, with the proviso that the invitation must come "through their own agents" and "with due formality." Clearly brother Gregory has little skill in managing church politics.

Gregory enters the stage once more in Basil's letter 215, probably written in the autumn of 375 to Dorotheus, who was a deacon and later a presbyter of Meletius, the new-Nicene bishop of Antioch. Basil's aim was to heal the schism in Antioch between the "old Nicenes" led by Paulinus and the "new Nicenes" led by Bishop Meletius, whom the Paulinians refused to recognize, supported as they were by Western recognition of their legitimacy. Basil, supporting Meletius, hoped to persuade Rome and the West to shift their support to the new Nicene cause. Dorotheus had already been sent as a legate to the West, and was destined to travel there again in 376.[10] Plans for this legation were already being made in 375, and Basil had also written to Terentius, a *comes* and *dux* of the emperor Valens (*Ep.* 214). He points out to Dorotheus the difficulty of traveling by land in the winter because the road from Caesarea to Constantinople is "full of enemies." Should a journey by sea be necessary, "it will be only opportune provided that our God-beloved bishop, brother Gregory, consents to both the voyage and the official mission in such important matters." Basil apparently can think of no one else to accompany Dorotheus, and he obviously has doubts about Gregory's competence:[11]

> I know that he is quite inexperienced in ecclesiastical matters;
> and that although his dealings would inspire respect with a
> kindly man and be worth much, yet with a high and elevated

8. Basil's letters 59 and 60 are addressed to uncle Gregory. The first letter is a plea for reconciliation, as is the second, which includes at its ending: "As to our most venerable brother, we have not constrained him to tell us anything by word of mouth; the reason is that his words on a former occasion were not attested by the facts."

9. Basil, *Ep.* 58 (LCL 1:357). "Simplicity" translates χρηστότητος, which Deferrari later translates as "fatuity." The word can, of course, mean "kindness"; but here some pejorative meaning must be found.

10. See Field, *Communion of Damasus and Meletius,* 119 nn. 6–7. For Dorotheus's legation to the West in 376, see 123–24, especially n. 22, and see 243 on the dating of Basil's letter.

11. *Ep.* 215 (LCL 3:237–39).

personage, one occupying a lofty seat, and therefore unable to
listen to men who from a lowly position on the ground would
tell him the truth—what advantage could accrue to our common interests from the converse of such a man as Gregory, who
has a character foreign to servile flattery?

In the event, Gregory did not accompany the legation in 376, perhaps because of Basil's lack of confidence in him. Basil gives the impression that
Gregory is both "kindly" in a somewhat simple-minded way and honest,
qualities that hinder his effectiveness as an ecclesiastical politician. Gregory
apparently finds it difficult to adjust his ideal of the Christian path to the
rough-and-tumble of the church's actual circumstances.

One other note of dissatisfaction with Gregory appears in Basil's letter
100, addressed to Eusebius of Samosata. He is answering Eusebius's letter
and begins by complaining of his ill health. He asks Eusebius to attend the
usual synod at the festival "in memory of the blessed Eupsychicus." The letter ends with a plea for Eusebius's help in establishing bishops and in "the
matter of investigating and deliberating about the actions meditated against
us by Gregory of Nyssa in his simplicity, who convenes synods at Ancyra,
and in no way ceases to plot against us." According to Loofs letter 100 was
written from Armenia in July or August 372.[12] But it is impossible to find
any evidence for Gregory's activity that would fit this date. Maraval suggests
that Gregory's work in Ancyra could possibly be understood against the
background of the council of Antioch that took place in the spring of 378
and before Macrina's death in July of that year.[13] The council of Antioch was
probably concerned to deal with the schism between Melitius and Paulinus, but its larger purpose was to reconcile the old and the new Nicenes.
Marcellus of Ancyra belonged to the older group, dominated by Athanasius
of Alexandria. His views were widely regarded in the East as an explicit
articulation of the supposed Sabellian tendencies of the old Nicene theology. But it is certainly possible that Gregory at some time made attempts to
reconcile the old Nicenes in Ancyra to the new Nicene party, dominated by
Basil. With what we might assume to be the best will in the world Gregory
seems to have failed in the enterprise and to have further alienated Basil.[14]

---

12. Rousseau, *Basil of Caesarea*, 7; he dates letter 100 to 373.

13. Maraval, *Lettres* (SC 363), 24, especially n. 4. On this conjectural reconstruction
Basil must have written letter 100 shortly before his death; and it should be correlated
with letter 243 addressed to the bishops of Italy and Gaul and meant to accompany
Dorotheus on his legation to the West in 376. For this mission and its relation to the
council of Antioch, see also Rousseau, *Basil of Caesarea*, 294–317.

14. For the council of Antioch in 379 or 378 and its subscription to Roman formulae, see Field, *Communion of Damasus and Meletius*, 121.

Yet it is obvious from Gregory's writings that he betrays no sense of any rift with his older brother. It is impossible to draw full conclusions. Perhaps there were also resentments on Gregory's part, but ones that were eclipsed by a recognition of his own limitations. As well, it is probable that family ties remained strong despite the stresses caused by ecclesiastical controversy.[15]

Despite the fact that reconstructing the historical background and dating of Basil's letters must remain conjectural, there can be little doubt that the evidence they supply for Gregory's interventions in ecclesiastical affairs show that they were more often attended by failure than success.[16] One of Gregory's letters (*Ep.* 1), addressed to a Flavian who was possibly Melitius's successor as bishop of Antioch, supplies his own account of one of his failures. It is not entirely clear why, but Gregory finds himself at odds with Helladius, the metropolitan bishop of Caesarea and, therefore, his ecclesiastical superior. Gregory tells Flavian that his earlier letter to him, as well as letters to many others, were all designed to enlist help in the matter of which, presumably, Flavian is aware. Gregory then tells the story of an unfortunate meeting with Helladius. Intending to leave Sebaste after the festival held there and to return to Nyssa, he then receives word that Helladius was holding services in a neighboring mountainous district. Deciding to see him, Gregory leaves his carriage and takes a long and arduous detour on horseback to find Helladius. Traveling with great difficulty and through the night he arrives at dawn in time to see the open air assembly, but also Helladius retiring to his own dwelling. Gregory is kept waiting until midday, and when ushered into Helladius's presence is not even asked to be seated. There is not a word from Helladius, but "a silence as profound as night." Gregory is deeply offended by the discourtesy he receives, partly because he regards himself as Helladius's social equal and partly because of their equality in Christ. Moreover, even the disparity of their ecclesiastical rank ought not to overturn their equality, since the Council had given them both the same privilege and commission for ordering the common life of the churches.

Gregory's last point must refer to the decision of the Council of Constantinople in 381, sanctioned by the emperor Theodosius, to designate those who were to be guarantors of orthodoxy. Gregory and Helladius were

15. Rousseau, *Basil of Caesarea*, 6–8, takes a dimmer view of Gregory's true attitude toward Basil. See also his discussion of the *Life of Macrina*, ibid., 9–11. See, however, Maraval's notes in his edition of the life (SC 178), 162.

16. Following Macrina's death Gregory was successful in restoring order to the church in Ibora; but success there was followed by failure at Sebaste (Gregory's letters 28–31). While the evidence of Gregory's letters is obscure, he seems also to have failed in his missions to Arabia and Jerusalem (letters 33–38). See Maraval's introduction in *Lettres* (SC 363).

two of the three bishops selected to perform this task in the civil diocese of Pontus.[17] It is likely that Gregory's attempts to fulfill this trust and mission were regarded as an infringement upon Helladius's rights as metropolitan. Gregory's letter 17 supplies a probable example of what was involved. The letter is addressed to the priests of Nicomedia and concerns the election of a new bishop to succeed the recently deceased Patricius. It merely alludes to Gregory's commission by the Council of Constantinople, and it seeks to persuade the Nicomedians that Gregory's intervention springs from the "debt of love" owing from one church to another. He recognizes that the church at Nicomedia remains divided, though we cannot be certain what the causes of conflict were. But, says Gregory, the situation requires the election of a good bishop. The rest of the letter describes such a candidate. Some wise and strong administrator is necessary in order to restore the "stream" of the church to its right banks and course. This must be someone who, like the Levites, has no earthly heritage and no attraction to worldly things. Birth, wealth, and worldly glory, even though they need not necessarily exclude a candidate, are not part of the apostolic definition of a bishop. Gregory cites the examples of Amos the goatherd, the fishermen Peter, Andrew, and John, Paul the tentmaker, and Matthew the tax collector. And he clinches his point by citing Paul's recognition that there are in the eyes of the world few wise, powerful, or well born in the church (1 Cor 1:26–27). The argument continues in this vein. A bishop must also be skilled in guiding the church into God's harbor by the cure of souls, and to this end his life must be "without reproach" (1 Tim 3:2). If "every disciple fully qualified will be like his master" (cf. Luke 6:40), then both disciple and master must be "humble, settled in character, moderate, superior to love of gain, wise in godly things, trained in virtue and gentleness in his manner of life."

Gregory's description of the ideal bishop spends as much time saying what he is not as describing what he is. He may well be contrasting his candidate with a rival one. As Maraval suggests, the rival candidate is probably a certain Gerontius. The only evidence is to be found in Sozomen's account of John Chrysostom's deposition of Gerontius, bishop of Nicomedia, in March of 402.[18] According to Sozomen, Gerontius had been a deacon under Ambrose in Milan. His public account of a dream in which he decapitated a demonic phantom or some other cause obliged Ambrose to order Gerontius's seclusion. Instead, Gerontius fled to Constantinople, where "in a

---

17. See Maraval, *Lettres* (SC 363), 103, n. 3; introduction, 38–41. The civil diocese of Pontus included the provinces of Galatia, Bythynia, Cappadocia I and II, Armenia I and II, Helenopontus, Pontus Polemonicus.

18. See Kelly, *Golden Mouth*, 177.

short time he obtained the friendship of the most powerful men at court."[19] Soon after he was ordained bishop of Nicomedia "by Helladius, bishop of Caesarea in Cappadocia, who performed this office the more readily for him because he had been instrumental, through his interest at court, in obtaining a high appointment in the army for that functionary's son." This must have happened in the 380s, and it is reasonably certain that Gerontius, rather than Gregory's candidate, succeeded Patricius at Nicomedia. The rest of the story, as Sozomen tells it, includes unsuccessful attempts by Ambrose and Nectarius (bishop of Constantinople, 381–397) to oust Gerontius, who was defended by the people of Nicomedia. After Chrysostom deposed him Gerontius joined those openly opposed to Chrysostom. Granted this reconstruction, once again Gregory failed because his ideal foundered upon the rock of worldly importance and power.

What seems to me of special interest is a section of letter 1 that describes Gregory's interview with Helladius and his own discovery of a conflict in his heart between his ideal and his ecclesiastical ambitions and social prejudices. Gregory finds himself so overwhelmed by his emotional reaction to Helladius's arrogance that "I was not in a condition to admonish myself to be unmoved, since my heart within me swelled up at the absurdity of what was happening and spat upon thoughts about putting up with it."[20] Immediately he remembers with admiration Paul's vivid description of the civil war within us between the law of sin and the law of the mind (cf. Rom 7:23). By God's grace his better inclination prevailed, and he broke the silence by speaking soft words to Helladius, asking whether his own presence interfered with measures being taken for Helladius's health. The conversation stumbles on for a short while, but to no purpose; and Helladius dismisses Gregory without even inviting him to the banquet about to take place. This small interchange between the two opponents, together with Gregory's admission of the civil war in his heart, suggests that Gregory well understands that he is far from reaching the goal toward which he aspires on the Christian path. The same recognition informs the opening of *On Perfection*. Gregory wishes that he could produce "instances to be found in my life for you to study so as to offer you the instruction you ask by deeds instead of words." But this is not possible, since "I am continuing to pray that this may one day come to be" (*Perf.* 173). Gregory, I wish to conclude, is well aware of the gap between the ideal of the new creation in the body of Christ and the realities found not only in the church but also in his own failure to embody that ideal in his own life. Yet he seeks to articulate that

19. Sozomen, *Ecclesiastical History* 8.6 (*NPNF*[2] 2:403).
20. *Ep.* 1.19 (SC 363:96).

ideal in his writings as one toward which he and all Christians, indeed all people, are moving.

THE TRANSLATIONS AND ESSAYS THAT FOLLOW

The translations that follow are of a number of Gregory's shorter writings; yet what he says in them, at least in my view, accords in broad terms with what may be found in the larger works more often consulted by those studying Gregory's thought. To be sure, the selection of writings to include is arbitrary, but they do reflect his ascetical ideals, his popular preaching and interest in ordinary Christians, as well as his theological concerns and his speculations on human destiny. In this way they cohere with themes in his larger works, even though they are not meant to be a basis for my general thesis. In the essays that follow my attempt in part is to show this by appealing also to the larger works. The first essay focuses upon *On the Christian's Profession* and *On Perfection*, and seeks to suggest that baptism is paradigmatic of the Christian life. The next essay is meant to assemble the various principal aspects of that life and employs *On the Dead* as a basis for describing how Gregory understands the Christian contest against Satan and the passions in order to gain the union with Christ that represents victory in the struggle. The third essay explores the way Gregory envisages the relationship between those who have made considerable progress on the Christian path and those who have not traveled as far. As well, the martyrs play a role in the lives of Christians, and I shall call attention to Gregory's homilies in their praise. The final essay argues for the importance of *On the Making of Man* for Gregory's view of the last things, and it ends by appealing to Gregory's universalism, particularly as found in *On Christ's Subjection*.

These short essays are not meant to deny the complexity and ambiguity found in Gregory's thought.[21] At the same time, they presuppose that, while his works function at various levels—polemical, homiletical, exegetical, theological—there is an underlying form of thought that is not quite as elusive as might be supposed. The tensions are creative ones, and since much of what he says is speculative, we should not expect a system of any kind. Instead, the various themes he pursues constantly interact with one another and invite the reader to supply some sort of coherent overview. The one I suggest represents, as it were, a bird's eye view of the landscape, a framework that might easily be filled out in detail and in such a way as to raise further questions. As Origen said, the answers we find have a way of

---

21. See Ludlow, "Introduction: The Elusive Gregory," in *Gregory of Nyssa*, 1–10.

becoming questions, and the pattern continues without any limit.[22] The idea is obviously related to Gregory's notion of perpetual progress in the good, or *epectasy*.

ACKNOWLEDGMENTS

Let me conclude by saying that I am grateful to two anonymous readers of an earlier version of this small book. I am very much in debt to Christopher Beeley, who encouraged me to rework that version. Most of all I am grateful beyond words to Warren Smith, who carefully examined my manuscript, made many useful suggestions, alerted me to secondary literature I probably would have missed, and gave me more of his time and help than he ought to have done.

22. See *De princ.* 4.3.14, where he cites Rom 11:33 and Phil 3:14.

PART ONE

Translations

On the Christian's Profession (De professione Christiana). Greek text, ed. Werner Jaeger, *GNO* 8.1:129–42. [*Prof.*]

On Perfection (De perfectione). Greek text, ed. Werner Jaeger, *GNO* 8.1: 173–214. [*Perf.*]

Homily in Praise of Theodore (De sancto Theodoro). Greek text, ed. J. P. Cavarnos, *GNO* 10.1.2:61–71. [*Th.*]

Homily 1 in Praise of Stephen (In sanctum Stephanum I). Greek text, ed. O. Lendle, *GNO* 10.1.2:75–94. [*St. 1*]

Homily 2 in Praise of Stephen (In sanctum Stephanum II). Greek text, ed. O. Lendle, *GNO* 10.1.2:97–105. [*St. 2*]

Homily 1a in Praise of the Forty Martyrs (In XL martyres Ia). Greek text, ed. O. Lendle, *GNO* 10.1.2:137–42. [*FM. 1a*]

Homily 1b in Praise of the Forty Martyrs (In XL martyres Ib). Greek text, ed. O. Lendle, *GNO* 10.1.2:145–56. [*FM. 1b*]

Homily 2 in Praise of the Forty Martyrs (In XL martyres II). Greek text, ed. O. Lendle, *GNO* 10.1.2:159–69 [*FM. 2*]

On the Dead (De mortuis). Greek text, ed. G. Heil, *GNO* 9:28–68. [*Mort.*]

On Christ's Subjection (In illud: Tunc et ipse Filius). Greek text, ed. J. K. Downing, *GNO* 3.2:3–28. [*Subj.*]

The arabic numbers in the translations refer to the pages in *GNO* and will also be used in the essays that follow, where they will be preceded by the abbreviations listed above and placed within the text rather than in footnotes.

From Gregory, Bishop of Nyssa, to Harmonius

CONCERNING THE MEANING OF THE CHRISTIAN'S PROFESSION

(De professione Christiana, GNO 8.1)

If those subject to daily tribute have failed to pay their debt to rulers for a good many days, they pay what is owing in a lump sum all at once, provided they are lucky enough to have the resources. This is what I shall do myself for you, honored sir. Indeed, since for Christians their profession is a debt, I owe it to you to send at once what by failing to write for some time past I have not paid, even though my failure was inadvertent. I want now to make full payment by writing such a lengthy letter that it may by comparison with the usual length of writing be thought defined as a substitute for many letters. But lest I should chatter idly and in vain by writing at length, I think it good to imitate our face to face conversation by this epistolary voice. For you surely remember that the topics of our discussions with one another were always themes that had to do with virtue and training for godliness. [130] For your part you always replied attentively to what was said and accepted nothing said without careful examination, while during the course of time on each occasion I tried to resolve the subject examined on the basis of the discussion's logic. And so, if it were possible for this to happen even now in such a way that a topic would be supplied for discussion from your understanding, this would be better in every way. For to contemplate at a distance and to awaken my old harp by the plectrum of your wisdom would be for both of us the profit of seeing one another. What one of life's goods would be sweeter to me? But since life's necessity contrives to separate us in body even though we are always bound together in our souls, it may

17

be necessary for me to assume your role also, if to some extent argument concluding the discussion may come to light for me in an orderly way. It would be a good thing first of all to set forth some topic helpful to the soul as a basis for the aim of my letter, and then in this way to engage myself in a discussion directed to what is proposed. Therefore, let me examine as the question proposed: What is the Christian's profession?

Indeed, it will probably not be without profit to ask this question. For if what is indicated by this name were to be discovered accurately, we should gain much assistance with respect to the virtuous life, since we should be eager to be truly also what we name [131] by means of a lofty way of life. If, say, someone should long to be called a physician, an orator, or a geometer, he would not receive proof of the title by want of education, since he would not be found by trial to be what he was named. Instead, someone who wants to be called by any one of these names in truth without being proved to be so called falsely, will prove the appellation trustworthy by his very practice. In the same way, if we should find by examination the true goal of the Christian's profession, we also would not deliberately fail to be what the name professes on our behalf, lest the story about the monkey circulating among those not Christian[1] should be applicable also to us. For they say that one [132] of the jugglers in the city of Alexandria trained a monkey to make a show of itself as a dancer by some sort of supple turning about. The juggler put a dancer's mask on the monkey and dressed it in clothing appropriate to that pursuit. He surrounded it with a chorus and gained quite a reputation by the monkey, which twirled itself around in time with the music and in everything concealed its nature by its actions and appearance. When the stage was set for the novelty of the spectacle, one of those present, wittier than the rest, by a kind of trick showed the people gaping at the sight that the monkey was really a monkey. For while they were all acclaiming and applauding the gyrations of the monkey, which was dancing in time with the song and the music, they say that this man threw onto the dancing floor some of those dainties that attract the greed of such beasts. Without the slightest hesitation, when it saw the almonds scattered in front of the chorus, the monkey forgot the dancing and its beat, forgot its ornamental clothing, ran after the nuts, and grabbed what it found with its paws. And so that the mask might not be a hindrance to its mouth, in its own eagerness the monkey stripped it off and with its claws tore the cleverly made form to shreds. The result was that all at once the spectators, instead of praising and marveling at it, burst out in laughter at the monkey, now displayed ugly and [133] ridiculous because of the shredded remains of the mask. Therefore,

1. Cf. Lucian, *Pisc.* 36.

just as the cleverly made appearance was not enough to make the monkey thought to be human, since its nature was exposed by its greed for the dainties, in the same way those who fail truly to form their own nature itself by faith will be easily exposed by the greeds of the devil to be other than what they profess. For instead of a fig or an almond or any such thing, vainglory, ambition, love of gain, love of pleasure, and whatever such things the evil market of the devil proffers for sale to human greeds in the place of dainties, easily bring to reproach souls that are monkey-like and which only act the part of Christianity by a show of imitation, since they destroy the mask of temperance or meekness or any other virtue when their own passions are stirred. Therefore, it may be necessary to understand what the profession of Christianity is; for we should probably become what the name means, lest, if we are formed by the bare confession and the pretext of the name alone, we should be exposed to the one who perceives what is hidden to be other than what we appear.

Therefore, let us first examine what Christianity is understood to be on the basis of the profession itself. It is, of course, something great and quite noble [134] according to the learned for a meaning to be discovered elevated in all respects to the loftiness of its name. But so far as we are concerned what we hold concerning this name is as follows. The name "Christ," if it is transferred to the sense of a clearer and better recognized word, signifies king, since holy scripture according to its special usage indicates by such an expression royal dignity. Nevertheless, since, as scripture says, divinity is ineffable and incomprehensible (cf. 1 Tim 6:16; John 1:18), transcending every comprehending thought, necessarily the prophets and apostles, inspired by the Holy Spirit, guide us to an understanding of the incorruptible nature by many names and concepts. This is because one of them sets us straight with respect to some other one of the concepts befitting God. As a result, authority over all things is hinted at by the name "kingship," while purity and freedom from all passion and all evil are specified by the names of virtue, each one both thought and spoken in a higher sense. And so Christ is righteousness itself (cf. Heb 7:2) and wisdom and power (cf. 1 Cor 1:24) and truth (cf. John 14:6), both goodness (cf. John 7:12; Mark 10:18) and life (cf. John 11:25; 14:6), and salvation (cf. Acts 4:12) and incorruption (cf. 1 Cor 15:53–57), both immutability and changelessness, and every lofty concept whatever indicated by such names—all these Christ both [135] is and is called. Therefore, the meaning that every lofty concept encompasses is apprehended by the name of Christ, for the ones not mentioned are also included in the more lofty meanings, since each of them is recognized by thinking of kingship. If this is so, it probably follows that we may have some means for understanding how to interpret Christianity. For if we, united to him by faith in him, are named together with him who excels the names interpretive of the incorruptible nature, it is entirely necessary that as many concepts concerning that incorruptible nature as are contemplated with the name should also become those conforming to our having the same name.[2] For just as we have obtained the title of Christian by participating in Christ, so too it is fitting that in conformity we should be drawn into sharing all the lofty names. Take, then, the example of a chain. The person who pulls the topmost link would draw up by this one the other links attached to one another. In the same way, since the other names that interpret that ineffable and manifold blessedness are, as well, naturally attached to the name "Christ," it would be necessary that the person grasping one of them would also draw up the rest by this one.

Therefore, if someone assumes the name of Christ but does not display in his way of life what is contemplated together with this name, such a person bears the name falsely just as in the illustration I have presented of the lifeless mask [136] fashioned in human form put on the monkey. For neither can it be that Christ is not righteousness and purity and truth and alienation from all evil, nor can it be that a Christian, at least one truly a Christian, should fail to display in himself his share also in those names. Surely, then, no matter how anyone may have interpreted the meaning of Christianity by giving a definition, we shall say this: Christianity is the imitation of the divine nature. And let no one attack what I have said as though it exceeds and oversteps the lowliness of our nature, for the definition does not go beyond our nature. Indeed, if someone were to take account of the first fashioning of humanity, he would find by the scriptural lessons that the definition has not exceeded the limits of our nature. For the first fashioning of humanity was in accordance with the imitation of the likeness of God. This is how Moses gives a philosophical account of humanity, when he says: "God made humanity, according to the image of God he made him" (Gen 1:27). And the profession of Christianity is that humanity be brought back to its original good inheritance.

Now if humanity was originally the likeness of God, I shall probably not have missed the mark in my definition by claiming that Christianity is the imitation of the divine nature. Therefore, promising to assume the appellation is in this way something great. And it may be convenient to consider carefully whether failing to be in this condition [137] in how one lives is without risk for the one who makes a show of the name. Let the question be clarified by an example. Imagine someone who professes the art of painting,

---

2. καὶ πρὸς ἐκεῖνα ἡμῖν τὴν ὁμωνθμίαν κατὰ τὸ ἀκόλουθον γίνεσθαι, literally, "that in relation to them the same name should become ours by consequence."

and suppose that the ruler commands him to paint a picture of him in his kingly office for those dwelling far away. If, then, he were to draw some ugly and misshapen form on the canvas and were to call this picture, this ugliness, the image of the king, would it not be likely to anger the authority, since because of that bad picture the beauty of the original would be insulted among those who did not know him? For it is necessarily supposed that the appearance of the original is like the form painted on the image. Therefore, if the definition states that Christianity is the imitation of God, the person who has not yet accepted the account of the mystery will suppose that the divinity is also such as the sort of life he sees in us, a life believed ordered according to the imitation of God. Consequently, if he should see examples of all goodness, he would believe the divinity we worship to be good. But suppose there is someone passionate and bestial, transformed from one passion to others and assuming in his character many forms of wild beasts; for it is possible to see quite openly wild beasts formed in the perversions of our nature. And suppose such a person were then to call himself a Christian. By his own way of life he would cause unbelievers to find fault with the divinity in whom we believe, assuming that it is obvious to everyone that promising to assume the name Christian professes the imitation of God. This is why scripture proclaims some quite fearful threat against such people, when it says: "Woe to those by whom my name is blasphemed among the Gentiles" (cf. Isa 52:5). And it seems to me that it was with this especially in mind that the Lord guides us [138] by saying to those able to hear: "Be perfect, as also your heavenly Father is perfect" (Matt 5:45). For when he called the true Father the father of those who believed, he wanted also those born through him to be like the perfection of goods contemplated in him. You will say to me, then, "and how can it be that human lowliness should strain forward (cf. Phil 3:13) to the blessedness beheld in God, since immediately with the command its impossibility appears? For how may it be possible for the earthly to be made like the One in the heavens, since the very difference in nature demonstrates that imitation is unattainable? For it is just as impossible to make ourselves equal in appearance to heaven's greatness with the beautiful things in it as to liken humanity from earth to God in heaven." But the explanation of this problem is clear, because the Gospel does not command the comparison of one nature to another, I mean the human with the divine. Instead, it commands the imitation in our way of life of good actions, as far as that may be possible. What, then, are the actions on our part that are like God's actions? Our being made strangers to every wickedness as far as may be possible, to be pure from its defilements in deed and word and thought—this is truly the imitation of the divine perfection and of what has to do with God in heaven.

Indeed, it does not seem to me that in the passage where the Gospel commands us to be made perfect in accord with the heavenly Father it is speaking of the element of heaven as something set apart for God's dwelling place. This is because the divinity is equally present in all things and [139] in like manner pervades the entire creation, and nothing would remain in existence if it were separated from the One who is. Instead, the divine nature takes hold of each one of existing things, as of equal value, since he encompasses all things with his own inner all-embracing power. This also accords with what the prophet teaches when he says: "Even if in thought I come to be in heaven, even if I examine things beneath the earth by going down there in my thinking, even if I stretch forth the intellectual faculty of my soul to the extremities of existing things, I see everything held fast by your right hand." The text reads this way: "If I go up to heaven, you are there; if I go down to Hades, you are present. If I should take my wings at dawn and take up my dwelling in the uttermost parts of the sea, even there, indeed, your hand will guide me, and your right hand will hold me fast" (Ps 138:8ff.). Therefore, it is possible to learn from this that the heavenly dwelling has not been marked out as a special place for God.[3] Instead, the portion above is understood as purity from evil, since in many places holy scripture indicates this to us enigmatically. As well, it is in this lower, quite material life that the passions are stirred up for vice, since it is here that the serpent that invented vice for earthly life crawls and creeps, as the passage about him says enigmatically (Gen 3:14). Because he goes on his chest and belly, and eats earth all the time, this form of motion and kind of food explain to us that this life, which is earthly and placed low down, is one [140] that admits into itself the crawling of vice in its many forms and that becomes the food of the wild beast that creeps upon it. On these considerations, therefore, by commanding the imitation of the heavenly Father (Matt 5:48) Christ is commanding purification from earthly passions. Removing them is effected not by a change of place, but only by free choice. If, then, estrangement from wickedness is naturally accomplished by the intention of the understanding alone, the passage in the Gospel enjoins upon us nothing toilsome. For exertion is not yoked together with the intention of the understanding, but it is possible for us by ideas to be present wherever we wish without trouble. Consequently, the person who wants it has the life of ease in heaven, even though he is on earth, just as the gospel explains by telling us to mind heavenly things (cf. Col 3:2) and to store up in the treasuries there the wealth of virtue. For it says: "Do not store up treasures on earth, but store up treasures in heaven, where neither moth nor rust consumes nor thieves break in and

---

3. τὸ μὴ ἀφωρίσθαι κατ᾽ ἐξαίρετον τῷ οὐράνιον οἴκησιν.

steal" (Matt 6:19). This passage proves that in the life above no power is introduced that would corrupt its blessedness. It is to damage life here that the one who in many ways puts his own changeable wickedness into action[4] against human life is given birth in our thoughts like a moth, rendering useless the spot where he is implanted by means of his [141] power to eat and destroy. Unless he is quickly shaken out of the spot, he creeps on to the ones next to it, and his movement is indicated by the track of corruption wherever he approaches. Or if what is within remains steadfast, he lays snares by means of outward circumstances. For he either has broken into the heart's treasury by pleasure or by some other passion has made the soul's receptacle empty of virtue, having secretly stolen away the reasoning power by anger or grief or some other such passion. Since, therefore, the Lord says that in the treasuries above there will be neither moth nor rust nor a thievish wickedness, teaching the things I have considered, we must transfer our merchandise to that place where what has been treasured up not only remains forever inviolate and undiminished, but also, like seeds, achieves increase by multiplying. Indeed, it is entirely necessary by nature that what someone who has received a deposit gives back should include interest. For just as we act according to our own nature when we offer poor things because they are such as we are by nature, so it is probable that the One who is rich in everything will return the favor to those who have previously given, with those things that are his by nature. Therefore, let no one be discouraged when he pays into the divine treasuries what is in accordance with his own ability, as though he would get back what was his in proportion to the measure of what he gave. Instead, let him wait according to the promise of the One who has said that great things will be given back for small ones, heavenly things for earthly, and eternal things exchanged for those that quickly die. Since what such things are by nature can neither be grasped by the understanding nor brought to explanation in speech, the inspired scripture teaches about them by saying that [142] "neither eye has seen, nor ear has heard, nor has it gone up to the human heart what things God has prepared for those who love him" (cf. 1 Cor 2:9). With this letter I am sending to you, my honored friend, not only have I filled up what was lacking in my letters, but I have also by way of a deposit paid ahead of time for the deficiencies to come after this letter. May you treat me agreeably in the Lord, and may what is both acceptable to God and agreeable to me be always agreeable to you.

---

4. ὁ . . . τὴν ποικίλην ἑαυτοῦ κακίαν. . . ἐνεργῶν.

From Gregory, Bishop of Nyssa, to Olympius

CONCERNING PERFECTION
(De perfectione, GNO 8.1)

It befits your choice of life to be eager for knowing how someone may be perfected by the virtuous life, with a view to your achieving an altogether blameless life. For my part, above all I would have produced instances to be found in my life for you to study so as to offer you the instruction you ask by deeds instead of words. For in this way guidance in good things would be trustworthy because life would correspond with words. But since I am continuing to pray that this may one day come to be, but do not yet now see myself such a person as could present his life instead of a word, and so that I may not seem to be someone entirely useless and without profit to you for your goal, let my purpose be to suggest what ought to contribute to a genuinely disciplined life, beginning the discussion after this preliminary remark.

Our good Master, Jesus Christ, has granted [174] us a share in the name that is worshipped, so that we are named after no one else of those around us—even if someone happens to be rich and well born, even if someone is base born or poor, even if he has distinction because of some accomplishments or honors. And since all such names are nullified, being named "Christian" is the one lordly title for those who have believed in him. Therefore, because this gracious gift has been ratified for us from on high, it may be necessary first of all to understand the greatness of the gift, so as worthily to thank God, who has given such great things, and then to show ourselves as those who by their life are such as the power of this great name requires. In this way the greatness of the gift of which we have been deemed worthy by being named together with the Master of our life would be clear

24

to us, provided we recognize what is signified by a name that corresponds to Christ so as to understand what sort of notion we are accepting in our souls whenever we call upon the Lord of all by this word in our prayers, or by what understanding of this name we believe he is called upon reverently. So whenever we understand this, it follows that we shall then learn clearly also what sort of character we should display in ourselves by a zealous way of life, using the name as a teacher and guide to this way of life. Surely then, by making Saint Paul our guide to these two things [175] we shall have the safest guidance to a clear understanding of what is being investigated. For he most of all both accurately understood what Christ is and led the way by what he did to the sort of character one named by Christ ought to have. Paul so visibly imitated Christ that he displayed his own Master formed in himself. By the most accurate imitation the pattern of his soul was changed to its prototype, so that it no longer seemed to be Paul living and speaking, but Christ himself living in him, just as by rightly perceiving his own goods Paul says: "since you desire proof that Christ is speaking in me" (2 Cor 13:3) and "it is no longer I who live, but it is Christ who lives in me" (Gal 2:20).

So then, Paul is the one who has also made known to us the meaning of the name "Christ," when he said: "Christ is the power of God and the wisdom of God" (1 Cor 1:24). Moreover, he also called him "peace" (Eph 2:14) and "the unapproachable light in which God dwells" (1 Tim 6:16), both "sanctification" and "redemption" (1 Cor 1:30), both "great high priest" (Heb 4:14) and "paschal lamb" (1 Cor 5:7), "the place of atonement" for souls (Rom 3:25), "the reflection of glory, the exact imprint of being, and the creator of the worlds" (Heb 1:2–3), "spiritual food and drink" (cf. 1 Cor 10:3–4), "rock" (1 Cor 10:4), and "water" (cf. John 4:10), "the foundation [176] of faith" (1 Cor 3:11) and "the head of the corner" (Matt 21:42; Mark 12:10; Luke 20:17), and "the image of the invisible God" (Col 1:15), and "the great God" (Titus 2:13), both "the head of the body of the church" (Col 1:18) and "the firstborn of the new[1] creation" (cf. Col 1:15) and "the first fruits of those who have fallen asleep" (1 Cor 15:20), "the firstborn from the dead" (Col 1:18) and "the firstborn among many brothers" (Rom 8:29), and "the mediator between God and humans" (1 Tim 2:5), and "the Only Begotten Son crowned with glory and honor" (cf. John 3:18; Heb 2:7, 9), and "the Lord of glory" (1 Cor 2:8), and "the beginning of existing things" (Col 1:18)—these are ways Paul has spoken of Christ. He is "sovereignty"[2] both as "king of righteousness" and additionally as "king of peace" (Heb 7:2) and

---

1. Note that Gregory has added "new" to the text, and has included Gospel texts with those from Paul.

2. ἀρχή, which could, of course, also mean "beginning."

the king who has unlimited power of reigning over all things,[3] and many other such names, the multitude of which is not easily numbered. Although each name's meaning contributes its own indication for what is signified, all of them put together with one another suggest for us some impression of what the name that accords with Christ means.[4] Insofar as we find room in the soul for understanding them, the more they point out to us his ineffable greatness. Since, therefore, the honored title of "kingship" excels every dignity and authority and domination, kingly power is properly and primarily indicated by the title "Christ"; [177] for the anointing of kingship takes first place, as we learn in the [scriptural] narratives.[5] And the entire meaning of the rest of the names is included in "kingship." For this reason the person who has understood the included names has with them also understood the meaning that embraces the individual names. And this is "kingship," which is the name indicated by the appellation "Christ." Now since from the good Master we have come to share in the greatest, most divine, and first of the names so as to be named "Christians," having been honored with the title of Christ, it would be necessary for all the interpretations of such a word to be seen also in us, since the title should not be falsely given to us as a name, but should be a testimony based on our life. For what something is does not come about because of what it is called; instead, the underlying nature, of whatever sort it happens to be, is recognized by a significance attached to the name. I mean something like this. If someone were to bestow the title "human being" to a tree or a rock, will either the plant or the stone be a human being because of what it is called? This cannot be. Rather, first it must be a human being, and then named this way by what the nature is called. For not even in the case of likenesses does what we call them have a proper sense, if, for example, someone were to call a statue or a horse a human being because it resembles one. Instead, if something were going to be named properly and without falseness, nature would by all means point out the true appellation. And the material that has received the resemblance, whatever it happens to be, will also be named this, whether it is bronze or stone or whatever other such thing [178] on which art has cast a form fashioned in relation to appearance.

Therefore, it is necessary for those who name themselves from Christ first to become what the name means, and then in this way to apply what

3. The best candidate for the scriptural text Gregory has in mind is Dan 7:14; Jaeger also suggests Luke 1:33 and Mic 4:7.

4. Gregory wants to underline the partial character of what we learn. Full knowledge of Christ would depend upon understanding all the names together, something that eludes our grasp. The word "impression" translates ἔμφασιν.

5. Jaeger suggests possible references to 1 Kgdms 9:16; 10:1ff.; and 16:12ff.

they are called to themselves. For example, if someone were to distinguish in the case of an image what is called by the same name from what is really a human being, he would make the distinction on the basis of specific properties; for he would name the one living, rational, and intelligent, but the other, lifeless matter that has assumed its form by resemblance. In the same way we shall recognize both the one who is truly a Christian and the one who only appears to be such by means of the specific properties that are displayed by characteristic marks. And the characteristic marks of one who is really a Christian are all those whatsoever that we conceive concerning Christ. As many of them as we grasp we imitate, but as many as our nature does not grasp for imitation we both venerate and worship. Surely then, all the names that interpret the meaning of Christ must shine forth in the Christian life, some by imitation and others by worship, if the person belonging to God is going to be sound, as the apostle says (cf. 2 Tim 3:17), on no account maiming his soundness by wickedness. For example, those who fashion mythic marvels either by words or by the art of painting,[6] when they construct out of different species people with the heads of bulls or centaurs or people with snakes for feet,[7] [179] do not draw a resemblance according to an archetype of nature. Instead, departing from nature by this irrational conceit, they fashion something else and not a human being. They give form in appearance to what does not exist, and no one would call what has been fashioned by this absurd construction a human being, even if part of what has been fashioned resembles some part of a human body. In the same way neither would anyone be accurately called a Christian who has the head of an irrational animal, that is, who does not have by faith the head of the universe, who is the Word (cf. Col 2:10), even if he is sound in other respects. Nor would anyone be called a Christian who does not display the body of his way of life as corresponding to the head of faith, either by assimilating himself to the anger of snakes, becoming bestial in the likeness of these creeping creatures, or by putting together with a human character the madness for women of horses and becoming a centaur with two natures, both rational and irrational. Many such people can be seen either leading a respectable life by the head of a young bull, that is, by idolatrous religion, such as they portray the Minotaur, or binding beneath a Christian face the body of a beast in their life, such as the fictions they compose of centaurs or people with the feet of snakes. Since, therefore, just as in the case of a human body the Christian is recognized by his completeness in every part, it is fitting [180] that the confirmation of all the goods discerned in Christ

6. γραφικῆς τέχνης.

7. Gregory's point is that these mythical creatures are half-human, half-bestial.

be expressed by the characteristic marks of his way of life. For to be such a person as the name means in one respect, but in other respects to incline to what is opposed to it, is nothing else than for him to be cut apart in himself for war, since he will find in himself a civil strife between virtue and vice and will be without a truce within himself and torn apart in his life. For, as the apostle says, "what fellowship is there between light and darkness?" (2 Cor 6:14).

Indeed, since the opposition of light to darkness cannot be harmonized and mediated, the person who takes hold of both and not one or the other of them, because of the hostility of things drawn up in opposition to one another, will himself necessarily be cut in two together with them. In his mixed life he will become both light and darkness at the same time, since faith sheds its light, while his darkened life quenches the brilliance of his reason. And so, since fellowship between light and darkness is impossible and irreconcilable, the person who holds fast to each of the two opposites will himself become his own enemy, since he has been divided in two with respect to virtue and vice and is setting himself up in a line of battle antagonistic to himself. And just as in the case of two enemies it cannot be that both should be victorious against one another—for the victory of one will inevitably bring about the death of his rival—so too in the case of this intestine battle [181] drawn up in the mixed life it is not possible for the stronger line of battle to win the victory unless the other has been utterly destroyed. For how will the army of true religion become stronger than wickedness, when the evil phalanx of the opposing powers is marching against it? Yet if the stronger is going to win the victory, the adversary[8] will inevitably be killed. And thus virtue will have the prizes of victory against vice whenever the entire hostile army withdraws to annihilation because of virtue's alliance with right thoughts. Then will there be fulfilled what was spoken by the prophet in the person of God: "I will kill, and I will make alive" (Deut 32:39). For there is no other way for the good in me to live, unless it is made alive by the death of the enemy. And as long as we try to hold fast to the two, grasping opposites by each hand, it is impossible to participate in both at the same time. For when vice has gained its grip, virtue has lost hold of its handle.

Therefore, let me take up again the point I made at the beginning—that for those who love virtue the one path to a life both pure and divine is to know what the name of Christ means. Our life must be conformed to this name, a life composed for virtue by the significance of the other names.

---

8. The translation understands "opposing powers" and "adversary" as references to the demons and the devil. The Greek need not mean this, and we could translate, "opponents" and "enemy."

And so as many words and names interpretive of the meaning of Christ as I assembled from Paul's holy voice in my opening discussion, these I have brought forward; and for the pursuit I have proposed I shall make them the surest guidance to the virtuous life, by imitating some of them, [182] as I have already said, while worshipping and venerating others. Let the list of the ones I have mentioned be the order⁹ of my discussion; and so, let me begin from the first. Christ, Paul says, is "the power of God and the wisdom of God" (1 Cor 1:24). Through these expressions we first learn the concepts befitting God indicated by the title Christ, concepts by which we venerate the name. For since the whole creation, both as much as is known by sense perception and what transcends the understanding of the senses, came to be through him and is held together in him (cf. Col 1:17), necessarily is wisdom combined with power for defining the meaning of Christ, who made all things. When we understand this by joining together these two expressions, I mean both power and wisdom, it is because these great and ineffable wonders of creation would not exist unless wisdom contrived their coming to be and unless power combined with wisdom for the completion of what was conceived, thereby enabling the concepts to become works.

Accordingly, what is signified by "Christ" is divided into a double meaning, into both wisdom and power, so that when we regard the greatness of the structure of existing things, we may understand Christ's ineffable power by what we have apprehended, while when we take account of [183] how what did not exist came to be, since the manifold nature in existing things was given substantial form by divine command, we may then worship the incomprehensible wisdom of the one who conceived these things, a wisdom whose conceptions are concrete realities. And it is not idle and useless for us to believe in Christ as power and wisdom in relation to the acquisition of good. For what someone calls upon in prayer, and what one looks at with the eye of the soul, this he draws into himself by prayer. In this way the person who looks at power (and Christ is power) is strengthened by power in his inner self, as the apostle says (cf. Eph 3:16), and the person who calls upon wisdom (which again the Lord is understood to be) also becomes wise, as the proverb says (cf. Prov 2:2–6).[10] Therefore, the person named together with Christ, who is both power and wisdom, is named together with power by having been empowered against sin; and he will display wisdom in himself by his choice of the better. When wisdom and power are displayed in us, with the first choosing the good and the other establishing what is intended, by the combination of both perfection of life is achieved. So too

9. τάξις.

10. Prov 2:3, 6: ἐὰν γὰρ σοφίαν ἐπικαλέσῃ . . . ὅτι κύριος δίδωσιν σοφίαν.

by understanding Christ as "peace" (Eph 2:14) we shall display in ourselves what it means truly to be called a Christian, provided we display Christ in our life by peace among us. Christ put to death "hostility," as the apostle says (Eph 2:16). Therefore, let us not bring this to life among ourselves, but let us show that it is dead [184] by our life. Let us never raise up the hostility that has rightly been put to death for our salvation by God. By doing so we would achieve for the destruction of our souls by anger and malice the raising up in ourselves of what has rightly been slain. If, instead, we hold onto Christ, who is peace, let us also kill hostility among ourselves, so that what we believe to be in him, this we may also achieve in our life. For just as Christ, having broken down the dividing wall, created the two in himself into one new humanity, making peace (cf. Eph 2:14–15), so let us also lead to reconciliation not only those who fight against us from outside, but also those who sow discord among ourselves, so that the flesh may no longer set its desires against the spirit, and the spirit against the flesh (cf. Gal 5:17). Moreover, with the mind of the flesh subject to the divine law (cf. Rom 8:6–7) let us be at peace among ourselves by being transformed into one new and peaceable humanity and by the two becoming one. For peace is defined as the concord of those who had been set at variance. Therefore, whenever intestine warfare is removed from our nature, then we become peace by being at peace among ourselves, displaying in ourselves the true and proper title of Christ. Now by understanding Christ as the light, true and unapproachable by falsehood (cf. 1 Tim 6:16), we learn that our life must also be illuminated by the rays of the true light. And virtues are [185] the rays of "the sun of righteousness" (Mal 4:2) that stream forth to enlighten us. By them there comes about laying aside the works of darkness and walking honorably as in the day (Rom 13:12–13) and renouncing the shameful things that one hides (cf. 2 Cor 4:2) and doing everything in the light and becoming light itself so as also to shine before others (cf. Matt 5:15–16), which is the property of light. And if we understand Christ as "sanctification" (1 Cor 1:30), let us show ourselves as truly sharers of the name by removing ourselves from every profane and unclean action and thought, confessing the power of sanctification in our life, in deed and not in word.

Now when we learn that Christ, who gave himself as a ransom for us, is "redemption" (1 Cor 1:30), we are taught by this word to learn that by furnishing us with immortality as an honor for each soul, he made his own possession those whom he ransomed from death by the life that came from him. If, therefore, we have become the slaves of the one who paid the ransom, we shall in all ways look to the one who is Lord so that we shall live no longer to ourselves, but to the one who bought us by giving his life in exchange (cf. 2 Cor 5:15). For we are no longer our own lords; instead, the one who bought is master of his own possessions, and we are his possessions. Therefore, the law of our life will be the will of the one who is Lord. [186] For just as the law of sin governed among us when death ruled over us (cf. Rom 8:2), so inasmuch as we have become the possession of life, it is necessary for our governed life to be changed in accordance with life which rules, lest by turning aside from the will of life we should again by sin desert to the wicked tyrant of our souls, I mean death. This meaning, then, will associate us with Christ whether we hear from Paul that he is the paschal lamb or that he is the high priest. Indeed, how truly was Christ sacrificed for us as the paschal lamb (1 Cor 5:7), and yet the priest who offered the sacrifice (cf. Heb 4:14) to God is no other than Christ himself. Indeed, it says, "he gave himself up as an offering and sacrifice for us" (cf. Eph 5:12). Surely, then, by these considerations we learn that the person who looks to Christ, who brought himself forward as an offering and sacrifice and became the paschal lamb, will also present himself to God as a living sacrifice, holy and acceptable, becoming a spiritual service (cf. Rom 12:1). And the manner of the priestly service is not to be conformed to this age, but to be transformed by the renewing of his mind by testing what is the good and acceptable and perfect will of God (cf. Rom 12:2). [187] For it is not when the flesh is alive and the priestly service is not performed according to the spiritual law that the good will of God is displayed in it. This is because the mind of the flesh is hostile to God and does not submit to God's law (cf. Rom 8:7). Nor, indeed, can it do so as long as the flesh is alive, since the priestly service performed by the life-giving sacrifice takes place through putting to death the bodily members on earth (cf. Col 3:5) by which the passions are aroused. Only then will the acceptable and perfect will of God be achieved in the life of those who have believed. Thus, since Christ is also understood to be "the place of atonement by his own blood" (Rom 3:25), Paul teaches whoever has understood this that each person should become a place of atonement for himself, purifying his soul by putting his bodily members to death. Now when Christ is called "the reflection of glory" and "the exact imprint of being" (Heb 1:3), we take the notions expressed by these words to refer to his greatness, which is worshipped. For Paul—how truly inspired and taught by God!—searched out the unseen and hidden things of divine mysteries[11] in the depth of God's riches, wisdom, and knowledge. The illuminations concerning the apprehension of things unsearchable and inscrutable came to him from God (cf. Rom 11:33). With a tongue too weak to express thought, as far as his hearing apprehended what he received, he marked out his

11. Cf. 2 Cor 12:2–4.

understanding in the mystery by certain [188] glimmers, saying as much as words were capable of serving his thought. Although he understood all such as human power may apprehend concerning the divine nature, he declares that an account of the transcendent being is both unattainable and unreachable by human thoughts.

For this reason Paul, in speaking of the things contemplated concerning the divine being as peace and power and life and righteousness and light and truth and such things, defined the principle of that being itself to be altogether incomprehensible, when he said that God neither has ever been seen nor will be seen. Indeed, he says that no one among humans has seen him or is able to see him (cf. 1 Tim 6:16). That is why when he searched out how he would name what cannot be grasped by thought, he failed to find a name to express and interpret what is incomprehensible; for this reason he called what transcends every good, what can neither be thought nor spoken of worthily, "glory" and "being." Therefore, on the one hand, he left the "being" that transcends all existing things unnamed; but, on the other hand, when he interprets the united and inseparable relation of the Son to the Father as well as the fact that Christ is contemplated in an unlimited and eternal fashion with the unlimited and eternal Father, he calls him "the reflection of glory" and "the exact imprint of being." By "reflection" he indicates the sameness of nature; and by "exact imprint," [189] the equal status of the two. For neither is any difference conceived between the ray and the nature that shares its radiance, nor is there any diminishment of the exact imprint with the *hypostasis* imprinting it.[12] Moreover, whoever has understood the nature that sheds brilliance has certainly by this also understood the reflection; and whoever has received in his mind the greatness of the *hypostasis* will certainly also measure the *hypostasis* by the exact imprint that has appeared. It is on this account that Paul also calls the Lord "the form of God" (Phil 2:6), not belittling the Lord by the idea of form, but indicating the greatness of God by the form in which there is discerned the Father's majesty, which in no way surpasses its own form nor is found outside the exact imprint which points to it. For there is nothing about the Father misshapen and deprived of beauty, nothing that does not glory in the beauty of the Only Begotten. This is why the Lord says, "Whoever has seen me has seen the Father" (John 14:9). By this he points out that there is

---

12. πρὸς τὴν ὑπ'αὐτοῦ χαρακτηριζομένην ὑπόστασιν. Literally, "with respect to the *hypostasis* characterized (or imprinted) by it." The problem is that the word in Heb 1:3 translated "being" is in fact *hypostasis*. Granted Gregory's understanding of the Trinity as three *hypostaseis* in one *ousia*, he must mean that the Father's *hypostasis* characterizes or imprints the Son's *hypostasis*, and the two are equal. The translation attempts to clarify this by using an active rather than a passive construction.

nothing less or more. Moreover, when Paul says that "he carries all things by his powerful speaking" (Heb 1:3), he undoes the perplexity of those who busy themselves with what cannot be searched out. They never stop busying themselves with investigating the explanation of matter, saying: "How can it be that matter is related to the immaterial? And how can quantity come from what is without quantity, and form from what is without form, and color from what is invisible, and what is limited by its own measures from what is unbounded? And if there is no [190] quality in the case of what is simple and uncompounded, how can it be that matter is combined with the qualities connected with it?" All these and other such questions are undone by the one who said that the Word carries all things from nonexistence to coming into being by his powerful speaking. For all things, whether they involve matter or have received the lot of an immaterial nature, have as the sole cause of their existence the speaking of ineffable power. And from this consideration we are taught to look to him from whom existing things came into being. For if it is thence that we have been brought into being and are held together in him (cf. Col 1:16–17), it is entirely necessary to believe that nothing escapes the knowledge of the one in whom we exist and from whom we came to be and to whom we return. And by this understanding what accords with the sinless life is in all likelihood helped to achievement. For who that believes he lives from him and through him and in him (cf. Rom 11:36) will dare to make himself a witness to a life inconsistent with the one who embraces each person's life in himself? And by naming the Lord spiritual food and drink the divine apostle presupposes the meaning thought expressed by these words to be that human nature is not one in kind; but since the intelligible has been mingled with the sensible, food is specifically adapted to each of the things discerned in us, with sensible food supporting the body and spiritual nourishment providing for us the soul's good health. Well then, in the case of the body both dry and moist nourishment mixed together become preservative of its nature, [191] since through mutual digestion they are combined with each of the elements mingled together in us. In just the same way, by analogy, Paul also divides spiritual nourishment, giving the same thing the names of food and drink adapted appropriately to the need of those who partake of it. And so, for those who are exhausted and weak it becomes bread, strengthening the person's heart; on the other hand, for those who have become weary of the hardships attached to this life and have for this reason become thirsty it becomes wine, bringing the heart to joy (cf. Ps 103:15).

Now from what has been said it is necessary to understand the power of the Word by whom the soul is nourished, receiving from him grace corresponding to its need, in accord with the enigma of the prophet, who indicates by the grassy place and by the water of refreshment (cf. Ps 22:2) the consolation that comes from the Lord to those who have become weary. If, then, someone were also to take into consideration the mystery of the eucharist, he would say that the Lord is properly named spiritual food and drink; nor would this be foreign to the proper meaning. For his flesh is truly food, and his blood is truly drink (cf. John 6:55). But in terms of the meaning mentioned earlier everyone according to his power has participation in the Word, who, when he is received without hesitation by those who seek him, becomes the food and drink offered. Yet in terms of the other sense [192] participation in such nourishment and drink is still not to be without examination and without hesitation, since the apostle adds a condition this way: "Let each one examine himself, and so let him eat of the bread and let him drink of the cup. But whoever eats and drinks unworthily eats and drinks judgment against himself" (cf. 1 Cor 11:28). It is with this in view that the evangelist also seems to me to be hinting at such a safeguard, when at the time of the mystery of the passion that noble councilor, wrapping the Lord's body in a spotless and pure linen cloth, put it in a new and pure tomb (Luke 23:53). As a result, both the apostle's command and the evangelist's observation about receiving the holy body with a pure conscience become a law for all of us, namely, that if anyone in the world should become stained by sin, they should wash it away with the water of tears. Moreover, by being called a "rock" (1 Cor 10:4) Christ will help us by this name to be steadfast and changeless in the virtuous life, to stand firm in enduring sufferings, and to display our souls resistant and unyielding to every assault of sin. For by these means and ones like them we shall also become a rock, imitating as far as possible in a changeable nature the changelessness and immutability of the Master. And if the same Master is named by the wise master builder both "the foundation of faith" (cf. 1 Cor 3:10–11) and the "head of the corner" (Luke 20:17), neither will this be shown a useless contribution to the virtuous life. For we are taught by these expressions that the Lord is both the beginning and the end of every good way of life and every education and pursuit. [193] Indeed, hope, which we understand as corresponding to "head" and as the end to which everything earnestly pursued according to virtue looks, is Christ, since he is so named by Paul (Col 1:27). And the beginning of this lofty tower of life (cf. Luke 14:28) comes about by faith in him, on which as on a kind of foundation we lay down the beginnings of our life and frame as laws pure thoughts and actions by daily good deeds. Thus, the head of the universe also becomes our head. Growing together with the corners, he fits himself to the two walls of our life, those of both body and soul, which are built up by what is becoming and pure. So whenever one of the structures is deficient, whether when what is outwardly becoming is not built together with purity of soul or when the soul's virtue does not correspond to outward appearance, then Christ does not become the head of this half-finished life. He fits himself only to a building both double and with corners, nor can he become the corner unless the two walls are joined. Therefore, the beauty of the head of the corner will be placed on our building at the time when from both according to the right [194] standard of life the double life has been stretched out harmoniously by the plumb line of the virtues and is both upright and immoveable, without anything crooked or bent out of shape.

Then Paul names Christ, who is "God over all" (Rom 9:5) and "great God" (Titus 2:13), "the image of the invisible God" (Col 1:15). (Indeed, it is by these words that he proclaims the greatness of the true Master, when he says "of our great God and Savior Jesus Christ" [Titus 2:13] and "from whom is Christ according to the flesh, who is God over all blessed forever" [Rom 9:5]). Therefore, by these expressions he teaches us through what is said that what the One who eternally exists as what he is—and this is what only the One who is knows, and what has always transcended the limit proportioned to human comprehension, even if someone who sets his mind on things above (Col 3:2) constantly progresses ever nearer to it—this One, therefore, who transcends all knowledge and comprehension, who is ineffable and unutterable and indescribable (cf. 2 Cor 9:15), in order to make you once more [195] the image of God, because of his love for humanity, also himself became the image of the invisible God. As a result, he has been formed in you in the form he assumed and made his own; and through himself you have again been conformed to the exact imprint of the archetypal beauty so as to become what you were from the beginning. Therefore, if we are going to become also ourselves the image of the invisible God, it is fitting that the form of our life be modeled in accordance with the example of life set forth to us (cf. John 13:15). What is that? Not to live according to the flesh, even though we live in the flesh (cf. Rom 8:12–13). For indeed, the prototype, the image of the invisible God, who came by means of the Virgin, was tested in all respects in the likeness of human nature, but did not admit the experience of a single sin (cf. Heb 4:15). "He committed no sin, and no deceit was found in his mouth" (1 Pet 2:22). Well then, suppose we were being taught the art of painting by the teacher's setting forth for us some shape beautifully formed on the canvas. It would be entirely necessary for each person to imitate the beauty of that form on his own painting so that [196] everyone's canvas would be embellished according to the example of beauty set forth. In the same way, since each person is the painter of his own life, and since free choice is the artist of this craft, and virtues are the colors used to complete the image, there is no small danger of drawing the copy of the original beauty amiss into an ugly and misshapen portrait, when we sketch by sordid colors the exact imprint of wickedness instead of the Master's form. Instead, as far as possible, we must take the pure colors of the virtues, combined with one another according to an artistic mixture for copying beauty, so that we may become an image of the image, modeling in ourselves the original beauty by effective imitation, as far as possible, just as Paul did by becoming an imitator of Christ through the virtuous life (cf. 1 Cor 4:16). And if it is necessary to elucidate in discussion one by one the things by which imitation of the image takes place, one color is humility. For, Christ says, "Learn from me, that I am meek and humble in heart" (Matt 11:29). Another color is forbearance. How great was the way it appeared in the image of the invisible God! Both sword and clubs, bonds and whips, cheeks struck, face spat upon, back given over to blows, an unholy judgment, [197] harsh denial, soldiers delighting in the sad denial with scoffing and mockeries and insults and blows from a reed, nails, gall and sour wine, and all those most terrible things brought upon him without a cause, or rather given in return for many kinds of beneficence.[13] What, then, does he pay back against those who were doing these things? "Father, forgive them, for they do not know what they are doing" (Luke 23:34). Would it not have been possible for him to rend heaven from on high against them or to destroy these violent people utterly by a yawning gulf of the earth or to hurl the sea out of its own bounds and make the earth covered with water by the depths of the sea or to hurl upon them the rain of fire of Sodom or to do some other terrible thing by command? Instead, he endured all these things in meekness and forbearance—he who gives the law of forbearance to your life through his own. This is how it is possible also to see all the other aspects of the prototype, the image of God. Whoever looks at it and embellishes his own form distinctly according to it becomes also himself portrayed through endurance as the image of the invisible God.

Now let whoever learns that Christ is the head of the church understand above all that every head is of the same nature and being as the body placed under it, and that there is a certain single natural union of the individual members with the whole, a union that by a single agreement[14] achieves for the members a sympathetic affection for the entire body. Therefore, if something is outside the body, it is in all respects also foreign to the head. [198] Therefore, by this the word teaches us that what the head is by nature, that also are the individual members, so that they may properly belong to the head. And we are the members that together complete

---

13. See the passion narratives in the gospels and Isa 50:6.

14. σύμπνοια μία. A medical term; see Daniélou, L'être et le temps, 52, 59.

the body of Christ (cf. Rom 12; 1 Cor 12). If, therefore, someone were to remove a member of Christ and make it the member of a harlot (cf. 1 Cor 6:15), invading the body with licentious madness like a sword, he would immediately alienate the member from the head by this base passion. In this way, as well, the other instruments of wickedness become swords by which the members are cut out of the natural body; and all those which the passions have succeeded in severing are separated from the head. Therefore, so that the body may remain whole in what it is by nature, it is fitting that the individual members, as well, should keep their proper relationship to the head. That is to say, if we assume that the head is purity by reason of its being, [199] the members completing the body under such a head must in all respects be pure. If we think of the head as incorruption, the members must in all respects unite in incorruption. In this way, too, whatever other concepts may be thought to apply to the head are also to be seen conformable in the case of the members—peace, sanctification, truth, and all such concepts. For it is by these and such things being displayed in the members that they bear testimony to their natural relation to the head, as the apostle said: "Christ is the head, from whom the whole body, joined and knit together by every ligament with which it is equipped, as each part is working properly promotes the body's growth" (cf. Eph 4:16). It is also fitting to be taught by the name "head" that, for example, in the case of animals the signal for the body's activities is given to it by the head. For it is by the eye and the ear that what each one does is directed—movement by the feet and activity by the hands. If, then, either the eye fails to oversee what engages its attention or the ear fails to accept direction as it ought, none of the proposed actions can take place. In the same way also for us the body must be moved to every impulse and activity in correspondence with its true head, moved wherever the One who formed the eye or who planted the ear (Ps 93:9) leads. And since the head looks up, [200] the members must in all respects follow what is suitable to the head by the head's guidance, and must keep their inclination directed to what is on high.

Whenever we hear that Christ is the firstborn of creation (Col 1:15) and the firstborn of the dead (Col 1:18) and the firstborn among many brothers (Rom 8:29), let us first dismiss the assumptions of the heretics, since their base manufacture of doctrine out of the above words has no support. Then, after this, let us consider what these expressions, as well, contribute to us regarding the moral life. Indeed, those who fight against God say that the Only Begotten God, the creator of the universe, the One from whom and through whom and in whom are all things (cf. Rom 11:36), is the work of God and a creature and something made. For this reason they give as their definition that he is called the firstborn of all creation because he is akin to creation and is first by the privilege of age alone, just as Reuben was ranked before his own brothers not by nature but by the privilege of age based on time. Since they say this, the first thing that must be said to them is that the only begotten and the firstborn cannot be believed to be the same person. For neither is someone only begotten understood to have brothers, nor is it apart from brothers [201] that someone is firstborn. Instead, if he is only begotten, he has no brothers; but if he is the firstborn among brothers, he certainly neither is nor is called only begotten. Therefore, these names are incompatible and have nothing in common with one another in referring to the same person, since it is impossible that the two names, both only begotten and firstborn, should be given to the same person. Yet truly from scripture it has been said of the Word who exists in the beginning that he is the Only Begotten God, and from Paul that he is the firstborn of all creation (Col 1:15). Therefore, it is fitting to assign meanings by the standard of truth, carefully distinguishing each of these names, so that "Only Begotten" gives an account of pre-existence, while it is the Word made flesh who became "the firstborn" of all the creation that came to be after this in Christ. And whatever concept has entered our mind by learning that he is the firstborn of the dead and the firstborn among many brothers, let us understand that also to conform to "the firstborn of creation." [202] Therefore, when he became "the first fruits of those who have fallen asleep" (1 Cor 15:20), he became the firstborn of the dead so that he might make a path to the resurrection for all flesh. And when he was going to make us, who were previously by nature children of wrath (Eph 2:3), sons of day and sons of light (1 Thess 5:5) by the new birth through water and the Spirit (John 3:3, 5), he led the way to such a birth himself in the stream of Jordan, drawing the grace of the Spirit upon the first fruits of our nature so as to give the title of brothers to all born to life from spiritual rebirth, since he was born as the first by water and the Spirit. When we understand him in the same way as the firstborn of the creation that came to be in Christ, we do not find ourselves outside what true religion assumes. For since the old creation has passed away because it was rendered useless by sin, necessarily the new creation (cf. 2 Cor 5:17) of life has superceded the passing of what has been destroyed. It consists of rebirth and the resurrection of the dead; its leader, the Author of life (cf. Acts 3:15), has become and is named the firstborn of creation. Yet how we must stand fast against the opponents ranged against us would be easy to say in a few words to the more industrious . . . to have sufficient alliance for the truth.[15] [203] On the other hand, how these words

---

15. The text appears corrupt at this point, and Jaeger posits a lacuna. The sense would seem to be that the more intelligent Christians will understand the theological point Gregory is making, but that it would be more difficult to persuade ordinary

may be seen to contribute to the virtuous life is what we shall briefly discuss. Reuben was the firstborn of those produced by birth after him, but what also bore witness to those born after him of their kinship with him was the character of a family resemblance displayed in them, so that they did not fail to recognize that they were brothers by the witness of a similarity of form. Therefore, if by the same manner of rebirth through water and the Spirit we have also become brothers of the one who for us became the firstborn among many brothers, it would follow that we display close kinship to him by various character traits, when the firstborn is formed in our life. What character, then, have we learned from scripture belongs to his form? We have often said of him that "he committed no sin, and no deceit was found in his mouth" (1 Pet 2:22). Therefore, if we are going to take the title brothers of the one who led the way to our birth, the sinlessness of our life will give proof of our kinship with him, assuming there is no defilement separating us from unity with purity. Moreover, the firstborn is righteousness and sanctification, as well as love and redemption and such titles. Therefore, if our life is also characterized by such things, [204] we shall present clear tokens of our noble birth, so that the One[16] who looks down upon these things in our life may confirm for us by his testimony kinship to Christ. For he is the one who has opened for us the door of the resurrection, and because of this has become "the first fruits of those who have fallen asleep" (1 Cor 15:20). That we shall all rise "in the twinkling of an eye at the last trumpet" (1 Cor 15:52) is what he has demonstrated both by what had to do with himself and by what he has done for the rest held under the power of death.

In truth no equal condition in the life hereafter awaits all those raised from earth's burial mound; instead, it says: "Those who have done good will go to the resurrection of life, and those who have done evil, to the resurrection of condemnation" (cf. John 5:29). As a result, if someone's life faces that fearful condemnation, this person, even if he happens by the birth from on high to be numbered among the Lord's brothers, pretends falsely to the name, since he denies close kinship with the firstborn by the appearance of wickedness. The mediator between God and humans (1 Tim 2:5), who through himself joined humanity with God, joins only that person who may be worthy of unity with God. For just as by the power of divinity he appropriated to himself his own man, who was part [205] of the common nature but did not in truth succumb to the passions of the nature that are

---

Christians. In any case, Gregory turns from the first of his themes regarding "firstborn" to the second, namely, its moral meaning.

16. God? Or the Spirit bearing witness with our spirit (Rom 8:16)? We could, of course, translate the word as "whoever" and think of the people who witness the Christian's life.

provoked for sin (for it says, "he committed no sin, and no deceit was found in his mouth" [1 Pet 2:22]), so too he will bring individuals to union with divinity provided they have brought forth nothing unworthy of unity with the divine. Still, if someone is truly a temple of God (cf. 1 Cor 3:16; 2 Cor 6:16), containing in himself no idol or image of wickedness, this person will be accepted by the mediator for participation in the divinity, since he has become pure for the reception of the mediator's purity. For neither will wisdom enter the deceitful soul, as the word says (Wis 1:4), nor will the one pure in heart see anything in himself apart from God (cf. Matt 5:8), since, firmly fastened to him by incorruption, he has received within himself the entire good kingly rule. And what this means may all the more be evident to us, if we take for our assistance in clarifying what has been said the Lord's saying, which he addressed to the apostles by Mary. "I am going," he says, "to my Father and your Father, and to my God and your God" (cf. John 20:17). For it is the mediator between the Father and the disinherited who says this, the one who through himself reconciled the enemies of God (cf. Jas 4:4) to the true and only divinity. So since, according to the prophet's word (cf. Ps 57:4), by sin human beings have been estranged from the life-giving womb and have wandered away from the place of generation in which they were fashioned, [206] having spoken falsehood instead of truth, because of this Christ, by assuming the first fruits of the common nature through both soul and body, made it holy, having preserved it in himself pure and incapable of admitting any wickedness. He did this so that, having dedicated the first fruits by incorruption to the Father of incorruption, he might through it draw along everything akin to it by nature and of the same kind, and might welcome the disinherited into the adoption of sons (cf. Eph 1:5) and the enemies of God into participation in his divinity. Therefore, just as by purity and impassibility the first fruits of the batch has been made his own for the true Father and God, so we too as the batch through similar paths will be made fast to the Father of incorruption by imitating as far as possible the mediator's impassibility and changelessness. For in this way, becoming honor and glory in our life, we shall become the Only Begotten's crown of precious stones. Indeed, Paul says that after Christ had made himself a little lower than the angels because of the suffering of death, he made through the dispensation according to death a crown for himself of those who had previously been changed into the nature of thorn by sin, having altered by his passion the thorny nature into honor and glory (cf. Heb 2:7–9). When once for all he was taking away the sin of the world (John 1:29), he received the crown of thorns on his head so that he might make the crown one plaited together from honor and glory. There is, therefore, no small danger for someone to be found by an evil life a thistle and a thorn (cf. Matt 7:16), [207] and then to be inserted into the midst of the Master's crown by fellowship with his body. The righteous voice will certainly say to him, "'How did you get in here without a wedding robe?' (Matt 22:12). How is it that you, being a thorn, have been plaited together with those who by honor and glory have been inserted into my crown? 'What fellowship does Christ have with Beliar? What portion belongs to a faithful person together with someone unfaithful?' (cf. 2 Cor 6:15). What is common between light and darkness?" Therefore, lest our life should ever summon such words as accusations against us, let there be careful heed that every thorny deed and word and thought be stripped away from our life, so that by becoming honor and glory in a pure life without passion we may crown through ourselves the head of the universe, becoming as it were a kind of treasure and possession for the Master. For it is of no one dishonorable that the Lord accepts being and being called the Lord of glory (cf. 1 Cor 2:8). Therefore, whoever is foreign to everything shameful and loathsome according to both his hidden and his apparent selves makes his own Master both to be and to be said the Lord of glory, not of dishonor.

Christ is also the beginning, and no beginning of something stands unrelated to what comes after itself. For if someone were to define life as the beginning, life will inevitably be also what is after its beginning. And if beginning is light, light and what follows its beginning will be understood. What profit, then, do we derive by believing him to be the beginning? [208] We have believed that we shall become such as we are in our beginning. For light is not named the beginning of darkness, nor when life has been posited as the beginning, shall we understand that death is continuous with the beginning. But unless someone keeps his natural relationship to what takes the lead by being joined to the beginning through impassibility and virtue, the beginning of things that exist would not become this person's beginning. The beginning of the darkened life, the cosmic ruler of darkness (cf. Eph 6:12), is the one who has the power of death (Heb 2:14), since sin is what brings death. It is impossible, then, for the one ranked under the beginning of darkness by a wicked life to say that the beginning of every good is his own beginning; and he is kept from having the same purpose as those who received for their proper good the divine words that name Christ the king of both righteousness and peace (cf. Heb 7:2). For the person who prays in accord with the teaching about prayer that the kingdom of God may come to him (cf. Matt 6:10), once he learns that the true king is the king of righteousness and peace, will in all respects accomplish righteousness and peace in his own life, so that the king of righteousness and peace may reign over him. Therefore, the whole of virtue is understood as an army of the king, for I think that it is by righteousness and peace that we must understand all the virtues. If, then, someone were to desert [209] God's army and enroll himself in the ranks of foreigners, becoming a soldier of the one who invented evil and taking off the breastplate of righteousness (Eph 6:14) and all the armor of peace, how will this person be ranked under the king of peace by throwing away the shield of truth? For it is obvious that the badge on his armor will indicate his ruler, a badge that indicates his leader by the character of his life rather than by the image inscribed on his arms. How blessed is that person who has taken his rank in the divine army and has been enrolled in ranks numbered by ten thousand times ten thousand and has armed himself against wickedness with the virtues that signify the image of the king for the one who puts them on!

And what need is there further to prolong an account of the words by which the name of Christ is interpreted, an account that has been presented by following a careful examination of those by which it is possible to be guided to the virtuous life, since each name by its own meaning certainly contributes something to us for the perfection of life? Nevertheless, I suppose it good to sum up a reminder of what has been called to mind, so that I may supply a kind of leading by the hand to the aim of the discourse, an aim I suggested by my question at the outset: how may someone achieve perfection in himself? For I suppose that if someone [210] were always to consider that by taking the name of a Christian he shares in the name that is worshipped according to the doctrine of the apostles (cf. Acts 11:26) and also necessarily in the other names by which Christ is conceived, then he would also display their force in himself by sharing in each appellation by his life. The sort of thing I mean is that there are three characteristic aspects of the Christian life—deed, word, and thought. Of these thought is prior to the others. For thinking becomes the beginning of every word; and word is second after thought, since it discloses by speech the thinking that has been imprinted on the soul. And deed, which brings thought to action, occupies third place after mind and word. Therefore, whenever the course of life advances to any one of these, it is good that as a whole, as word and deed and thought, these divine concepts by which Christ is understood and named should be observed with exactness, lest either our deed or word or thought should be carried outside the force of those lofty names. For when Paul says that everything that does not proceed from faith is sin (cf. Rom 14:23), it is to show clearly in this way what he has thought out by implication, that everything [211] that fails to look to Christ, whether spoken word or deed or concept, inevitably pays heed to what is opposed to Christ. For it is impossible that what comes to be outside light or life should fail to be entirely in darkness or in death. If, therefore, what is not done and spoken and thought according to Christ belongs properly to what is opposed to the good, it is obvious to everyone that what this makes known is that whoever comes to be outside the good abandons Christ by whatever he thinks or does or says. Therefore, the prophet's divine voice is true in saying: "I have reckoned all the sinners of earth apostates" (Ps 118:119).[17] For just as the person who has denied Christ in persecutions is an apostate of the name that is worshipped, so too if someone should deny truth or righteousness, or sanctification and incorruption, or if under the control of the passions he should cast away from his life any other one of the names understood in accord with virtue, he would be named an apostate by the prophet, since by each of these names he would be an apostate in his life from the one who is these names. What, then, must the person do who has been made worthy of the great title of Christ? What else than at all times to distinguish precisely in himself thoughts and words and deeds, to see whether each of them looks to Christ or is foreign to Christ; and it is quite easy to determine such things. For whatever is set to work, or thought, or said by means of passion has no agreement [212] with Christ, but bears the mark of the adversary, who by smearing the passions like mud over the pearl of the soul thoroughly spoils the luster of the precious stone. But what is pure from every impassioned disposition looks to the founder of impassibility, who is Christ. Anyone who draws to himself the thoughts taken from Christ's name, like someone drawing water from a pure and incorruptible spring, will display in himself a likeness to the prototype, one such as that between spring water gushing forth and water then placed from it in a pitcher. For there is a single purity by nature, whether seen in Christ or in the one participating in him; but Christ is the spring from which the water gushes forth, while the one participating in him draws the water by transferring the beauty of the concepts to his life. As a result, there is agreement between the hidden self and the one that appears, since the fine appearance of life agrees with the thoughts set in motion according to Christ.

This, therefore, in my judgment is perfection in the Christian life: to keep in soul and word and in the pursuits of life fellowship with all the names by which the name of Christ is signified, so as to receive in oneself, according to Paul's fine statement, entire sanctification in a sound body and soul and spirit (cf. 1 Thess 5:23), guarding it perpetually outside the admixture of evil. [213] Suppose someone were to say that the good is hard to achieve, since only the Lord of creation is immutable, while human nature is mutable and prone to changes. How, then, is it possible for steadfastness and freedom from change to be achieved in a mutable nature? Well then, this

---

17. παραβαίνοντας would usually be translated "transgressors," but the context shows that Gregory is understanding the word to mean "apostates."

is what we say to such a view. No one can be crowned in the games unless he contends lawfully (cf. 2 Tim 2:5), and there would be no lawful contest unless he struggled. If, then, there were no rival, neither would there be the crown; for victory does not take place by itself unless there is something defeated. Therefore, let us contend against the mutability of our nature itself, as though we were wrestling with some rival through our thoughts, becoming victors not by overthrowing our nature but by not permitting it to fall. For it is not only for evil that a human being makes use of change. Indeed, it would be impossible for him to come to be in the good if the only inclination he had from nature were to its opposite. But as it is, the finest work of change is growth in good things, since alteration to the better always transforms the person rightly altered to what is more divine. Therefore, what seems to be something to be feared—and I mean that ours is a mutable nature—the word has indicated to be like a kind of wing for flight to greater things (cf. Isa 40:31), so that loss for us is being unable to accept alteration to the better. Therefore, let whoever sees in our nature its tendency to change not be vexed, but by always being altered toward the better and [214] being transformed from glory to glory (2 Cor 3:18) let him be changed this way, at all times becoming better by daily growth and always being perfected and never attaining the limit of perfection. For this is what perfection truly is: never to stop growing to the better or to draw boundaries around perfection by some kind of limit.

Gregory, Bishop of Nyssa

IN PRAISE OF THEODORE, HOLY AND GREAT MARTYR[1]

(De Sancto Theodoro, GNO 10.1)

You are Christ's people, the holy flock, the royal priesthood (1 Pet 2:9). You have streamed together from all sides, both city dwellers and those from the countryside. What has moved you to accept the signal for a journey to this holy place? Who is it that has enjoined upon you the zeal and urgent necessity for coming here? Is it not winter time when war is quiet and the soldier has taken off his armor, when the sailor has put his rudder aside by the smoking hearth and the farmer has taken rest serving his plowing oxen at the manger?[2] Was it clear ahead of time that when the holy martyr from the military rolls sounded the trumpet, he would move many from different fatherlands and summon them to his own place of rest and home, not to win them over to preparation for war, but to assemble them for a peace sweet and surely fitting for Christians? For it was he, as we believe, that last year stilled the storm of barbarians and put a stop to the savage Scythians' war by threatening them with something terrible and fearful when they were already seen and close at hand—not with a three-crested helmet or a well-sharpened sword gleaming like the sun, [62] but with the cross of Christ which wards off evil and is all powerful, and for which he also suffered and gained this glory.

---

1. Delivered at Euchaita, a day's journey from Amaseia where Theodore was martyred, probably on the date of the Greek feast, 17 February, and in 376 or some few years before.

2. Cf. Hesiod, *Op.* ll. 45 and 629.

45

Well then, you who serve this pure worship (cf. Jas 1:27) and who love the martyrs, pay attention to me and consider how great a treasure the righteous one is and of what responses he is worthy, I mean on the part of those still in this world and those present with us. Indeed, no one is competent to reckon up the magnificence of those unseen martyrs; yet, you who are acquainted with the fruit of true religion, be eager for a judgment about those who have so been specially honored. And desire the gifts that Christ distributes to his athletes according to their worth. For the time being, if it seems right—since the enjoyment of the good things to come tarries and is stored up for the righteous as a good hope until the time when the judge of our lives comes here—let us turn our sight to the present condition of the saints, how very beautiful and magnificent it is. For the soul that has gone up delights in its own inheritance and lives without a body together with those like it, while the body, its revered and spotless instrument, which never harmed the incorruptibility of its indwelling soul by its own passions, lies with reverence in this holy place, cherished with much honor and worship. It is kept for the time of the new creation like some highly valued treasure, quite incomparable to other bodies. For it was not destroyed by the chance death that happens to all in common, even though it existed in a material nature like the others. Indeed, other bodies of the dead are even disgusting to many, and no one gladly comes to their grave, or, if unexpectedly someone chances upon it uncovered, he runs off after casting his sight on the ugliness of what lies there, filled with entire nausea, and mourning for the burdens of humanity.

But when someone comes to a place like this one where we have assembled this day, where there is a memorial of the righteous one and his holy remains, at first [63] when he sees how God's shrine has been brilliantly adorned by the greatness of the building and the beauty of its decoration, his soul is lifted up by the magnificence of what is seen. There both the carpenter has shaped the wood into the appearances of figures, and the stone mason has polished the flat stones to the smoothness of silver. As well, the painter has colored the flowers of his art, depicting in an image the martyr's valorous deeds—his constancy, his sufferings, the bestial shapes of the tyrants, their insults, that fiery furnace, the most blessed perfection of the athlete, and the figure of the contest's judge, Christ in human form. By artistically working out all these things for us through colors, as though in some book endowed with speech, the artist has clearly told the story of the martyr's contests and has decked the shrine with glory like a meadow in bloom. For even painting, though silent, knows how to speak on a wall and to bring the greatest help. Even the mosaic worker has made the floor we walk on worthy of the story.

Even when someone has delighted his sight by the works of art so perceived, he still longs afterward to draw near to the tomb itself, believing that touching it brings sanctification and blessing. And if someone were to grant him permission to carry away even the dust lying on the surface of the resting place, the soil would be taken as a gift, and the earth would be stored up as a treasure. For to touch the remains themselves, supposing such luck were ever to supply the right—those who have experienced and fulfilled such a desire know how greatly to be desired is this gift of the highest prayer. For those who look at the body as though it were living and flourishing kiss the eyes, the mouth, and the ears, approaching with all the senses; and then, shedding tears of reverence and emotion, they offer supplication to the martyr as though he were in complete health and appearing, asking him to be their ambassador and beseeching him as God's attendant, [64] as the one receiving gifts and, once summoned, bestowing them when he is willing.

From all these things, people of true religion, learn that "precious in the sight of the Lord is the death of his saints" (Ps 115:6). For there is one and the same body of all human beings, constituted from a single batch; but part, simply dead, is cast out as chance has it, while part, graced with the passion of martyrdom, is thus beloved and sweet and unrivaled, as my earlier words have taught. This is why we put our trust in those unseen on the basis of what appears, from what they experienced in this world by the promise of things to come. There are, indeed, many who, by giving first place to the guidance of the belly and vainglory (cf. Phil 3:19) and the trash of all the fine things that come from them, have no regard for what is to come and suppose that everything is finally concluded by the end of life. Yet, whoever you are who think this way, learn about great things from small ones; from the shadows consider the originals. Which of the emperors is given such honor? Which of those who appear high and mighty among humans is glorified by such a memorial? Which of the generals who have captured fortified cities and have enslaved ten thousand nations is so famous in song and story as this soldier—a poor man, newly recruited, whom Paul armed (cf. Eph 6:11–17), whom angels anointed for his contest and Christ crowned when he won the victory (cf. 2 Tim 4:8)? But rather, since I have come near to an account of the martyr's contests, let us leave behind general considerations and give a particular account of the saint. For dear to each person is what is his own.

Well then, the noble man's fatherland was a land toward the emerging sun [65], for he like Job was a wellborn man of the east (cf. Job 1:1–3), and in his outward character he was no different from those who shared his fatherland. But now he is a martyr in the whole world, a fellow citizen for all who dwell beneath the sun. It was when he left his home and enrolled himself as a foot soldier that he came in this way to our land with his own legion, since those in charge had appointed this place as a winter camp for the soldiers. But war suddenly broke out—not because of a barbarian attack, but because of a satanic law and a decree fighting against God; for every Christian was carried off by the ungodly rescript and led to death. Then, indeed then, this thrice-blessed man was well known for his religious devotion, and he was proclaiming faith in Christ everywhere, all but writing his confession on his forehead. He was no longer newly recruited in courage, nor was he unacquainted with war and battle; but he was noble because he had made his soul strong for steadfastness in the face of dangers; he was unyielding; he was without fear; he did not put forth a word without confidence. For when their evil demon took his judgment seat and when the governor and the military commander came together in agreement, just as Herod and Pilate once did (cf. Luke 23:12), they brought the servant of the crucified one to a similar despotic judgment. "Now speak," they said, "where has your boldness and daring come from that you insolently despise the imperial law? [66] Why do you not tremble and bow down before the decrees of the emperors? Why do you not worship as the rulers see fit?" For those in Maximian's circle were then in charge of the empire.

Theodore, with a firm countenance and an undaunted purpose, gave a straight answer to what they had said. "I do not know how to speak of the gods, for that is not truthfully what they are; and you are in error by honoring deceitful demons with the title of god. My God is Christ, God's Only Begotten Son. Therefore, for the sake of true religion and my confession of him, let the torturer wound, and let the flogger lacerate, and let the burner apply the flame, and let whoever is offended by these words of mine cut out my tongue. For in each of its parts my body owes its creator the debt of endurance." The tyrants were overcome by his words and did not endure the first assault of the valiant one, when they saw the young man vigorous for suffering and drawing to himself the end of his life as some kind of sweet drink.

When they held back a little while because they were at a loss and were debating what should be done, at last a certain one of them, a soldier, thinking he was clever and at the same time mocking the martyr's answer, said, "Does your God, Theodore, have a Son? And does he beget with passion like a human being?" Theodore said, "My God did not beget with passion, but I do confess his Son also, and I speak of his begetting in a way suitable to God. But you, childish in thought and wretched, do you not blush, or are you not ashamed when you confess even a female god and worship her as the mother of twelve children, as some kind of demon with many children [67] like rabbits or like those a sow easily conceives and bears?"

Now when the saint in a double way had thus turned the ridicule back upon the idolater, the tyrants, pretending an appearance of kindliness, said, "Let a short time be given to the madman for reflection. Perhaps by restraining himself he may change his opinion for the better." For those who were out of their senses called soundness of mind madness, and religious devotion drunken excitement and frenzy, just as when those who are drunk revile the sober with their own condition. But the devout man, the soldier of Christ, used the respite given him for a courageous deed.

What was that? It is time to recount for you the story with gladness. In the metropolis of Amaseia the fabled mother of the gods had a temple which those who were then in error had built in their vanity somewhere on the banks of the river. This temple, in the safe time granted him, the noble one set on fire and burned up after watching for an opportune time and a favorable breeze, thereby giving in deed the answer that the wicked were certainly waiting for after examining him. Now when what had happened quickly became obvious to everyone—for the fire was kindled with the greatest brightness in the middle of the city—Theodore did not conceal his undertaking, nor was he eager for it to escape notice. Instead, he was discovered both taking great pride in his accomplishment and rejoicing at the confusion with which the atheists were confounded when they were greatly pained because of the temple and its idol. And, of course, it was reported to the rulers that he was the one who had caused the conflagration. Again there was a tribunal, more fearful than the first, as was indeed likely since such a great event provoked it.

And so they ascended the judgment seat, while Theodore with utmost confidence and courageous in the midst of the authorities was interrogated as one standing condemned; [68] and he quickly cut short the interrogation by his confession. Since he was undaunted and paid no attention to any of their terrible threats, they changed to the opposite approach and tried to trip up the righteous one by speaking kindly to him with promises. "Know this," they said, "if you are willing with ready obedience to accept our advice, we shall set you up as distinguished rather than obscure, honored instead of contemptible; and we promise you the dignity of high priest." But when he heard of the dignity of the high priesthood, the thrice-blessed one laughed aloud and said, "For my part I judge even the priests of idols wretched, and I lament them as ministers of a vain practice; but still more do I pity and abominate high priests. For in the case of those who are worse, the one who is greater and ranks first is still more wretched, just as among the unrighteous there is one still more unrighteous, just as among murderers there is one more savage, just as among the licentious there is one more wanton. Therefore, on this reasoning what you offer by your deadly promises already falls to the ground. For you, my opponents, are mistaken in me when you offer the promises of the choicest of evils. But for one who has chosen to live devoutly and rightly 'it is better to be cast down in the house of God than to dwell in the tents of sinners' (Ps 83:11). I also pity these emperors whose lawless law you constantly read clause by clause, because, having imperial power as a sufficient dignity among humans, they have attributed to themselves the title of high priest; and on the basis of that they put on mournful and gloomy purple, carrying about dark clothing for the bright dignity in imitation of the high priests possessed by evil demons. Sometimes when they approach the polluted altar, they become butchers instead of emperors, sacrificing birds and [69] scrutinizing the entrails of wretched cattle and defiling their clothes with bloody gore like some kind of sellers of meat."

After the righteous one had spoken the rulers no longer at all displayed a feigned and formally assumed kindliness, but calling him extremely sacrilegious toward the gods and still insolent and blasphemous to the emperors, they first hanged him up on a wooden beam for torture and tore his body to pieces. But while the people were greatly stirred up, he was strong and unyielding; and in his tortures he sang a verse from the Psalter: "I shall bless the Lord at every time, always his praise will be in my mouth" (Ps 33:2). All the more they tore off pieces of his flesh, but he kept on singing the psalm as though it were someone else undergoing punishment. Prison followed this chastisement. And again wonders were accomplished there because of the saint. At night the sound of a multitude singing was heard, and the light of lamps shining as though in a night vigil were seen by those outside, so that even the jailor, disturbed by the marvelous sight and sound, rushed into the chamber and found nothing but the martyr at rest and the other prisoners sleeping (cf. Acts 12:7; 16:25–28).

Now since with all this happening he flourished all the more in his confession and his religious devotion, the sentence of condemnation came to him; and, commanded to be brought to his end by fire, he departed on his fine and blessed journey to God. But for us he left the memory of his contest as a school, since he gathers peoples together, teaches the church, puts demons to flight, brings down angels of peace, seeks advantages from God on our behalf. He has made this place a hospital for many kinds of diseases, a harbor for those tempest-tossed by afflictions, a thriving storehouse for the poor, [70] a free lodging place for travelers, an unceasing place of assembly for those celebrating festivals. For if we even observe this day by annual festivals, surely there will never be a time when the multitude of those eagerly coming here will stop. The highway leading here bears a resemblance to ants, some approaching, others making way for those who are coming.

For our part, then, blessed one, having concluded a yearly circle by the kindness of our creator, we have gathered for you the festal throng, a sacred assembly of those who love the martyrs. We are worshipping our common Master and accomplishing the memorial for the victory of your contests, while you, here indeed with us wherever you are, are the overseer of the festival. For we are in return summoning you who have summoned us. And whether you are dwelling in the lofty ether, whether you circle some vault of heaven, you worship as a faithful servant, placed and ranked by the Master either in the choruses of angels or with the principalities and powers. You have come here for a short time at the appeal of those who honor you as their unseen friend. Give an account of the rites being accomplished so that you may double thanksgiving to God, who in return for a single passion and a single devout confession has given you such returns, and so that you may rejoice in the blood you shed and the pain of fire. For as many people as you had then as spectators of your punishment, so many are there now as ministers to your priceless honor.[3] We need many services. Be an ambassador on behalf of our fatherland to our common King. For the martyr's fatherland is the place of his suffering; and his fellow citizens, brothers, and kindred are those who have cherished it and who hold and honor it. We suspect there will be afflictions; we expect dangers. The wicked Scythians, who are in the birth pangs of war against us, are not far away. Fight for us as a soldier; as a martyr use your boldness on behalf of your fellow servants. Although you have passed beyond this life, yet you know the sufferings and needs of humanity. Ask for peace, so that these festivals may not cease, so that the raging and lawless barbarian may not break in like a reveler against shrine or altars, so that the profane may not trample down the holy places.

Indeed, even on behalf of those of us who have been kept free from suffering, we count on you [71] for your service, and we ask for safety in the time to come. If there is need for more importunity, bring together the chorus of your brother martyrs and make supplication together with all of them. Let the prayers of many righteous peoples and lands loose sins. Remember Peter, rouse Paul and likewise John the theologian and beloved disciple, so that they may be anxious for the churches they founded (cf. 2 Cor 11:26, 28), for which they bore chains, for which they endured dangers and deaths, lest idolatry should raise its head against us, lest heresies should sprout up like thorns in a vineyard, lest tares should spring up and choke the wheat (cf. Matt 13:7, 25), lest any rock left without the richness of the true water should be against us and show the power of the word's fruitfulness to

---

3. Gregory plays with the words he is using: "punishment" (τιμωρίας) is contrasted with "priceless honor" (τιμῆς).

be without root (cf. Matt 13:5, 20). Yet, you who are regarded with wonder and are more than brilliant, by your power as ambassador and by that of your companions may the commonwealth of Christians be shown thriving among the martyrs, remaining until the end in the rich and fruitful field of faith in Christ, and always bearing the fruit of eternal life in Christ Jesus our Lord, with whom be glory, might, honor to the Father together with the Holy Spirit now and forever and to the ages of ages. Amen.

Gregory, Bishop of Nyssa

IN PRAISE OF STEPHEN, SAINT AND PROTOMARTYR I

(In Sanctum Stephanum I, GNO 10.1)

How beautiful is one good thing following another; how sweet is the succession of gladness. For see, we are receiving a festival from a festival and grace in return for grace. Yesterday the Master of the universe gave us a feast; today, the one who imitated his Master. How did the one or how did the other do this? The former clothed himself with a man for our sake; the latter stripped off a man for the sake of the former. The former came beneath the cave[1] of life for us; the latter came from beneath the cave through the former. The former was wrapped in swaddling clothes for our sake; the latter was stoned for the sake of the former. The former destroyed death; the latter entered it when it was laid low.

Well then, my brothers and sisters, let us also assemble in the theater for a speech [76] telling how the great athlete, stripped for action in the arena of his confession, competed with the evil rival of human life. For truly in accordance with Paul's words Stephen became a spectacle in the theater to the world and angels and mortals (cf. 1 Cor 4:9), the first to put on the crown of martyrdom, the first to make a path as an entrance for the chorus of martyrs, the first to resist sin to the point of shedding blood (Heb 12:4). And it seems to me that for the whole host of those above the world, for all the thousands of angels, both ministering and attending, and—if we should hear anything of those honored in accord with their lot on high as rulers

---

1. σπηλαίου. The reference is to the cave of the nativity in Bethlehem. See Daniélou, L'être et temps, 174.

and powers and thrones and authorities and dominions (cf. Col 1:16; Eph 1:21)—for the entire festal throng in heaven the athlete locked in combat with his opponent was at that time a spectacle.

Indeed, human life is spread out like a kind of arena for contestants, with the two sides attacking each other. From the fall of the first humans until Stephen's times the evil opponent of human life practiced himself in victory against humans, but the great champion of faith[2] judged the assault of his rival as worth nothing. But both had weapons against each other—the inventor of death had the threat of death, while the disciple of life had the confession of faith. Indeed, who would not marvel at this new [77] form of contest, when truth was determined by life and death, and death became the proof of truth? For the herald of the life, hidden till then and unknown, announced to humans by his deed its proclamation, since his willing abandonment of this life proved for those with right judgment that the life more greatly honored had taken the place of the one he abandoned.

Well then, it would be a fine thing to paint in words as though on a canvas an accurate portrait of the combat, so that the list of marvels through the sequence of events could be displayed in its relation to our path. Even now the violent wind from on high, having scattered all the demons' power, aloft and deceitful, has filled the house of the apostles; and the Spirit, distributed like fire to their tongues according to the number of those receiving his grace, has come upon each of them. And already amazement and bewilderment because of the unexpected marvel with respect to the sound and the speech have overtaken those of every nation dwelling in Jerusalem. Though they were all speaking the same tongue at the same time, the tongues had come to the disciples divided into many different kinds of tongues. This was when the power of speech came, not by previous instruction and any study, but by the Spirit's inspiration of the apostles all at once with the sudden rising of his grace (cf. Acts 2:2-5). For it was necessary that those who had destroyed the unity of language at the time when the earthly tower was built (Gen 11:1-10) [78] should come again to unity of language at the time of the spiritual building of the church. For this reason the Holy Spirit's dispensation rightly began his grace from this point, with the result that it distributed the benefit common to humans to every differing human language, lest the preaching of true religion, by being restricted to only a single language, should remain unavailing and ineffective for those of other tongues.

And so, the Pharisees were already both disbelieving their own ears and preparing to overturn utterly those who had been struck with wonder at the miracle, as though it was new wine that had brought about such frenzy

2. That is, Christ, who defeated Satan by his death and resurrection.

(Acts 2:13). On the other hand, Peter by the single compass of a speech had caught in his net three thousand souls for Christ (Acts 2:41); and afterwards the church continually increased its multitude by the addition of those being saved. And the man lame from birth opened once more for those being saved the Beautiful Gate of the temple, where he used to sit (Acts 3:2–10), and led to faith those lame of soul by the miracle of healing he received. Therefore, since a great many were streaming to the preaching of faith, and since need required many more hands to minister to the grace, at that time Stephen, a man great in wisdom and grace (cf. Acts 6:5), was called by the Spirit to assist the apostles. And let no one suppose that because of the name of the diaconate he fell short of apostolic worth, since even Paul knows he is himself a deacon of Christ's mysteries (cf. 1 Cor 4:1); and the Lord of the universe, who through his flesh dispensed [79] human salvation, was not ashamed to be called a deacon, since he said that he was in the midst as one who is a deacon (cf. Luke 22:27), and it is he who activates the varieties of diaconates, as the apostle says (cf. 1 Cor 12:5–6).

Just as fire taking hold of suitable wood lifts its flame aloft and makes its blaze very evident all around, so the Holy Spirit, present in Stephen's noble nature, made the rays of his grace quite conspicuous. Therefore, all, as many as shared in some knowledge and training, looked to him. And group by group those others who thought he was claiming too much, in close formation with one another as though into phalanxes, tried in this way to withstand Stephen's impact. But he was equally unwilling to fight with all of them, even though many, even those inferior, joined forces against him. At this time, therefore, it appeared that the Alexandrians, the Libertines, the Cyrenians, and people from everywhere were banded together against the contestant for truth (cf. Acts 6:9), while what was discerned through this appearance was the father of falsehood (cf. John 8:44) rousing himself by means of human actors against the truth spoken by Stephen. But truth bore the trophy of victory against falsehood, since the valorous one overturned all the champions of deceit. And the deacon [80] of truth was the victim of plots from the enemy of truth who did not manifest what is, but made what is not the truth. "Why do you prepare these things against the herald?" I would speak to the devil. "If you have any power, harm the truth within Stephen. If the power of your devices is so very lofty, why do you keep employing your malice on the vessel of truth, and why do you try to destroy the enclosure and leave behind what is within it, just as dogs do when they take into their mouths the stones thrown at them, but do not touch the one throwing them?" Therefore, since falsehood had been refuted by what is most true, and since it would no longer be possible to find any other champion of deceit when all were gazing at the manifestation of truth, he remembered his own struggle, and after distributing his own activity to the accusers and the judges, and becoming present in both, he led some to speak lies against Stephen and others to accept their slander with anger. And in various ways, by insinuating himself with the Jews, he became everything for Stephen—accuser, judge, people, and the rest of what served death, not realizing by what a fall he would be brought down after such a sentence against Stephen. For just as experienced athletes, by going underneath the body of those with whom they are wrestling, prepare for them a more difficult fall by some kind of artful twisting, [81] so too great Stephen, though fallen to the ground, worked a difficult ruin upon the adversary.

Indeed, it was from this that the course raced by the apostles into the whole world took place; this was the beginning of the word's spreading everywhere. For if the people of the Jews had not raged against the apostles by their bloodthirsty murder of Stephen, the grace of the gospel would probably have been restricted to the inhabitants of Jerusalem alone. But as it is, when they were persecuted by the Jews, they were scattered one to one and one to another of the nations throughout the world, driving the devil out everywhere by their teaching of the mysteries. In this way Samaria received the word (cf. Acts 8:14); in this way the eunuch's salvation took place beside the road from Philip (cf. Acts 8:26–40); in this way that great chosen vessel Paul (cf. Acts 9:15), though fully armed by the devil with anger and threats, turned his arrows against the warrior himself, banishing him from the whole world so that he left no place without a footing for faith in Christ. From then on Egyptians, Syrians, Parthians and Mesopotamians, Galatians, Illyrians, Macedonians—indeed, the word in its course brought nations everywhere to faith. Do you see Stephen's athletic skill, with how many falls the one who wrestled against him was ruined, even though he thought that by slandering Stephen he would be stronger than the one with whom he struggled?

But let us return once more to the arena. What were the words with which [82] the slanderers stirred up the people? Scripture says: "he never stops saying things against this holy place and the law; for we have heard him say that this Jesus of Nazareth will destroy this place and will change the customs that Moses handed on to us" (Acts 6:13–14). Such, then, was the accusation of the devil's spokesmen. What was the folly of those who heard it? Why were they angry with the accused? What wickedness did they discover in what was said? Indeed, the charges they brought forth against him later on came about. For they asserted that he had said that the place would be destroyed and that the customs of Moses would be altered. What, then, was wrong with this whether he told the truth or said what was false? For if what he said was false, the distressful event would not come about, while if he told the truth, why were his words a crime since they predicted the outcome? Surely what was going to be would come about in any case whether people kept silent or not. What correction of distressful things did the murder of the one who predicted them bring? Next, it was Jesus of Nazareth who was accused, but the sentence of punishment was brought against Stephen. Even if, indeed, the one who committed the crime stirred up anger—and the crime concerned changing the place and the customs—since the prosecutor said that these charges did not come from Stephen but from Jesus, the court certainly ought to have been moved against the one actually accused. What an unjust sentence on the part of those who heard this! Since Jesus will change the law, the prosecutor said, let Stephen be stoned to death. [83] But how would Jesus try to destroy the law when he had such an attitude toward the law that he put down so many laws of those of ancient times in order to confirm them? Jesus said, "I did not come to destroy the law, but to fulfill it" (Matt 5:17). He confirmed for his disciples the law forbidding murder by saying there should not even be its beginning in anger (cf. Matt 5:21–22); he cast out adultery together with lust (cf. Matt 5:28); by commanding that whoever first suffered pain should not defend himself he prepared the argument that one should not even give the first blow (cf. Matt 5:39); by commanding us to share our belongings he banished the passion of covetousness (cf. Matt 5:40–42).[3] How is it that these things were neither remembered nor examined in the trial? Would that the council of those bloodthirsty judges were now present with me, and that I could learn what they have to say about the topics that angered them. Where is that far renowned temple? Where is the magnificence of its stones? Where is that gold that almost equaled the rest of the temple's fabric? Where are the sacrifices prescribed by the law, the ram, the calf, the lamb, the heifer, the pigeon, the turtledove, the goat carrying away evil (cf. Lev 16:20–23)? If it was for this reason that they condemned Stephen to death, so that none of those melancholy things would come to fulfillment, let them show how many of them were prevented by their own bloodthirstiness. [84] But if none of these things exist, let them say what it was for that they delivered that sentence, in return for what was the murder?

But let us go on to consider the contests, how Stephen, overwhelmed by showers of stones, defended himself against those bloodthirsty murderers, what were the missiles he sent back against those who were throwing stones as missiles. Let the children of the Jews learn what the Christians' weapons are. By using them to defend himself against those who were injuring him great Stephen has made his deed a law for our way of life. For

---

3. Lendle (*GNO* 10.1:2) instead suggests a comparison with Matt 6:19ff. He also places the question mark here rather than after the sentence introducing the discussion.

those standing in a circle around the saint with a kind of bestial and cruel rage, all of them were throwing stones for one aim, making of everything that came to hand a weapon against Stephen. In contrast, like some priest performing a pure sacrifice according to a spiritual law, not with something else, but offering his own body and sprinkling his blood instead of a drink offering, he gave himself as a propitiation to God, whom he saw in the heavenly sanctuary, on behalf of those in error, repaying their bloodthirstiness with kindness, crying aloud in the hearing of his murderers, "Lord, do not hold this sin against them" (Acts 7:60). By prayer he wiped away from them the sin that the bloodthirsty murderers had guaranteed in writing by their lawless hands. In contrast, they were provoked at his prayer and did not stop throwing stones until great Stephen, as though he were showered with tender blossoms or some sort of light dew, fell into a sweet and most blessed sleep.

Yet it was before the contest that victory came, and we see Stephen crowned before his struggles.[4] For before considering the contest we have been brought to the end of his struggles by the word of scripture. [85] Indeed, I think it was necessary not to pass over speaking about those things by which the martyr's virtue was especially displayed—what the murderers' council was like, and how anger inciting them to murder was stirred up equally in all of them, how great an agreement for evil those convicting him had, what the look of each one was like, how they appeared, what emotion showed in their teeth, just as divine scripture points out, when it says, "they became enraged and ground their teeth at him" (Acts 7:54). Stephen, standing even in the midst of such and so many people and rousing himself in opposition to all the hostile power at work in the bloodthirsty murderers, prevailed throughout all this by the noble nature of his purpose. He resisted anger with forbearance, threats with disdain, the fear of death with contempt for life, hate with love, enmity with beneficence, slander with disclosure of the truth. For it was not in a single way that the contestant for truth was proved a victor; but by resolving himself into various kinds of virtue against every form of evil worked by the Jews at that time, he both combined them all and prevailed over everything. I hear that so also in gymnastic contests those stripped naked in the whole gymnastic arena often have a powerful advantage and carry off the prizes of victory against all their rivals. This was what the first to enter the martyrs' arena was like; having set himself against all the power of the adversary he was proved illustrious by his victory over all. The falsely called wisdom expressed by the Libertines, the Cyrenians, and [86] the wise men of Alexandria wrestled against him; but he prevailed

---

4. "Stephen crowned" is a play on words: Στέφανος, στεφανίτην.

by the true wisdom, struggling against fear by boldness, against threats by disdain, against bitter enmity by beneficence, against falsehood by truth. They were intent upon murder and were already arming their hands with stones, and giving signs of their bitter enmity by looks, hard breathing, and grinding their teeth; but he looked at them as though they were brothers, and greeted them as though they were fathers. For he said, "Brothers and fathers, listen to me" (Acts 7:2).

They fabricated slander persuasively, but for him the council of murderers was a lecture room of truth. He did not cut his speech short, nor was he paralyzed with the expectation of dangers, nor did he regard death; instead, keeping his soul aloft and looking around at all of them at his feet as though they were foolish little children without reason, he taught them by his speech, making use of those of them who had entrusted themselves to his accusers in order to prove that they were in error about his doctrines. In his speech Abraham was introduced, and his story was briefly given attention, then the succession of holy people after him. After this Moses was born, raised, educated, initiated into mysteries on the mountain, striking the Egyptian, saving the Israelite, predicting the mystery with respect to the Lord. This especially stirred up the council and [87] increased their fevered madness, because even Moses, whom they, of course, pretended to take quite seriously, was exhibited as agreeing with Stephen's doctrine. Roused to anger by this, they brought about an end worthy both of their own bitter enmity and of Stephen's longing. For he, having left his nature and before leaving his body, looked with pure eyes at the heavenly gates opened to him and at what appeared within the inner sanctuary, the divine glory itself and the reflection of God's glory (cf. Acts 7:55–56; Heb 1:3). No one can describe in words the exact imprint of the Father's glory, but its reflection in the form that appeared to humans was clearly seen by the athlete, since it appeared so as to be grasped by human nature. Therefore, when Stephen had come to be outside human nature and had been transformed to angelic grace, with the result that he astonished the bloodthirsty murderers when the form of his countenance was changed to the dignity of the angels (cf. Acts 6:15), he both saw what is unseen and proclaimed aloud the grace that appeared to him. But they covered their ears (Acts 7:56) and would not hear his account of the vision, at least doing this of all things rightly. For the ears of the profane were certainly not worthy to receive accounts of a divine manifestation. Stephen, therefore, communicated with those who had attained grace, imparting those visions in his account only to those he thought worthy of them, and saying, "I see the heavens opened and the Son of Man standing at the right hand of God" (Acts 7:56). But, "crying out with a loud shout and covering their ears, they rushed [88] against him all together" (Acts 7:57).

The narrative about him rightly added the shout to their deeds, in order to show the kinship of their free purpose with the Sodomites. For, indeed, the lawless shout of those people was mentioned by the One judging. For it says, "The shout of Sodom and Gomorrah has come up to me" (cf. Gen 18:20–21). Therefore, these people also shouted so that their shout against Stephen would be heard.

Surely the athlete was not unaware that he was being benefited by the bitter enmity of the bloodthirsty murderers. For crowned by the circle around him of those stoning him to death, in this way he accepted what was happening like a crown of victory woven by the hands of his opponents. That is why he defended himself against the bloodthirsty murderers with blessing. He did not think it right that what was done to him should be divided into opposite outcomes, bringing life to him but destruction to his opponents. Instead, he thought it right that even his enemies should not be deprived of being joined with him in asking for good things. Thus, by looking to Christ he knew how to offer himself for those fighting against him. For when he saw the lawgiver of forbearance, he remembered the laws commanding us to love our enemies, to do good to those who hate us, and pray for those who fight against us (cf. Matt 5:44). Yet the athlete was not glorified by human praises. For his aim in being an athlete did not at all look to glory from humans; but after mounting above the whole world by the noble nature of his achievement, he also ran beyond the measures of human power, having cast away behind himself every power to praise him.

Therefore, let him have the victory prizes over every human speech, [89] but let him contend for us by his own story in order to save our souls. For in the case of bodily athletes those who have retired from contests train the young by athletic exercises, teaching them how to escape the holds of their wrestling opponents by some artful twisting. In the same way I think we also must be trained by great Stephen for true religion, so that through him we may avoid the holds of those who fight against the Spirit. To be sure, those enraged against the glory of the Spirit say that Stephen agreed with their outrageous view because "he gazed into heaven and saw the glory of God and Jesus standing at the right hand of God" (Acts 7:55). Therefore, overturning the doctrine of true religion, they say that if the Spirit must certainly be numbered with the Father and the Son, how is it that in his vision Stephen did not see the Spirit also with the Son? How, then, will Stephen stretch out his hand to those tripped up by such words? How will he correct by his skill in contending those who bow the knee to this view? Surely, at once there is help to overthrow the disbelief of someone wrestling with this. Do you ask, you who fight against the Spirit, where the Spirit was when the glory of the Father was seen and the Son was standing at his right hand? If the Spirit were within you, you would not run to one side of the account concerning him that lies before you (cf. Acts 7:55), like blind people who unaware of it pass by the gold lying at their feet. But at any rate listen to me now, at least if your hearing is not impaired like that of the Jews.

How was it that Stephen saw the glory above heaven? Who was it that opened wide for him the gates [90] of the heavens? Was it an achievement of human power? Was it one of the angels who caused that nature lying below to mount up on high? Not so. For the narrative about him does not say in this way that Stephen saw what he saw because he was great in power or because he had been filled with angelic help. What does it say instead? Stephen "filled with the Holy Spirit saw the glory of God and the Only Begotten Son of God" (cf. Acts 7:55). For it is not possible, as the prophet says, for light to be seen unless it is beheld in light; for "in your light," he says, "we shall see light" (Ps 35:10). What is not in light does not admit the sight of light, for how could the sun be in view without its rays? Since, then, the Only Begotten light is beheld in the light of the Father, that is, in the Holy Spirit who proceeds from him, for this reason it was when Stephen was first illuminated by the glory of the Spirit that he apprehended the glory of the Father and the Son. And yet, how shall we say that the Gospel is telling the truth when it says that no one has ever seen God (John 1:18)? How can it be that the apostle does not cry aloud what contradicts the narrative about Stephen, when he says, "neither has any human seen nor can he see God" (cf. 1 Tim 6:16). For if it has been established that the glory of the Father and the Son can be comprehended by human nature and power, whoever declares that the vision of God cannot be comprehended by humans is certainly making a false statement. Nevertheless, it is quite necessary that such a person is not speaking falsely, and also [91] that the narrative about Stephen is telling the truth. The obvious conclusion is that the villainy of those who fight against the Spirit has been detected, because scripture testifies that like is beheld by like. For Stephen did not look at the divine by relying on human nature and power, but it was after being mingled with the grace of the Holy Spirit that he was exalted by him to the contemplation of God. Therefore, if apart from the Spirit it is not possible either to see the Lord Jesus, as the apostle says (cf. 1 Tim 6:16; 1 Cor 12:3), or to contemplate the Father's glory, it has been clearly demonstrated that where the Spirit is, there also the Son is beheld, and the Father's glory is grasped.

Moreover, another weapon, one against the ungodliness of those who fight against Christ, is set before us from what has been narrated. They indeed say that the narrative points out the inferiority of the Only Begotten, for they make the fact that he stands beside the glory of the Father a proof of his being subject to the Father's authority. Let me, then, tell them what

Paul said and what before him the prophet David said, both of whom by the Spirit's instruction describe the glory of the Only Begotten.[5] For David says, "The Lord said to my Lord, sit at my right hand" (Ps 109:1); and the apostle says that the Lord has taken his seat at the right hand of God's throne (cf. Col 3:1; Heb 1:3). If, then, his standing is a sign of inferiority, and if certainly his sitting is a sign of his sameness of honor, then either let them cancel out [92] the magnificent deeds of martyrdom by which the excellence of its dignity is indicated, or let them also accept this dignity reverently.[6] For the Spirit's grace equally taught each of those I have mentioned. For it was when he was filled with the Holy Spirit that Stephen saw what he saw, and gave voice to what he saw. And it was in the Spirit that David called Christ Lord, as the Gospel says (Matt 22:43). And it is in the Spirit that Paul, as he says himself, speaks mysteries (cf. 1 Cor 14:2). If, then, there is one teacher, never contradicting himself, and if the teacher is the Spirit of truth present in those who were inspired, how would anyone suspect any contradiction in his doctrines? But, my opponent says, sitting and standing have different meanings when understood in their obvious sense. And so say I. Nevertheless, what the meaning of the words indicates in the case of bodies is not to be considered apparent in the case of an incorporeal nature. Indeed, in the case of a human being sitting describes the position of the body on its haunches, whenever the straightening of the bended joint that bears on itself the weight of the body does not entirely do its work. And, contrariwise, standing explains the person upright supported by his knees, not resting on his haunches by sitting. But in the case of the transcendent nature sitting and standing are free of such notions, both equally separated from a meaning understood in an obvious way. For we shall not admit either that standing supported by the knee joint [93] belongs to what is incorporeal, or that sitting on the haunches belongs to what is without form or figure. Instead, by both words we have understood in a reverent way stability in every good and immutability in everything. In speaking of the divine as standing and sitting there is no difference conceived between the two expressions because of the distinction of the words, since our doctrine is that the divine has walked without moving, while being seated immutably in the good. And just as the prophet David and the apostle Paul, when each of them describes in his own words the sitting of the Only Begotten, have not given us to understand that the Son is seated while the Father is standing—in fact they mention only the Son's sitting—in the same way in the

5. Lendle (*GNO* 10.1:2) makes this sentence a question.

6. That is, they must either reject Stephen's vision of the standing Lord or accept the verses from David and Paul.

case of Stephen, after hearing that the Son is standing, you would no more reasonably suppose that this implies that the Father was sitting. For as in the case of Paul and David the Father's sitting is also acknowledged because of the Son's sitting at his right hand—even though their accounts taught nothing about the Father explicitly—in the same way also in the case of Stephen the Son's standing is indicated as equivalent to the Father's glory. For the account of the image would thus be preserved, if everything whatsoever conceived and contemplated in the Son [94] were believed to be the same in the archetype. And as good is exactly imprinted in good, and light in light, so too in the Son's sitting—whatever concept this name gives—the Father's sitting is also comprehended; and the Father's standing is comprehended in the Son's standing, lest the account of the image should fall apart, alienated by a deviation from the characteristic properties of the archetype.

Let what I have just been saying by way of a digression from my proposed topic be kept in consideration by us, even though such consideration has entered my speech as additional comments on Stephen's vision. And may it turn out that we have not only become spectators of Stephen's struggle, but also partakers of his grace by being filled with the Holy Spirit for putting down those at law against us and for the glory of our Lord Jesus Christ, to whom be glory and might to the ages of ages. Amen.

Gregory, Bishop of Nyssa

ANOTHER IN PRAISE OF SAINT STEPHEN, THE PROTOMARTYR

(In Sanctum Stephanum II, GNO 10.1)

Christ came into the world for our salvation, and after him the fruits of the church grew up. The martyr of truth shed light, and the martyrs of the great dispensation shed light with him. Traveling in the Lord's footsteps the disciples followed their teacher—those bearing Christ after Christ, the lights of the world after the sun of righteousness (cf. Mal 3:20; Phil 2:15). And the first who blossomed for us was Stephen,[1] not woven from Jewish thorns but offered to the Lord as the first fruit of the church's plenty. For the Jews wove a crown of thorns and put it on the Savior's head (cf. Matt 27:29), displaying fruits worthy of their wicked husbandry to the Lord of the vineyard (cf. Matt 21:33–41), just as the verse of prophecy predicted by saying, "The vineyard of the Lord of hosts is the house of Israel, and the man of Judah his newly planted beloved. I expected it to yield grapes, but it yielded thorns" (Isa 5:7, 2). But the workers of the gospel's truth offer to the Master, as a first prelude of true religion and the first of the first fruits of their husbandry, the holy man Stephen, truly put together out of many and various virtues, quite like a kind of crown. Indeed, at first this amazing man was entrusted with the care of widows, testified to by the apostles' judgment and choice to be a man [98] faithful and filled with the Holy Spirit (Acts 6:5), and then with the power of spiritual wisdom. Indeed, he showed such advocacy for the divine word on behalf of the preaching that great wonders of divine working also

---

1. Throughout the homily there is a play on words that cannot be reproduced in English. "Stephen" (στέφανος) is not only the martyr's name, but also means "crown."

coincided with his teachings. For it says, "Stephen, full of faith and power, did great signs" (cf. Acts 6:7–8). Now he did not think it right that his care for the widows should be any obstacle for him, but he eagerly maintained this and did not abandon the other. He was both greatly admired, and he excelled in painstaking thought. He was entrusted with widows; and he guided souls, feeding some with bread, teaching others with the word, and setting a bodily table for some, while holding a spiritual feast for others. For he was a good man and filled with the Holy Spirit (Acts 6:5). By the goodness of his purpose he undertook the service of the poor, while by his boldness of speech and by the power of the Spirit he stopped the mouths of truth's enemies. At least he resisted all of them, and he struggled with all of them by the word of truth, "destroying arguments and every proud obstacle raised up against the knowledge of God" (2 Cor 10:4–5). He had such great might in speaking that, according to the testimony of holy scripture, no one could "withstand the wisdom of the Spirit with which he spoke" (Acts 6:10). But the herald of truth was brought before the council of unbelief. Indeed, we who have so hurried to the protomartyr's side must render the commemoration owed him, which weakness of body did not permit us to fulfill yesterday. And today we must accomplish their own commemoration for the holy apostles. For, first, the praises of the saints are not limited by days or times, for it says, "The righteous person will be for an eternal memorial" (Ps 111:6). Next, what belongs to our purpose is not divided among them. Accordingly, neither are the martyrs without the apostles, nor again are the apostles apart from them. For the apostles are the teachers of the martyrs, while the martyrs are the images of the apostles. [99] In any case, blessed Stephen, by bearing the cross as the image and exact imprint of the apostles, was also the first to put on the crown of martyrdom by his death. But for all that, through his endurance of martyrdom he extolled his teachers and became truly a crown. For the crown of fine teachers was not an honor for good repute, but it was a success for the church, just as the divine apostle says, "My beloved, joy and crown, stand firm in this way" (cf. Phil 4:1). But let us return to the topic before us.

The Christ-bearer entered the council of the Christ-killers; the sheep rushed into the assembly of wolves. But he was not simply like a sheep caught by wild beasts, but was a sheep shepherded by Christ and one contending with wolves. For they were maddened and goaded with rage, gnashing their teeth at the little flock with accusations and threats, while he tore them in pieces by refutations rather than by threats and accusations, as they did. Let us not pass over what was said simply and superficially. For this Stephen, in the face of such a great assembly of wicked people and in the face of such a great attack of injustice from wolves, was not afraid to speak boldly and

to say, according to that mighty teaching, "You stiff-necked people, uncir-
cumcised in heart and ears, you are forever opposing the Holy Spirit, just
as your fathers, and the rest" (Acts 7:51). In this way he appeared on earth,
while, seeing as in a mirror what is in heaven, he was transformed into the
appearance and form of an angel (cf. Acts 6:15). And there was nothing
unlikely in this; for it was truly fitting [100] that the dignity of the martyrs
should be displayed in the protomartyr, and that all should know thereafter
the works of the new grace. The longing for martyrdom not only bestows
angelic worth, but also opens the gates of the heavens, no longer escorting
souls to death, but commending the spirit into Christ's hands. For the Savior's dominical man called upon his own Father on the cross, when he said,
"Father, into your hands I commend my spirit" (Luke 23:46). And Christ's
servant, Stephen, reaching up to the Master, said, "Lord Jesus, receive my
spirit" (Acts 7:59). With these words he put off his soul. Angels took away
their own devoted follower, hurling him up with praises rather than down
with stones like the Jews. Still, Stephen, after fighting the good fight this way
(cf. 2 Tim 4:7), received a lot in the heavens. And to this Stephen all the precious stones have suddenly been joined (cf. 1 Cor 3:12; 1 Pet 2:5)—the most
divine heralds of the Gospels, after them the martyrs, and after them again
those brilliant with saving virtue, and especially those much remembered at
the present time and who flash forth the radiant beauty of true religion. Of
course, I mean Peter, James, and John, the leaders of apostolic harmony and
the crowns of ecclesiastical fame. For I am not done with the title "Stephen."
Instead, though I have said it often, thousands of times, and since I still
have a thirst for it, I am repeating it. For those who are awaiting the blessed
goal of "crowns" have no surfeit of "Stephen." Therefore, if we must speak as
lovers of truth, we are again feasting on crowns from Stephen, and we are
having fellowship in their commemorations, since we are surely hoping to
have fellowship and [101] to stay here, and since we are joined together in
giving glory. For when profession is steadfast, the fellowship of our faith is
multiplied.

Moreover, my brothers and sisters, we have the enjoyment of good
things because the Lord's day of the resurrection shines together with the
commemoration of the martyrs. For it is especially in this that the light of
Christ's gospel has illuminated our thoughts, because by shining with the
saving rays of righteousness it has obliterated the darkness of ungodliness,
and it has brightened souls with knowledge of the truth. Observe for me
what a marvelous and exceptionally great service it has performed. For this
perceptible sun, rising at dawn and ushering in day as the light of its rays
runs forth, covers and encompasses what is beneath heaven with its gleams;
but at the same time it hides and obscures all the choruses of stars, so that

it alone is seen traversing its vault in the heavens. On the other hand, our Lord Jesus Christ has risen upon us from on high, according to the prophecy spoken of him: "By which the day spring from on high has visited us" (Luke 1:78). Not only did he not hide those who before his coming were saints shining like stars and who became his forerunners, but he also made them brighter and made for himself other luminaries to shine with them. For the prophets spread their light more after his presence than before it. Since prophecy was still obscure in the evangelical interpretations of the scribes, when the Savior came into the world, he illuminated and clarified all of them (cf. Rom 13:10) by becoming the fulfillment of the law and the prophets. For he did not come to destroy the law and the prophets, but to fulfill them (Matt 5:17). And of the new grace concerning himself the Savior says, "I am the light of this world" (John 8:12). When the spring of goodness came forth from the good Father, he did not refuse to share his own title with those who serve him. Instead, he said to his disciples, "You are the light of the world" and "Let your light shine before others" (Matt 5:14, 16). And we shall once more explain by the Lord's grace what is a greater introduction for reminding us of what has been said. John [102] the Baptist was called a lamp both because he was named this ahead of time in the Psalms and because of the Lord's testimony. For the prophet in the person of the Father says of him by the hymn, "I have prepared a lamp for my Christ" (Ps 131:17), that is, "I have prepared a servant and forerunner of the light." And the Lord in confirmation of the Father's words says, "He was a burning lamp" (John 5:35). But, though he was a lamp, he nevertheless was so far from being obscured by the presence of the Lord, who was the sun of righteousness (Mal 3:20), that he spread his light all the more as at once the herald and theologian of the Savior himself when he became the Baptist. John, therefore, was named a lamp because he gave light to one house alone, that of Israel (Matt 5:15). On the other hand, the Savior's apostles were not lamps or beacons or stars; but they were proclaimed as lights (Phil 2:15), shining not in one region or in one corner, but illuminating the whole world beneath heaven. Their leaders and chiefs were Peter, James, and John, who today are venerated for their martyrdoms on behalf of Christ, since they ran in concord to the end of life, while they contested by different forms of martyrdom. For the one appointed first in rank and chief of the apostolic chorus gained a glory appropriate to his worth by being honored with a passion like the Savior's. When nailed to a cross he modeled the Master's image of a king (and I mean by kingly image the cross), unashamed of his passion, but exalted on the great trophy of victory. For may neither he nor we nor those after us nor anyone else "[boast save in the cross][2] of our Lord Jesus Christ," as Paul says (Gal 6:14). In the following way, indeed, Peter is also seen to hold in honor that venerable crucifixion. For because of great godly fear he asked to be hanged head down by those crucifying him, so that he would not seem to be equal to the Savior, who was crucified for all mankind and with hands stretched out, and who encompasses the world with his hands, just as he did with his hands stretched out on the cross. And James's head was cut off [103] when he was urgently pressed to cut off what was really his head, Christ (Acts 12:2). For Christ is the head of a man, according to the apostle, and at the same time head of the entire church (cf. 1 Cor 11:3; Eph 5:23). And blessed John, after struggling in many and various contests throughout his life, and after becoming conspicuous in all the achievements of true religion . . .[3] he was numbered with them, judged to be in the chorus of martyrs. For people determined that he belongs with them, not because the end of his life resulted in his passion, but his martyrdom is judged from his purposeful yearning love. Yet such a kind of death belonged to those who by death bestowed a deathless commemoration also to the churches. But how truly was it fitting to celebrate at the same time the commemorations of the men just mentioned, not only because of their agreement in true religion, but also because of their equally honored worth. For they alone were always fellow students of the Lord, and they had a special place, as it were, compared with the other apostles, as well as a freedom of speech not acquired by human friendship, but by the divine determination of truth.

Therefore, it is possible to discover that at the time of the greatest miracles these men alone were taken by the Lord as the most faithful and most true witnesses of what happened. This is the case with the vision on the mount (cf. Matt 17:1ff.). For only Peter, James, and John were there when the Lord transfigured his own body into a glorious one and transformed it to a brighter divinity. After setting Moses and Elijah beside himself, and overshadowing them with a cloud of light, he revealed that great image of kingship. This is also the case with Jairus's daughter, whom he raised when she was dead. For there, too, he had these men as eyewitnesses of the wonderworking that took place (cf. Mark 5:37). Moreover, lest I spend time speaking about the details one by one, also at the very time of his saving passion he took the same men with him (cf. Matt 26:37), and was not afraid to say to them as faithful and quite steadfast men, "Now my soul is troubled" (John 12:27). We have said these things not to demote the other apostles,

---

2. The manuscripts omit the first part of the citation.

3. The text is corrupt at this point, and Lendle identifies it as a *locus obscurus* with a possible lacuna.

but to testify to the virtue of those mentioned. But if it is necessary [104] to speak as a lover of the truth, my praise is to be shared with the other apostles. For to define superiority and gradations among the saints would not depend on human examination, but on God's determination and truth. And for our part, since we have been deemed worthy of having fellowship with such great men, it is necessary to give thanks, not as much as we ought (for that is impossible), but as much as we can (for that is well accepted). The saints require these honors from us not so that they may profit in any way when they are praised, but so that we may have fellowship with them when we are benefited. Moreover, I think that no devout person is unaware of the fact that we are celebrating the commemorations not only of Peter, James, and John, but also at the same time of the entire concord of the apostles. For if according to the truth of their doctrines it is by preserving the order of their members that they complete the form of a single body, it is obvious that when one member is glorified, as the apostle says, "all the members are glorified with it" (cf. 1 Cor 12:26; Rom 8:17). And this is especially the case for those blessed and most perfect men for whom everything agrees together with truth. Their manner of life has the same purpose; their faith has the same belief; and just as the gains of true religion are common to them, so also their solemn discourses of truth are common. Who would not with good reason be delighted, who would not be filled with the Holy Spirit himself, once he were deemed worthy of having fellowship with the apostolic chorus? It guided the whole world to knowledge of the truth; it spread the nets of true religion throughout the whole world and fixed the traps of truth everywhere, so that by catching together all humanity when it was grown wild by wickedness it might offer it to the One who tames and saves. Therefore, "Their sound has gone out into the whole earth" (Ps 18:5; Rom 10:18). The foundations of the church (cf. Eph 2:20), the pillars and bulwarks of the truth (1 Tim 3:15)—these are the ever-flowing springs of salvation that pour forth the plentiful, rich, and godlike stream of teaching. To these men it is also the prophetic voice that sends us, when it says, "Draw water with joy from the springs of salvation" (Isa 12:3).

Peter is remembered as the head of the apostles, and the other members of the church are glorified with him, and the church of God is strengthened (cf. Luke 22:32). For according to the gift given him from the Lord he is the unbreakable and firmest rock on which the Savior has built the church (Matt 16:17–18). Again, James and John are remembered; and [105] since they were given the title "sons of thunder" by the Savior (Mark 3:17), they carried along with them all the rain-producing clouds. For when thunder breaks out, clouds are necessarily gathered together. Therefore, "clouds" must be taken as the words of the apostles and prophets, which, even if the times of their preaching are different, are nevertheless the laws agreeing with true religion. For the gifts were set in motion for them by one and the same Spirit (cf. 1 Cor 12:4). But what is it to dare undertaking the impossible and try to celebrate the memory of the apostles' virtue as they deserve? We are ambitious to praise Simon, not because he was known for his fishing, but because of his firm faith and as the foundation of the whole church together. Nor, again, do we have a speech for the sons of Zebedee, but for the Boanerges, which means "sons of thunder." Where now will the puny sound of my speech be noticed when such great thunder echoes in everyone's ears? Therefore, striving for this very thing alone, namely to satisfy prudence toward the saints, we are taking refuge in a silence without danger, in full knowledge that in this one thing we are deemed worthy to share in the commemorations of the saints, that is, by imitating and being zealous for their virtues, not publishing their life in words, but preserving their manner of living in our purpose. For what will demonstrate us to be their genuine disciples is not the habit of speechlessness, but devotion with reverence, a life formed in the same school, and a manner of living by the same zeal. Do you honor the memory of the martyrs? Honor also their purpose, for agreement with their purpose is sharing in their memory. Indeed, has the light of the knowledge of the glory of Christ's gospel shone upon them alone (cf. 2 Cor 4:4, 6)? Has grace been sent forth to them alone? The commandments are in common; the manner of life is in common; there is one judge of the contests; there is one prize of truth, of which may all of us be deemed worthy by the prayers and embassies of the saints we have remembered, by the grace of our Lord Jesus Christ, to whom be glory and might to the ages of ages. Amen.

Gregory, Bishop of Nyssa

IN PRAISE OF THE HOLY
FORTY MARTYRS 1a

(In XL Martyres Ia, GNO 10.1)

I guess at what distresses many of you, but for myself I glory in thinking about it. For being pressed together with one another is probably unpleasant for many, but for me this is the chief point of my gladness. Indeed, the shepherd's eye is gladdened when he sees the flock crushed by its multitude and overflowing its fold. And yet the sheep's quarters are not small; but the flock, thriving in its numbers, makes the large space narrow. When Peter saw something like this happening to the Lord, he responded by saying, "Master, the crowds surround you and press in on you" (Luke 8:45). In fact, as the divine apostle somewhere says, this is to be afflicted and not crushed.[1] For he says, "We are afflicted in every way, but not crushed" (2 Cor 4:8). But what speech shall I undertake before such an assembly? Who will give me a voice louder than a trumpet, so that I may shout over the multitude and place my words in the hearing of those assembled? To which of the readings shall I turn my own thoughts and find a suitable speech for those present? Job gives much instruction for a courageous life by his own example; the author of Proverbs, much by riddles. And what would someone say about the holy apostle, who from those ineffable words, which he says are beyond human understanding (cf. 2 Cor 12:4), by [138] what he taught the Ephesians has probably also whispered to us, revealing by riddles the ineffable word found in the cross (cf. Eph 3:18)? And the mysteries[2] from the psalmody are

---

1. στενοχωρεῖσθαι, the same word used above, where the flock *is* crushed.
2. The three expressions that follow are found in the LXX titles of the psalms.

also other such things—"memorial" (Pss 37, 69), "inscription" (Pss 15, 55, 59), and "at a wine press" (Pss 8, 80, 83). For after considering these words in the titles of the psalms we have read aloud, I see no small opportunity given by the riddles for a speech. But it seems to me that to pursue what I have said is suitable to be stored up for a later time. And I want to find some speech suitable to the present gift and appropriate. What, then, is this? I know a certain law of nature inscribed as his own in the divine tablets themselves by the giver of the natural law, who commands us to pay in full every good recompense to our own parents, so far as our ability admits. For it says, "Honor your father and your mother—this is the first commandment with promises, so that it may be well with you" (Eph 6:2–3). If this law takes first place according to its promise,[3] and if successful observance of it becomes the proper gain of the one keeping it—for honoring parents amounts to having kept the law—then it would be right for everyone, at least everyone with sense, to pay attention to this commandment, the end result of which becomes the beneficence and grace of the One who made it. On the one hand, then, our fathers of the flesh, having served in their own generation according to the time determined for them from the beginning, are not in need of our honor, since long ago they departed life. As a result, it is not possible to fulfill such a law, when those meant to receive its benefit do not exist. But still the law does command us to be active in attaining the promise. For it is not at all possible for those who are idle to have the prizes that belong to those who are active. What, then, must someone do if he loves his forebears who are not, as well as the promise, and who lacks the means for exercising this zeal? Surely, what we see solves this difficulty; for when I look at you, I have no need to busy myself with any other fathers. Indeed, you are for me fathers, you who are also fathers of my fathers themselves. For the fatherland of those who have been begotten includes in itself also [139] the dignity of those who have begotten them. What, then, shall I do to fulfill the law of honor for you? For any considerate and affectionate child, when he renews his father's old age by his own care, supports the unsoundness of his weakness, since he has himself become all things to his father. From this it is possible to see the father made young again by his son. And to some degree even the aged and trembling hand rests itself with the strength of youthfulness and enjoys the power of youth; and the movement of the feet, now with bent knees because of the stiffness of the members, becomes active because of the child's diligent care, and is propped up by his support. Even if his sight has grown dim through time, the old man becomes again

---

3. See Exod 20:12: "so that your days may be long in the land that the Lord your God is giving you."

clear-sighted because of the child, since he is led by his hand to the necessities of life. But you all, my fatherland, are not in this condition so as to need any of these things.

What, then, shall I do to enjoy the commandment's blessing? What gift of those that have been bestowed on you shall I bring, when not one of the good things is lacking for you? Would merely describing the fine things present be part of the honor owed you? Therefore, let there be time to speak of these things—in what kind and how many things your life takes pride. Rather, it is possible not to speak of them but to show them; and, indeed, I am showing them. I suppose you think I am speaking of these common and ordinary things—the fertility of the land, the abundance of crops, the river that determines where to dwell. I mean the one that circles the plain, confining its own stream and becoming a lake, the one that both before it forms the lake and after that, cut short for the use of each of the inhabitants, flows through, artfully arranging groves and meadows.[4] And it furnishes those who dwell there with thousands of gifts for every desire, dividing itself from the habitations of the city. Let others speak of these things—those for whom speaking serves their self-importance and for those trained in such matters brings some sort of ambitious display, when the speaking magnifies praise of the fatherland. [140] But let some worldly man and one who knows how to judge the fine things in this life add to the praises, if he chooses, even some other of the rivers. I mean this neighboring river, which because of its size is counted as one of the notable rivers throughout the world. Beginning from our land, it eventually passes by the city, introducing from itself no small gift for the addition both of beauty and of its own assistance for life. Even if I ought to list the city founders, even if I ought to extol the kinds of habitations resulting from colonization, even if I ought to extol some of the achievements gained by the hand of war as told in the narratives concerning us—the trophies of victory, the battles, the wonderful deeds of valor, as many as the servants of the historians have stored up in books—these things are far removed from my choral chant. For a Christian speech is ashamed to curry favor with those who love Christ by praising what is to one side of the faith, just like those who extol the shadow of a valorous man before the trophies of victory. Therefore, let my speech be turned to what is present, and bring to attention for us your profit. And let it be silent about the fine things of the world, even though such a theme for praises in a speech would be lengthy because of the abundance of its topics. For not even the entire heaven, which is surely the most beautiful and greatest of all the things in creation, nor the beams of the luminaries, nor the breadth of the earth,

---

4. Cf. Basil, *Ep.* 14.

nor any other of the things that underlie the universe as elements—none of these does my inspired speech recognize as something great and worthy of admiration. I have been taught by divine command not to compose speeches in admiration of any of the things that perish.

If, then, all of heaven and earth will perish, and the entire form of the world is passing away (1 Cor 7:31), as the apostle says, how would anyone suppose it fitting for us to propose the enduring power of earth and water as an occasion for praises? For even if there is more to be added with respect to your place or to such advantages of land in other places,[5] yet my speech knows how to hurry over them as worth nothing by comparison with yours. Therefore, [141] I turn myself in praises to things more honored in nature. And these will no longer be shown to us by words, but it is possible to see in this the chief of your goods. For who does not know your fruit, that you have produced this prolific sheaf of martyrs, and one amplified beyond three hundred in the abundance of its fruits (cf. Matt 13:8; Mark 4:8)? See this sacred field; from it is the uncut wheat of the martyrs. If you are seeking to learn what I mean by the field, please do not look around far away from what is present. What is the place that includes the assembly? What does the annual recurrence of the cycle mean to you? What sort of stories does the return[6] of this day come bringing to your mind? Are not some of them "speeches," as the prophet says, and "words" (Ps 18:4), the sounds of which are not merely heard, since they describe wonders more forcefully than any word? If you look at the place, it says that it is the arena of the martyrs. If you consider the day, like some loud-voiced herald it proclaims the crown of the martyrs. I think I hear the day shouting these things, because one day prides itself in the creation of the luminaries, another in heaven, but still another glories in the fashioning of the earth. But for me the wonders of the martyrs are enough to outweigh the world. They are enough because they are adorned with the beauty of crowns. They are enough to be extolled by trophies of victory against the devil. What stories have come about in me! What an addition to the angels has come about through me! What a fruit from it has the earth given to God (cf. Ps 84:13)! What a planting has the Lord planted in me! From this almost the entire world, as well, has been planted with offshoots of the branches here, just as some flourishing vine makes other vines through itself and yet remains itself complete. These and such things are those that the day's gift seems to me to proclaim as good news, and the place of assembly is another such gift.

---

5. Following the conjectural emendation of an obscurity in the text.

6. ὑπόμνησις, which could also mean "reminding," "mention."

But what is to become of me in the face of so great a people, since my voice is weak, my tongue is slow, and when I am speaking I am hardly heard by those standing by within earshot because your sound drowns out my speech? Am I to understand that I have delayed speaking about good stories, [142] how the company of the forty had a common contest, and how they procured for themselves a common migration everywhere, and were distributed everywhere, and were welcomed as guests one with another in these places? Therefore, no one who has taken up a partial gift of their remains has failed to receive in its entirety the manifestation of the martyrs. For since all of them became one in the Lord, they make their dwelling through one with the whole of their full number. But how is it that I have not been wrong in my speech by keeping silent about the beginning of the stories about them? What, then, is the beginning? They were a goodly and admired band of youths, all chosen for their noble merit, distinguished for their beauty, nearly equal in stature to young shoots in the bloom of springtime. Do you notice the sound stirred up in the assembly's uproar and the speech interrupted by the sound, so that tempest-tossed by the sound of the people as in some billowing sea, I necessarily take refuge in silence for a calm harbor? If there may be by God's grace a second leisure time for speaking with quiet hearing, what has now been omitted will be completed with the help of God, because to him glory is befitting to the ages of ages. Amen.

Gregory, Bishop of Nyssa

IN PRAISE OF THE HOLY
FORTY MARTYRS 1b

(In XL Martyres Ib, GNO 10.1)

Yesterday the martyrs invited the people to themselves; now of their own accord they are being entertained as guests in the church's lodging. And there is a certain custom for banquets that the guests should give these recurring feasts to each other in turn. Therefore, it is necessary also for me to fulfill my turn in the same custom, by freely giving a meal to the martyrs. But since my fortune of speech is a poor one, it is right for me to welcome with their own leftovers those who were hosts yesterday, but are guests today. For even a small portion from a rich table is enough to become a provision for great feasting, when there are such leftovers. What, then, are these leftovers? You certainly remember at what point I was in my speech when that prayerful and sweet uproar from the multitude of those assembled prevented hearing what was said, when that living sea of the church, in flood tide with the multitude of those pouring in, seethed with the motion of people constantly hard pressed. It even imitated the sound of the real sea, beating with the noise of its waves against our ears as though they were seacoasts. Therefore, when I abandoned my speech, since it was tempest-tossed by the uproar, you certainly remember with what it was concerned for keeping the martyrs in remembrance. And, so I think, this was the logic of the speech: that those chosen for this contest were not any ordinary men, nor was it as some [146] motley and nameless mob, urged on by base pursuits, that they were raised up to this dignity. Instead, first, it was because they excelled the rest in beauty and power and superior strength on account of the natural goodness

76

of their bodies that they were enlisted in the military rolls. But next, it was because they were eminent in their virtuous life and sober conduct that they received, once perfected, the grace of martyrdom as some gift and prize for valor. And assuming that I am quite welcome, let me take up in order all the deeds of the martyrs as though they were holding their contest in the sight of the present theater.

Long ago there was a certain legion of soldiers from every nation[1] camped opposite a nearby city to defend it against the assaults of the barbarians. The faith of the legionaries was all the more earnest because of a certain manifestation from God that had earlier taken place for them. Perhaps it is not untimely to recount in passing one achievement of those men's faith. For once, when they were set at war with the barbarians, when all their resources had previously been captured by their opponents' army, when the supply of water came to be in the enemies' control, they had come to the uttermost danger, whether because of the inexperience of those who are in charge of our affairs or because of some more powerful and more divine dispensation with the special purpose that even by this the difference between Christians and foreigners might appear. When they had nothing to provide for those who were there, and when there was great helplessness because there was no spring or stream of waters to be seen by them in the place, and there was the risk they would stoop beneath the yoke of their enemies, forced to capitulate by thirst, then the noble ones, abandoning the help of weapons, recognized the assistance that is unconquerable and uncontested in fearful circumstances. For, leaving those in the camp that had not yet been admitted to the faith and going off by themselves, they imitated the wonder worked by Elijah the prophet (cf. 1 Kgs 18:41–46), [147] beseeching with a common and combined voice that they would be freed from the helplessness of their misfortune. They prayed, and all at once the prayer became a deed. For while they were still persisting on bended knee, a cloud brought up from somewhere by a violent wind stood aloft above the camp of the warriors. Then, after clashing with extraordinary thunderings and kindling fiery lightnings against those below, the cloud poured down water more plentiful than rivers. The result was that for those on the enemy side both the continuous thunderbolts and the quantity of heavy rain became the cause of utter ruin, while for those standing side by side through prayer it was sufficient for two purposes—for victory over the enemy ranks and for the assuagement of thirst, since the flowing of the torrents furnished them with drink abundantly. And so, our chorus of the army was ranked with the latter; and from those events, both strengthened concerning the

---

1. Or the phrase "from every nation" could modify "city."

faith and respected for similar achievements, they were exalted to such great nobleness of nature that they raised up envy against themselves when news of their virtue got around. Indeed, in what has now been read aloud to us from the story of Job we learned that the rival of human life worked his own injustice on Job's good repute and for this reason demanded his torture because Job, since he was true and righteous and blameless, vexed Satan. In just the same way, the one who fastens himself on good people with his evil eye saw these great contestants and could not bear it when he saw gray-haired customs in youthful years. He saw the bloom of their bodies adorned with continence. He saw them set up as a kind of armed chorus, leading their choral dance to God through the army, beautiful to look at, digni-fied of eye, splendid in thought, swift of feet, mighty in power, harmonious of limbs, in all the advantages belonging to them outshining bodily good fortune with the virtue of their souls. The one who walks up and down the world walked up and down with envy because of them (cf. Job 1:7; 2:2). He saw not a single true man, but a divine company [148] of such men, all true, righteous, and god-fearing. He demanded them, too, for his own purpose. And first of all he became counselor to the commander of the army, who was maddened by idol worship, advising him that he would in no other way prevail in victory against the barbarians unless he sacrificed those who worshipped the name of Christ.

Now when these people were identified as quickly as possible by their good confession and came of their own accord to perfection through suf-fering, the enemy demanded that they be led immediately to death by the sword, as though that were something humane; but after binding them with iron chains he made that the beginning of their punishment. But for them, as one might expect, the chain was an ornament and a sight elegant and sweet for the eyes of Christians. Such a numerous distinguished band of youths, conspicuous for its nobility, in stature above the others—all of them at the same time were joined together with one another by the chain, like some crown or necklace having pearls of equal size distributed in a circle. Such were the saints, both united in faith and bound together with one an-other by the chains. Since they were all beautiful individually, they became an additional beauty for one another. Just as happens in the case of heavenly wonders, when by a clear night sky the grace of the stars is diversely embel-lished when each star brings its own radiance into the common ornament of heaven, such was the sight of the saints; it was really just as Ezekiel the prophet somewhere says, "a vision of torches collected together" (Ezek 1:13). Speech is fond of dwelling upon the beauty of the bloom of youth, for it knows, as Wisdom says, that "fom the greatness and beauty of created things the beauty in secret is also reckoned" (cf. Wis 13:5), since the soul's purity also shone through what appeared, and the human being that appeared was the worthy dwelling place of what was unseen. How beautiful, then, was the sight for those who saw it at that time, beautiful I mean to those willing to look at beautiful things, [149] beautiful to the angels, beautiful to the powers that transcend the world, but bitter to the demons and as many as welcome what belongs to the demons. The martyrs were human beings, if at least those who stood so high by their greatness of nature were such; they were Christ's soldiers, the Holy Spirit's armed men, faith's champions, the divine city's towers. They mocked every punishment meted out by tortures, every swelling up of fear, every threatening assault, as though they were some childish folly. It was as though they gave over to tortures not their bodies, but the shadows of their bodies. Though in the flesh, they wrestled against the flesh; and despising all the fearsome acts of the tyrants by their contempt for death, they were displayed as people far above human limits. How nobly did they practice for bodily trophies of victory! How nobly did they transfer their experience of warfare to the line of battle against the devil, not arming their hands with a sword nor holding a wooden shield in front of them nor protecting themselves with a bronze helmet and greaves. Instead, they put on the whole armor of God, which the church's general, the divine apostle, describes—the shield, the breastplate, the helmet, and the sword (cf. Eph 6:11–17); in this way they advanced against the opposing power. Heavenly grace was their general, while the devil, who has the power of death (Heb 2:14), was drawing up his battle line. And the place of their battle line was the court of bloodthirsty men. Standing together in it they contended, one group hurling threats as missiles, the other warding them off by endurance.

The first proposal was from the opponents—forswear faith in the Lord or pay the penalty of death. The answer from the heroes was that they would remain steadfast to death in their word. They were threatened with fire, the sword, the pit, and whatever other instruments of torture could be named. In response to all this a single voice was heard, as Christ was confessed by the mouths of the saints. This was a blow to the opponents; they held it forth against [150] the enemy as a spear; by this sound the adversary was wounded in the midst of his heart. This is the stone thrown from the sling in David's hand that struck the helmet of his adversary (1 Kgdms 17:49).[2] For the confession of Christ becomes the noble soldier's sling; the enemy falls, and his head is cut off. But my speech, after disobeying its reins, is carried to one side of its course and leaps above the mountains. It makes a daring attack on what cannot be spoken and goes on to speak, as though it

2. The LXX refers to the helmet.

had become a spectator seeing what is unseen. This is because in response to such a voice confessing Christ with bold speech there was applause and praise from above—acclamation from the citizens of the heavenly city who applauded the achievement, and joy from the entire festal throng in heaven. For it was as though a theater for the angels was set up at that time in the world of humans (cf. 1 Cor 4:9). The spectators of our life saw what sort of binding together there was of the devil and human beings, and how this opposition had its formation in the first wrestling match, when the serpent overthrew Adam. At that time the man did not bear up under a single attack of the evil one, an attack introduced by something good in appearance and enticing to him; but he both fell at once and was overthrown by his fall. But for these martyrs all the wrestling tricks of the enemy were fruitless and ineffective. He held out hopes; but they trampled them under their feet. He threatened them with fearful things, but they laughed. Only one thing was fearful to them—to be parted from Christ; the one good thing was to be with Christ alone. Everything else was a joke and a shadow and nonsense and the fantasies of dreams. This is why my speech is making a daring attack on what cannot be seen and is declaring that the entire power of those transcending the world glories in the achievement of the athletes. Still my speech is emboldened to attack what should not be dared; still it dares to describe things above the world, because the righteous judge of the contest has held forth the crowns for the victory of those men who succeeded here in their struggle with the enemies, and because the chief general has prepared for the victors the prizes of divine power, and because [151] the Holy Spirit has welcomed them with manifold gifts. For when faith in the Trinity is confessed, for this reason grace has also in turn been measured out for them from the Trinity. What was the grace? The very fact that they were proved to be loftier than the first contestants, I mean Adam and Eve. They were the ones who through sin brought down human nature when it was standing; these men, when it was lying with the fall of those who first received it, raised it up again by their endurance. The former were driven out of paradise into the earth; the latter from there have found again their dwelling in paradise. The former armed death by themselves, for it says that sin is death's weapon (cf. 1 Cor 15:56; Rom 6:13); the latter by their own courage disabled death which was armed with sin, blunting the point of the goad by enduring sufferings, so as to say rightly, "Where, death, is your goad; where, hell, is your victory?" (1 Cor 15:55). What is more wretched than the fruit of a tree? What cheaper than a tree? A fruit, tinged on the surface with a good appearance and a sweet taste, caused the grace of paradise to be dishonored.

For these great contestants not even the sun itself appeared sweet; rather they were willing to be deprived even of it in order not to fall away from the true light. What does the word say about Eve? For I am carrying on even beyond what is necessary in my pursuit of our first parents. "She saw," it says, "that it was pleasing to the eyes and ripe for taste" (Gen 3:6). Then they exchanged paradise for the gift in these things. And, as it seems, what is seen is endowed with a pleasant taste in these things—heaven, the sun, the earth, humans, the fatherland, mothers, brothers, friends, kinfolk, comrades. Which of these is sweeter to be seen? Which is more prized to go and taste? You know, children, affection for your parents. You know, parents, your disposition toward your children. You know, you who look at it, the sweetness in the sun. You are not unaware, you who love your brother, of your natural relationship with brotherhood. You understand, young man, the gift of comrades, [152] how much they make life pleasant for you. But for those martyrs all of this was hated, all foreign to them. There was only one good thing, Christ; they denied everything so that they might gain him (cf. Phil 3:7–11). They spent no small time in chains, and their desire for perfection ripened for the saints because of the punishment's delay. And just as those who exercise their bodily condition, when they acquire sufficient strength from their training, emboldened in this way go forth to the contests, in the same way these men, too, sufficiently trained for true religion by their chains and by prison, were brought forth to the crown of their contests. My speech in due course has come to its conclusion, or rather to the summit of the entire noble achievement. This was the critical moment; these were the days of the contest; this was the prelude to the Passover, the mystery of the holy period of forty days. We have forty days of propitiation, the same number as the crowns for the contests. Do I somehow seem to you superfluous and speaking idly when I recount your own wonders among you and greet your hearing with your own affairs? So that, however, my speech may not pass over you if you are not initiated,[3] I shall hurry along to the end of the contests for the saints. There was frost that day. Certainly, you do not need to learn anything about what frost is like, since you can guess at that from the present day; frost has slipped through even the very walls. You know it in its excess, both you who are strangers to these places and you who are native to them, and so have no need to learn about it by being told. Well, let someone else speak of the wonders worked by your winters, how the ever-flowing rivers stand still when ice resists their stream and petrifies their waves. The nearby lake lacks any signs to show that it is a lake, since it has been made into dry land by the ice; those who wish are accustomed to ride their horses on it above its waves. I know that water is often contrived

---

3. The reference appears to be to baptism, though we could translate instead "if you are not accomplished" or "if you are imperfect."

by the local inhabitants through the use of fire, when, by breaking off a lump of ice as though it were some kind of bronze or iron and by melting it, they make what was hard as stone water. Such was the moment at the time of the combat, [153] when the evil one seized from the north winds an unnatural intensity of cold, as we can hear from those who described the wonders.

When, then, after brilliantly preaching the Lord's name in public and after already displaying themselves crowned by such a public proclamation, they went forth to their perfection through death, this was the kind of combat devised for them. The tyrant's decree was that they should be punished by freezing. Alas for the weakness of both my words and thoughts; how far short does my speech fall of what the story deserves—the decree of death, the freezing, the punishment, and the expectation of such a chastisement. And the blessed band of youths seized upon the place of their punishment with laughter and amusement and cheerfulness. The racecourse of the athletes was one that led to suffering; the racecourse was both sacred and intense, and the competition was to carry off the crown in return for their confession. They had the same zeal for victory. No one was seen lagging behind in eagerness, but all of them with one accord, seized this place which was then reserved for public bathing. And as though they were about to cleanse their bodies thoroughly by washing, they readily took off the covering of their tunics, all of them quoting Job's words, "Naked we came into the world, naked we shall go to the One who brought us here. We brought nothing into the world, nor ought we to take anything out of it. But rather, though we came into it naked, we shall leave it filled with the treasures from our good confession" (cf. Job 1:21; 1 Tim 6:7). Saying this and emboldening themselves with such words, they gave their bodies to the ice. The nature of the elements was subdued by the ice, while the nature of the martyrs was unsubdued, or rather, their proper nature suffered and admitted painful torments, while the nobility of the athletes struggled even against nature itself. Indeed, their power was dissolved little by little, since it was quenched and consumed by the ice, while the intensity of their souls became greater. [154] Their bodily bloom of youth was darkened, and its beauty faded, and the healthy complexion of their flesh withered. Their fingers fell off, gradually cut off by the freezing, and all their limbs and senses were pounded to pieces by the bitter cold. For their flesh, discolored little by little, swollen, and torn from their limbs, fell away from their bones and admitted feelings of deadness in their sensation. And so death, gradually advancing upon them, was delayed, protracted for three days. For, while sensation held out for them for such a long time, they remained steadfast in the rank to which they had been posted from the beginning, becoming in all respects victors over the opponent.

But who may recount for me in its true worth their circumstances? What speech will describe that divine procession, when their holy bodies were led in triumph to the fire on wagons, how instead of being stolen by the devil the jailor was led into our number by grace? Who will tell me the story of that mother, the worthy root of a martyr? Her son was left behind by the public executioner because he was still breathing, and for that reason was not put up on the wagon with the others. When she saw the humane act of the public executioner toward the hero, she did not put up with the insult. Instead, she reviled him because he had separated the athlete from his fellow contestants. And she stood beside the martyr, who was already numb and motionless because of the ice; and she saw him hard pressed by cold and weak breathing, only alive so much as to feel his pains, looking up at his mother with a wasting glance, beckoning and encouraging her with a dead and enervated hand, exhorting her to bear up nobly. When his mother saw these things, what were her feeling as a mother? Was she inwardly disturbed, or did she tear her garments, or did she embrace her child, comforting the dying man with her warm arms? Far from it. Even to say such a thing is absurd. In truth, it is from its fruit [155] that we know the tree; a bad tree cannot bear good fruit (cf. Matt 7:16–18). Since, then, the fruit of martyrdom is good, I have been praising the mother who bore the best child and who was "saved through childbearing," as the apostle says (1 Tim 2:15). Indeed, when she presented such a fruit to God, she gave an account of herself above the common nature of women. "You," she said, "are not my child, not the offspring of my birth pangs. By receiving God you were begotten according to God. You have received power to become the child of God (cf. John 1:12–13). Hurry to your Father lest you be left behind your comrades, lest you come in second place to your crown, lest you make your mother's prayer ineffectual. You will not grieve your mother when you are crowned and a victor and the bearer of victory's trophy." When she had said this and braced herself above nature, or rather was braced by the Spirit, she put him away from herself into the covered chariot[4] with the rest, marching before the bright countenance of the athlete. What happened next? The saints contended in the air; they sanctified the fire, becoming fuel for the flame by adding themselves to it. They also brought a blessing upon the water. By all this the divine oracles were fulfilled, the ones spoken when the three children included cold and heat in their common hymn of praise,

---

4. λαμπήνην. This may be simply another word for the wagon (or wagons); cf. Num 7:3, ἁμάξας λαμπηνικὰς. The word is also the synonym for one meaning a four-wheeled wagon or any car or chariot. It is tempting to see the change of word as a hint that the victims are really the victors, now carried in the triumphal chariot rather than in the wagons that carried the captives in the triumph.

cold because of the ice, heat because of the burning (cf. Dan 3:66–67). And so, "they went through fire and water" (Ps 65:12).

But my speech wishes to pass over these things as well known, and to examine for a moment now something about the topics for inquiry mentioned earlier. When humanity was banished from paradise, a sword flaming and turning was assigned to guard the entrance (Gen 3:24). The reason for such a precaution on the part of God was to prevent humanity from approaching the tree of life, making use of it and remaining immortal. You certainly remember my inquiry, and you probably remember what I found as an answer to my question. Yet if I were intending to go back over everything from the beginning and treat the entire account, [156] the extended discussion would go beyond the time available. The question, then, was this: if paradise cannot be entered even by the saints because of the turning sword, and if the athletes are excluded from paradise, what promise is there then for which they submitted to contests for true religion, and will they have less than the thief to whom the Lord said, "Today you will be with me in paradise" (Luke 23:43)? Even though, of course, the thief did not come to the cross willingly, nevertheless, when he was near the Savior, the keen and good-natured thief saw the treasure, and, seizing the opportunity, rightly won life by his thievish art; and he successfully used it to the full, when he said, "Lord, remember me in your kingdom" (Luke 23:42). With that he is deemed worthy of paradise, but in the case of the saints does the flaming sword still bar the entrance? Surely, the problem has an immediate solution. For because of this story the word has demonstrated that the sword does not always stand in the face of those trying to enter; but God made it "turning" so that it might appear in front for those unworthy, but might be turned back for the worthy, opening for them an unhindered entrance into life. Those martyrs came to be within life by the boldness of their contests after passing through the flame without feeling it. May we, too, come to be within paradise after passing through it unafraid, strengthened by their embassy for the good confession of our Lord Jesus Christ, to whom be glory to the ages of ages. Amen.

Gregory, Bishop of Nyssa

A SPEECH IN PRAISE OF THE FORTY MARTYRS DELIVERED IN THE MARTYRION

(In XL Martyres II, GNO 10.1)

According to ancestral law and the ancient custom which children received from their forbears and continue to observe to the present time, the soldiers of the Romans equip themselves with full armor at the beginning of the present month and go to some plain sufficiently broad and level, where it is possible to spread out a race course for horses and to practice drilling and be trained in every martial exercise. They make a memorial of the year and observe the day as special. But for my part, in celebrating the memory of the martyrs, yesterday I proclaimed it to you and armed through memory Christ's soldiers, the forty, who excelled all eagerness in their contests. Today for those able to see I put them before you as marvelous, the ornament of the church, the delight of the people, and the glory of God who strengthened them. It is in every way best and quite profitable for youths to be brought up and men to flourish by stories of virtue. For hearing is the most vital of the senses and is no less instructive than sight. Indeed, through the ears it introduces learning to souls; and there is no small risk in encountering good or bad stories. For whatever is said must bring a comparable impression to the thoughts, and the conception and consideration held together in the mind leads a person to a desire to do what is thought. Therefore, [160] prepare to hear me calmly and attentively, so that the blessed martyrs may be honored with what is fitting and so that you may be taught devotion and the love of God by their memory.

A double contest lies before me, and I am afraid that I may abuse the theme by the weakness of my exposition. For one thing, if someone were to consider the magnificence of the very subject at hand, it would carry off the prizes of victory against every speech. For another, suppose he were to consider the one who before me has crowned the saints by his own wisdom—a man admired throughout the whole world, an exact model of learning both that among Christians and that of those outside, an image of philosophy, a type for bishops and a challenge[1] for them, a teacher who harmonized deeds and words, one who had an unassailable good repute with everyone, unless it were with those for whom even Christ is the object of blasphemy. For just as no one denies that the sun gives light and heat, so no one will deny that the great Basil was adorned with all the beauty of virtue. Exalted, then, he praised those who were exalted; a saint, he was the servant of saints because in accordance with his own power he completed the prize for those who gained it by their valor. But I must not be silent for this reason, seeing that my predecessor has greatly proclaimed the marvelous deeds of the martyrs. For my aim now is not rivalry with the one who spoke before me, but a concern for what will profit you who hear me. Each person is certainly of use as far as possible by enjoying the greater things furnished him by those richer than he.

Now the forty soldiers obtained as their rank in life serving in the army for the emperor of the Romans, but they were Christians in their faith and devout in their worship. And when the ruler at that time, since he was one of the polytheists (the demons proposing to him that bitter purpose), persecuted the Christians with a new law and decree, he commanded all his subjects either to make a sacrifice of incense to the demons, or if they failed to do this, to be condemned to death and before their end to endure many mutilations in their entire body. Then, indeed then, the blessed ones made the tyrant's savagery and the God-hating law their own courage. Breaking away from the other soldiers and organizing a separate company, one based on the love of Christ and with the power of the Spirit as their general, they openly drew themselves up in opposition to the foul decrees. And [161] all of them in harmony, as though from a single tongue, proclaimed aloud our faith, saying that they cared little for this transient life and would allow their bodies to be handed over to various kinds of torture. Therefore, when the officer, more tyrannical than the violent law, found out that the saints had set up a company in opposition, he hastened to devise a punishment for

---

1. κίνδυνος.

their zeal, since he supposed that it was a strange and unexpected cowardice for stubborn souls. "If I should threaten them with the sword," he said, "it would be a small fear to strike terror in them; and they would by no means submit. For they are men who have lived with weapons from their childhood and are accustomed to bear steel. If I apply tortures to them, they will hold out nobly, since they are not without experience of blows and wounds. Nor would fire be fearful to men as stubbornly disposed as these are. Therefore, it is right for a punishment to be found that will cause painful suffering, and for a long time and prolonged." What, then, did this wise deviser of evils decide with deliberation against the saints? After careful thought he found a perilous trial in the open air, one that the time and place supplied to him ready at hand. For the time was winter; and the place, Armenia, the neighboring place which, as you know, has harsh winters. It does not even furnish its inhabitants with the hot season of summer, but is barely warmed enough to raise wheat. The planting of vines has not been known among them, and whoever has not traveled far away has no knowledge of grapes. He would ask about a bunch of grapes the way we would about what is grown among the Indians. In Armenia the sower ploughs the earth while there is snow, and falling snow overtakes the harvest. The winds strip the reaper's clothes off unless he struggles against the force of the winds by binding himself up tightly with clothes. Autumn and spring scarcely exist, since they are swept away by their evil neighbor, winter, to its domination.

Therefore, in that place and in the present month the officer, after stripping the saints of their clothing, placed them with completely naked bodies in the open air, taking a vengeance on the disciples of true religion quite opposite to that of the king of the Assyrians and the Babylonian furnace (cf. Dan 3). Freezing congealing to ice and wasting with numbness was nothing like painful burning fire. For by its harshness fire has the property of leading quickly to death, while freezing, though it has [162] an equivalent pain, prolongs the end. Indeed, the sufferings caused by cold are in general slower to work, like quartan fevers, cancers, carbuncles, and whatever physicians investigating the subject have declared produce cold matter in bodies. Thus, those who are too cold or fat and too sluggish also have a body hard to manage, as is likewise the case with irrational animals. Some of them, because they are warmer, are swift and easily moved to urgent need, while others, in the opposite condition, are slow and bound fast by torpor. Thus, a swift horse is urged down the racecourse by whistling rather than by a whip; the ass is slow and scarcely completes its journey by being beaten by clubs. The leopard is quick, flying through the valleys with a dry and warm body; in contrast the bear plods along slowly with thicker limbs. I have given you this natural instruction not pointlessly, but so that you may understand the steadfastness of the men by considering the kind of punishment they endured. Winter makes the navigable rivers paths to be walked on, and it changes flowing water to the hardness of stones. It even breaks up rocks when it reaches its depth. And it has an equally damaging effect on the bodily substances it opposes, turning soft ones to stone and breaking up hard ones. Thus, wine, when frozen, is shaped to the jar that contains it; and soft olive oil is set hard, fashioned to the form of its vessel. Glass and earthenware, bursting by the fluids, are broken in pieces. As for the animals allotted a life on the mountains and in the open air, some perish, while others escape the worst of the evil and of the savage weather. Indeed, the deer and the antelope take shelter in enclosed spaces, neither then fearing hunters nor fleeing from them when they approach. For what is more to be feared always drives out cowardice in the face of lesser fears. And the birds enter the houses of human beings and stay beneath their roofs. People quarry for drinking water and cut the water off with stone-masons' tools; neighbors do not associate with one another. Such a season became the tyrant's weapon against the martyrs. For it was necessary, as was likely, that the great and harmonious company of blessed ones should enter a contest with a novel mode of punishment, so that they might acquire a glory for true religion surpassing that of many of the martyrs. Therefore, they took their stand and were frozen, [163] trembling in their limbs and unshaken in their purpose, offering a spectacle in their contest for angels, humans, and demons (cf. 1 Cor 4:9). The angels were waiting for the separation of their souls so that they might receive them and take them up to their own allotted place. Humans were waiting to see the end, testing the power of the nature common to theirs to see whether on account of the fear and expectation of what was going to happen we[2] would be strong enough to overcome such great sufferings. The demons paid extremely close attention to what was happening, since they were eager to see the fall of the athletes and a cowardly denial in the face of the perilous trials. But their hope was put to shame because of God who strengthened the martyrs. For they looked at the mutilations, both each one at his own and all of them at one another's. One lay with his foot or fingers broken off; another lay with his natural warmth completely chilled. Just as the strongest winds blowing at a wooded place then shake the tops of the trees and bring them down to the ground root and branch, so the company of blessed ones was laid low from the winter weather. They were a noble planting, the ornament of paradise, the roots of our sprouting, Paul's soldiers, Christ's bodyguards, those who broke up altars, those who

---

2. The idea appears to be that the human bystanders, including Gregory and his audience, are measuring themselves against the martyrs. Would "we" be able to imitate the martyrs in their endurance of suffering?

built churches. They were enrolled to make war on the barbarians, and they completed their contest against the common enemy of humanity.

Death came to them not by force and unavoidable necessity, but salvation was both more ready and in command provided they were unwilling to show weakness in their steadfastness. For there was a bath near at hand which was by design adjacent to the place of punishment. Its door was open, and those who stood by were summoning them. For since the tyrant was clever in persecuting and in various kinds of deceit, he put nearby an enticement to escape for the frozen comrades; and he advised them to desert for healing, just as his father enticed the first formed humans to taste [164] of the tree. But then they even more intensified their courage, since they knew that steadfastness submits to testing at a time when it tries to refrain from an advantage placed before it with permission. This is what in earlier times Daniel, divinely inspired, is shown to have done (cf. Dan 1:8–16). For when he was summoned to partake of abundant and sweet food and drink, by hating and turning away from things sacrificed to idols he was contented with a vegetarian diet. Even though he was fasting, he flourished; and though he abstained from food in contrast to those who fared sumptuously, he was in good condition. For this is the special gift of God, to bestow what is beyond hope to his faithful servants in their difficulties.

Since, however, grudging feelings for what they had done had fastened upon the lofty ones, there was a risk that the blessed company would be mutilated; and we all but lost the full number of the forty. For one of them, after renouncing the completion of his victory because of the icy cold on him—alas—left his fellow soldiers. Because of the tyrant's craftiness he went to the bath when his flesh was already wasting away, spared because he loved his own life. In fact he was deprived of his hope and did not gain the life that passes away, since he died the moment he transgressed. He was the wretched Judas among the martyrs, neither a disciple nor a wealthy man, but one dragged, indeed, to the hangman's noose. Let no one be surprised. For this sort of villainy against those who submit to him is habitual to the devil. He uses deceit and flattery in various ways to overthrow someone; and when he has overthrown him, he tramples upon him and derides him lying there. Boasting, he adds shame to misfortune and delights in the shame of the one enticed. This is also why the psalmist used the expression "enemy and avenger" (Ps 8:3), indicating by the contradictory words the untrustworthy character of the devil's behavior. For he never becomes a person's ally and friend, but he then pretends to be [165] friendly whenever he wishes to put on a mask of deceit toward him. But the one who helps our weakness and is the husbandman of good things, both words and deeds, found, as was the case with Abraham (cf. Gen 22), a sheep for himself as a fitting sacrifice, one from among the enemies, a confessor from the blasphemers and a martyr from the company of persecutors. For one of the servants of tyranny was deemed worthy of a vision of angels, who came to the martyrs. He was illuminated by the manifestation of the holy spirits just as Paul once was by Christ's glory when he was traveling to Damascus (cf. Acts 9). Immediately he changed his purpose, and after stripping himself of clothing he was included with the frozen comrades. All this happened together in a brief moment of time—the convert, the confessor, the martyr, washed with the water of rebirth (cf. Titus 3:5) in his own blood, a blood deadened and not flowing. He was a man crowned as victor, a man worthy of the whole. By him I have forty for the church of God; by this noble man the company of martyrs was not mutilated. Because of the convert we are celebrating a complete festival with a complete number. And the devil experienced an event that returned his favor and one worthy of laughter. For since he stole a soldier, he was robbed of a persecutor and servant.

Then, what happened after this? The thrice blessed ones arrived at the place toward which they were hastening. But the lord of the punishment, refusing to put up with or tolerate the victory of the martyrs, made war against their dead bodies. He commanded these dwelling places of the holy souls to be handed over to fire, and in one deed he imitated wild beasts and vindictive men. For beasts tear to pieces the clothing thrown to them by people pursued in flight, while men set on fire and destroy the houses of their enemies after they have left. One of the martyrs might justly have said to him, "No longer, you fool, do I fear your savagery. For I was afraid, as long as our souls were present in our frozen bodies, that [166] excessive torture would conquer the courage of the devout. But now that this fear has passed, use the clay that remains as you wish. Even if you taste our flesh, I do not care. For as much as you display your raging savagery, so much the more do you display victory for the crowns of those who have gone away. For the genuine assaults of those arrayed against us are sure proofs of the courage of those who have prevailed."

Yet why do I spend more time? The bodies were burned, and the fire received them. We divided those ashes and the remains of the furnace, and almost the whole earth is blessed by these holy relics. Even I have a portion of the gift; and I have deposited the bodies of my forbears beside the relics of the soldiers, so that at the time of the resurrection they may be raised with helpers speaking with the boldest freedom. For I know how strong they are, and I have seen clear proofs of their bold freedom with God (cf. 1 John 3:21). Indeed, I want to speak about a single one of the wonders accomplished by their activity. Neighboring the village that belongs to me where the relics of these thrice blessed ones have been laid to rest there is a small town they call Ibora.[3] Now since in this place according to the customary rule for the Romans a list of soldiers was drawn up, a certain one of the armed foot soldiers came to the village already mentioned. He had been assigned by the company commander to guard the district, in order to restrain his own fellow soldiers' attacks and outrages, the ones which armed foot soldiers were accustomed to inflict by their arrogance on the country dwellers. This man was lame in one of his feet and limped. His affliction was chronic and hard to heal. When he entered the martyrs' shrine and the saints' resting place, after praying to God he also implored the saints to be his ambassadors. At night a certain distinguished man appeared to him, and after he had spoken of certain other things, said, "Are you limping, soldier, and do you need [167] healing? But allow me to touch your foot." The dream he had received drew his close attention. And since the vision at night had this effect, it actually became such a noise as happens when a bone slips out of its natural joint and then is forcefully put back in joint. As a result, it woke up those who were sleeping with him, as well as the soldier himself. The man immediately got up and began to walk in a sound way according to nature, as he used to do. For myself, I saw this wonder, since I happened to be near the man himself as he told the good news to everyone, proclaimed the good deed of the martyrs, and praised the kindness of his fellow soldiers.

Now if it is necessary to add something of events that concern me in particular, I shall tell about it. For when we were about to celebrate the first festival for the relics and to lay the urn to rest in its sacred burial place, my mother—for she was the one assembling and organizing the festival for God—ordered me to come and share in the rites, even though I was living far away, was still a youth, and numbered among the laity. Such was her fondness for hurrying things along that, even though I was quite busy, I thoughtlessly accepted her invitation, despite secretly blaming my mother because she would not put off the festival to another time but had removed me from many responsibilities and dragged me to the festival even one day before the assembly. I came to the place; and while there was a vigil in the garden where the relics of the saints happened to be honored by the singing of psalms, a dream appeared to me while I was sleeping in some nearby chamber. This was the vision. I thought I wanted to enter the garden where the vigil was actually being celebrated. But a crowd of soldiers keeping watch at the entrance appeared to me when I came to the door. At once standing up, brandishing rods, and looking at me in a threatening way, they all refused to permit me entrance. I would have received blows had not one

3. See SC 178:39, n. 1: "Ce panégyrique . . . nous fait connaître qu'à cette date [383], trois ans après le décès de Macrine et l'élection de Pierre au siège de Sébastée, le village où a vécu Macrine [Annisa] appartient à Grégoire." See *Life of Macrina* 34.15–16.

of them who was more kindly, as I thought, interceded for me. Now when the dream left me and I came to a reconsideration of the faulty way I had accepted the invitation, [168] I perceived the point of the fearful vision of the soldiers; and with many lamentations I bewailed my own vanity. I shed bitter tears on the very cask of the relics, so that God would be kindly disposed toward me and the holy soldiers would grant me amnesty.

I have told this so that we may be persuaded that the martyrs are alive and are God's guards and attendants, those who today have benefited and adorned our church. Brighter and greater, this fortieth day keeps the memory of the forty martyrs; and the month is more brilliant than other months. Harsh winter no longer seems difficult to me, nor do I make complaints against the savagery of the present time. For this time, though it has become a weapon of banishment, has consecrated for me the sacred company. Consider the mother of the seven Maccabees (2 Macc 7). Because she kept her soul loving God rather than loving the flesh, she neither blamed the savagery of Antiochus, the tyrant of Syria, nor was unable to endure the tortures and unhappy fates of her sons. She accepted her destitution as a benefit and the loss of her children as help. Nor, indeed, did Stephen, when he was stoned, suppose that he was harmed, but rather that he was made alive (Acts 7). In the same way I also owe thanks to those who fight against God because of a good outcome. Despite themselves they have stood as causes of so many good things, even if they worked with the aim not of benefactors but of enemies. For even enemies unintentionally give benefits no less honorable than genuine friends. The devil helped Job more than he hurt him (Job 1). The king of the Assyrians became Daniel's benefactor (Dan 2). And let the three boys in the furnace give thanks (Dan 3). Let Isaiah sawn asunder (cf. Heb 11:37) hymn the Hebrews. Let Zechariah [169] slaughtered between the sanctuary and the altar (Matt 23:35) honor his murderers. Let John whose head was cut off (Matt 14) proclaim Herod his benefactor—and the apostles, those who bound and beat them. Let all the martyrs love their persecutors, for unless they had opened the arena, the athletes would not have made a public display of their courage. What would someone most admire about the men placed before us for our praise? Their great number or their courage or their concord free from deceit? Let me not pass over without feeling or thanks, chiefly, their number. For whoever has so many ambassadors would never leave prayer and supplication without success, even if he were quite heavily weighed down with sins. Even God in his conversation with Abraham is a witness of this thought and hope. When he accepted Abraham's supplication for the Sodomites, it was not forty righteous persons but ten that he required for sparing the city that was about to be destroyed (Gen 18:32). But as for us, according to the apostle, "since we have so great a cloud of martyrs surrounding us" (Heb 12:1), let us bless ourselves, rejoicing in hope, persevering in prayer (Rom 12:12), sharing in the memorials of the saints. For the forty martyrs are strong defenders against our enemies and faithful advocates of our prayer to the Master. With hope in them let the Christian take courage against the devil when he contrives temptations, against evil people who rise up against us, against tyrants seething with anger, against the sea when it becomes wild, against the earth when it does not bear what it is ordered to produce for humans, against heaven when it threatens disasters. For the power of these martyrs is sufficient for every need and circumstance, since it has received rich grace from Christ, to whom all glory is befitting to the ages of ages. Amen.

An Address of Gregory, Bishop of Nyssa

IN REGARD TO THOSE FALLEN ASLEEP

(De Mortuis, GNO 9)

[28] Those who treat the necessary consequence of our nature in those who depart from life as a disaster and mourn deeply for those who are changed from this life to one spiritual and incorporeal do not seem to me to have examined what our life is, but to have the experience of many who through some irrational habit love their present life as good for them whatever it may be like. At any rate, it is at least proper that what has been assigned to rule over the irrational nature by reason and understanding should have an inclination only to what is declared by the judgment of reason to be good and to be chosen, and that what appears sweet and desirable to them because of some habit and an uncritical passionate emotion should certainly not be chosen. And so I think it right by attempting to think this through to remove them from their disposition toward what is habitual and to lead them as far as possible to a better understanding and one fitting for people who have considered the matter. For in this way there may be excluded [29] from human life the irrationality eagerly pursued by many with respect to the passions. May an eagerness for reason be what accompanies us in the subject that lies before us. First, the quality of what is truly good must be examined, and then we may consider what properly belongs to life in the body. And in addition to these considerations what is stored up for us by hope may by comparison be contrasted with what is present. For in this way our consideration may proceed by reference to the aim of reason, so as to change the opinion of the many from common usage to

a good understanding. Indeed, since some natural relation to the good is innate in all humans, and every free choice is moved toward this, proposing to itself aiming at the good of every pursuit in life, because of this it is a mistaken judgment concerning what is really good that customarily causes many mistakes to be made, so that if what is truly good were at least obvious to all, we would never make a mistake about that one in whom goodness is nature, nor would we willingly be constrained by the experience of evils, at least if circumstances did not make use of some falsified illusion of the good. Therefore, first of all let us consider by reason what the truly good is, lest by error concerning this the worse should ever be pursued instead of the better. Therefore, I say that something must be presupposed by reason as a kind of definition and characterization of what is sought, by which an understanding of the good may be convincing to us.

Therefore, what is the characteristic mark of true goodness? It is not only to have a usefulness in relation to something, or at certain moments, or [30] to appear now helpful, now useless, or to be good for one person but not such to another. Rather, it possesses what is good both of itself according to its own nature, and likewise for everyone and at all times. This is, at least in my judgment, the characteristic mark of the good, one without error or deceit. For what is good neither to all, nor at all times, nor of itself apart from outward circumstance would not be judged properly to belong to the nature of the good. Because many without examination have been attentive to what exists in the elements of this world, they have imagined that they are the good; in none of them would one find by careful examination any good of itself and always and for everyone. For there has been mixed with the usefulness of each one of these also the opposite activity. For example, water preserves health for those nourished by it, but it destroys those on dry land if it should become a flood. Likewise air preserves those who have been born by nature to live in it, but for those allotted a life in water it is found ruinous and destructive when any one of those living under water comes to be in it. So too fire, though useful to us in some respects, is ruinous in more ways; and one would find the sun itself neither to everyone nor always nor in all respects good for those exposed to it. For there are times when it even becomes quite harmful, becoming hotter than its due measure, and by its excessive heat drying up what lies beneath it, often producing the causes of disease and afflicting those whose eyes are weak with disease and generating by the pollution of waters harmful and nauseating effects by the corrupted putrefaction of the waters. Therefore, as has been said, of all things only one must be chosen as good, [31] what is seen always and likewise by all to be in the nature of the good, always existing as such and unchanged with respect to outward circumstances. For concerning the rest, as many as seem

good to humans by some quite irrational presupposition—and I mean what
concerns the body and externals such as strength and beauty, distinguished
birth, property and ruling offices, distinctions, and all such things—I think
it necessary to omit them from discussion, since what they are is plain to all
of themselves and they need not be introduced in vain as an obstacle to my
argument from matters agreed upon. For who does not know that beauty
and power are short-lived, or that ruling offices are easily overthrown,
or that reputation has no substance, or that the passionate attachment to
property of people who consider the good to be in certain kinds of material
things because of their fine appearance or rarity is vain. Concerning the
present life—and I mean the one actualized through the flesh—it should be
examined whether such a thing should be considered as in the characteristic
mark of the good or in some other condition. Indeed, what is found about
the present life by reason will certainly guide the understanding of what has
been passed in review so as to include how it is necessary to consider the
passage from this life.

Therefore, the life of our body is actualized in two ways, both by filling
and by emptying, in one way by food and drink, in another way by drawing
in and expelling breath, without which life according to the flesh would
not have the capacity to sustain its nature. For when the succession of these
opposites no longer crowds into the nature, then the human being ceases
to live. [32] Indeed, after this such activity completely stops, since there is
nothing from outside that either flows in or goes out in those who have died,
but the body is divided and dissolved into the kindred elements from which
it was composed. Thereafter the nature is quiescent through its stillness,
because it has caused what in it is akin and of the same kind to rest on its
own element, earthy to earth, what is proper to it to air, what belongs to it
to water, and what corresponds to it to heat. For the mass of the body, composed forcibly of heterogeneous parts and woven together by constraint, no
longer exists but has gone away to its own home, distributed according to
the power of each of the parts in us. Because of this the nature that forcibly
holds together in itself the growing together of different kinds puts a stop to
its activity. And if someone were to compare both sleeping and waking in
the form of this life with what has been said, he would give an account not
to one side of the truth. For it is also by these that our nature toils, always
being drawn to opposites, now relaxed by sleep and again stretched tight
through waking, by both of which there is furnished what corresponds to
emptying and filling. If, therefore, both filling and emptying are the specific
property of our life, it would be right to reexamine what was said earlier
about the character of judgment concerning the good, now with respect to
the specific properties of life, so as to discern whether this life is the true

good or even something contrary to it. Because, then, filling by itself would not likely be judged to be in the nature of the good, [33] it is obvious to all that such is the case because of the fact that its opposite as well (and I mean emptying) might be supposed to be good. Of course, in the case of things that have been opposed to one another as contraries it is impossible to apply an account of the good equally to the things that are opposed, but if the former were good according to its own nature, its opposite would certainly be evil. But surely here nature has something useful equally from each of them. It seems that neither filling nor emptying has the possibility of receiving the definition of the good. Therefore, filling has been demonstrated to be something other than the good. For it has been admitted on the part of all that such a thing is to be chosen neither by everyone nor at all times nor in every form. For not only does the fact that surfeit comes to be among harmful things make filling destructive, but also, because when what is useful slips into appropriate things in excess, it often becomes the cause of dangers and destruction. And if, even when the condition of fullness was seeking an emptying, some other fullness were to overload the one existing, such a case would be a piling up of evils leading to incurable suffering. Therefore, filling is something good neither for everyone, nor in all ways, but it becomes useful in relation to something, at some time, and according to the quantity and quality that comes from it. And in this way one may also find an understanding of the opposite (I mean what has to do with emptying). Emptying is dangerous to those who submit to it if what is useful exceeds its limit; and it becomes not without profit once more, if it corresponds with what belongs to beneficial things—time, quantity, quality taken together for the usefulness of emptying. Therefore, since the form of this life by which we live does not correspond to the characteristic mark of the good, [34] it may be admitted as a consequence of what has been said that removal from such a life is a separation from nothing good. For it is plain that what is truly, properly, and first of all good is neither emptying nor filling, which have been demonstrated to be useful at some time, in relation to something, and for some people; the characteristic mark of what is truly good is not found in these.

Since, therefore, the truly good is opposed to what is not truly good, and since the opposition of these two is without a middle term, what would follow with respect to the separation from what is not truly good to what is good by nature is the belief that the removal from this life becomes something good always, for everyone, and in all respects, and is neither good at certain moments, nor in relation to something, nor for some people, nor because of something, but is always in the same and like condition. Therefore, with regard to this the human soul leaves fleshly life, taking some other condition of life instead of the present one, which is impossible for those still mingled with flesh to see accurately. But by taking away things recognized in this life, it is possible to adopt some guess by analogy. For the soul will no longer be implicated in bodily thickness or living its life by the equal rule of forces arrayed against one another. The equally balanced struggle of them with one another is what makes our constitution and health (for it is the excess [35] of one of the opposites and the deficiency of the other that becomes the suffering and sickness of our nature). In the soul nothing is contracted when emptied or distressed when burdened, but it even becomes in every respect outside the unpleasant aspects of the atmosphere (I mean cold and heat). It is delivered from everything understood in relation to opposition, and it comes to be in those conditions where life is free and released from all constraining toils. There it does not suffer distress by farming; it does not endure toils at sea; it is not busy with commerce and trade, with building houses and weaving, and it is separated from the misery of handicraft arts. It leads some "quiet and peaceable life," as Paul says (1 Tim 2:2), not fighting on horseback, not fighting on ships, not bound closely ranked in a battle line of infantry, not busied with the preparation of weapons, not gathering tributes, not digging ditches and building walls. Instead the soul is something exempt from and free from all such things, neither having nor producing business. There is no place in the soul for slavery and lordship, poverty and wealth, noble and ignoble birth, private lowliness and dignified ruling power, and all such irregular diversity. For that life,[1] since it lacks nothing and is immaterial, detaches itself from the necessity of all these things and such others; in it what maintains the substance of the soul is not partaking of anything dry and moist, but the apprehension of the divine nature. And instead of the spirit that blows through the air [36] we do not doubt that there is a sharing in the true and Holy Spirit. The enjoyment of these does not change in a way similar to this life through acquisition and deprivation; the soul does not admit and reject things, but it is always filled and never limits its fullness by satiety. For spiritual bounty is not burdensome and is always unsatisfied, overflowing insatiably with the desires of those who share it. Because of this that life is something blessed and undefiled, since it no longer wanders about in the pleasures of the senses for its judgment of the good. What, then, is sorrowful in the fact because of which we look gloomily at the removal of our provisions? Unless, of course, anyone should consider it grievous that their removal is to a life without suffering and untroubled, a life which does not introduce the pains of blows, does

---

1. ζωῆς. In the next sentence "this life" translates βίου. Sometimes the two words do refer, respectively, to the next life and to this one, but Gregory often appears to use them as synonymns.

not frighten with the threat of fire, does not have wounds made by the sword, does not have the disasters of earthquakes, shipwrecks, and captivities, does not have the assaults of carnivorous wild beasts, does not have the stings and bites of creeping things and poisonous ones, a life in which no one is either heaped up with luxury or trampled down in humiliation; where no one is either made savage by rashness or frightened by cowardice; no one either swells in anger blazing into wrath and raving madness or is driven to confusion by fear since he is unable to resist the impetuousness of the ruler who has no consideration. Such is the case of certain laws codified as customary by emperors. For example, in this way those appointed over the magistrates issue such tax lists [37] for how much the annual tribute should be, but take no account of whether there has been too much rain, flooding by its excess the land being farmed, or whether hail has rendered useless the hopes of those who work the land, or whether drought has overpowered and dried up everything sown. Moreover, that life has entire freedom from fear of the rest of the evils of earthly life. For sorrow of being an orphan does not grieve that life; the evils of widowhood have no place; the many forms of bodily sickness lie idle; envies against those who prosper and contempt against those who are unlucky and all such things are banished from that life, while a certain equality of speech and rights in all peaceful freedom is made the common citizenship for the assembly of souls, since each person has what he has prepared for himself by free choice. But if something worse instead of something better were to have been prepared for anyone because of some thoughtlessness, death would not be responsible for such things apart from the power of free choice to elect what seems good. For what reason, then, are those who lament someone departed unhappy? Surely even if the one who has divested himself of both pleasure and pain together with the body has not in all respects become pure of every passionate disposition, that person who mourns would more justly lament those who go about, who have the same experience as those who spend their life in prison, whom their habitual exposure to gloomy things and their familiarity with darkness make them suppose that the present life is gentle and free of pain. [38] Perhaps those people also look darkly upon those cast out of prison because of their ignorance of the brilliance awaiting those delivered from darkness. For if they had known the sights in the open sky—the beauty of the sky and the heavenly height, the rays of the luminaries, the chorus of stars, the cycles of the sun, the course of the moon, the earth's springtime and its diverse produce, the sweet sight of the sea in the bright rays of the sun rippling elegantly because of a gentle wind, the beauty of the private and public buildings in the cities, through which the splendors and great riches of the cities are adorned—if, then, those who have been shut up in prison had known these and such things, they would not have loudly bewailed those leaving confinement as though they were departing from some good. And so what those outside the prison likely thought about those still confined, namely, that they were enduring hardship in a piteous life, this seems to me what those leaving the prison of this life would suppose, if it were at all possible for them to show by tears their compassion for those in distress, to lament and weep for those being tortured by the pains of this life, because they do not see what is above the world and its immaterial beauties, the thrones, rulers, powers, dominions (Col 1:16), the hosts of angels, [39] the church of the holy ones, the city on high, and the festival gathering above heaven of those enrolled (cf. Heb 12:22–24). For the beauty of these things, placed above, which the word that cannot lie declares those pure in heart see (Matt 5:8), is better than every hope and higher than any likeness one could guess. This by itself would be thought not to deserve our lamentation and grief for those departing from us, apart from the fact that since such great suffering besets this life, such a great disposition for wretched things has stood in people's way that they do not bear their onset as some enforced service, but make them the object of their zeal so that they may remain forever. For the desire for positions of power, for the objects of greed, and for these appetites that bring advantage, and if there is any other such thing pursued because of which there are weapons and wars and mutual slaughters, and all that misery and deceit willingly bring about—all this is nothing else than a kind of piling up of disasters introduced into life from free choice exercised eagerly and willingly. But there is no passion of tears in the departed because there is no passion of any kind; and the mind and spirit, when they happen to be delivered from flesh and blood, do not have a nature to be seen by those buried in the thickness of the body, nor to admonish by themselves people to depart from their erroneous judgment about existing things. Therefore, let our own mind discuss the matter in their place, and let us speak as though it were possible to be outside bodies by thought and to separate our soul from its passionate attachment to matter:

·[40]² "My friend and everyone who shares my nature, 'pay attention to yourself,' according to Moses' instruction (Deut 15:9), and know yourself accurately as who you are, by having separated in reasoning what you truly are from what is seen of you superficially. May you never suppose that when you look at what is outside you, you are seeing yourself. Learn from great Paul, who examined our nature accurately. He says that we have an outer self and an inner one, and that when the former wastes away, the latter is renewed (cf. 2 Cor 4:16). Therefore, when you look at what is wasting away,

---

2. Note that this "speech" does not conclude until p. 44 of the *GNO* text.

you should not think you are looking at yourself. (For that will at some time be free of corruption, when in the regeneration what is mortal and dissolved is changed to what is immortal and indissoluble, when what now is in flux falls away, when our outward appearance perishes [cf. 1 Cor 15:42, 53–54].) Therefore, it is necessary not to look at this outer self, because it does not concern us to see anything else of what is looked at, since Paul speaks as follows, 'We look not at what can be seen, but at what cannot be seen; for what can be seen is temporary, but what cannot be seen is eternal' (2 Cor 4:18). Instead, having turned our contemplation to the invisible aspect of what is within us, believing what we truly are escapes understanding by sense perception.

"Therefore, let us become, as the saying in Proverbs puts it, 'knowers of ourselves' (Prov 13:10). For knowing oneself becomes a cleansing of transgressions committed by ignorance. But it is not easy to see oneself clearly, at least if one wishes to see what is truly himself, unless some power of thought makes what is impossible for us possible. For what [41] nature has done in the case of bodily eyes, which while looking at everything else remain without sight of themselves, in the same way the soul also searches through all other things, busies itself with and tracks down what is outside itself, but is not in a condition to see itself. Therefore, let the soul imitate what happens in the case of the eyes. Indeed, even they, since they do not have by nature the power to contemplate themselves, by turning around the power of sight and by seeing themselves clearly in a mirror (cf. 2 Cor 3:18; Wis 7:26), gazing at the form and fashion of their own pupil, they see themselves clearly by an image. In this way the soul as well must look away to its own image, and what it sees in the characteristic mark to which it has been likened is to be gazed at as proper to its own self. But it is fitting to alter the example in some small way so that my thought may be appropriate to my words. For in the case of the outward form in the mirror, the image is fashioned according to its archetype, but in the case of the soul's characteristic mark we have understood the contrary. For the form of the soul is imaged according to divine beauty. Therefore, when the soul looks at its own archetype, then it sees itself clearly and accurately.

"What, therefore, is the divine to which the soul has been likened? Not a body, not a shape, not a form, not size, not a surface, not weight, not place, not time, not any other such thing—nothing by which the material creation is recognized. Instead, when all these and such concepts are taken away, it is certainly necessary to understand what remains as something intelligible, immaterial, impalpable, incorporeal, without intervals of time and space. If, therefore, such a characteristic mark of the archetype is accepted, it would certainly follow that, since it has been shaped according to that form, [42]

the soul is recognized by the same characteristic marks, so that it too is immaterial, invisible, intelligible, and incorporeal.

"Therefore, let us consider when human nature draws closer to the
archetypal beauty, in living by the flesh or when we come to be outside this.
But the kind of answer to be given is obvious to everyone, because just as
the flesh, since it is material, belongs to this material life, so too the soul
partakes of intelligible and immaterial life at the time when it shakes off
the matter that surrounds it. What, then, in these considerations is worth
calling a disaster? For if the body were the truly good, we would need to
have a hard time putting up with the estrangement of the flesh, since when
we fall away from the body, the flesh is certainly lost with the body and its
relationship to the good. But since the good that is above every conception,
in whose image we came to be, is intelligible and incorporeal, it would follow that we must be persuaded that when by death we pass over to what is
incorporeal, we draw near to that nature which has been separated from
all bodily thickness, and that when we strip off our fleshly robe like some
ugly mask, we ascend to our proper beauty by which we were shaped in the
beginning when we were made according to the image of the archetype.
Such an understanding would be by what has been said a basis for joy rather
than sorrow, because by having accomplished this enforced service a person
would no longer live in an abnormal condition when he gave back to each
of the elements the particularity that was contributed from them, and when
he returned to the pure and incorporeal home proper to him and according
to nature. For the material of the body is really something alien and foreign
to incorporeal nature. [43] When the mind is by necessity combined with
bodily material in this life, it endures persistent hardship, since it is living in
a foreign life. For sharing in the combination of elements with one another
is something forced and discordant, since each is drawn by its own nature
to what is proper to it, just as some persons with different languages and
alienated by their customs make up a single assembly out of different races.
Since it is uncompounded and exists in a single and uniform nature, the
mind when mixed with bodily things lives in alien and foreign conditions,
being unlike the assembly from the elements that surrounds it. When by
some necessity it is sown in the body with its many parts, the mind con-
strains its own nature, since it is united with foreign elements. And when
the elements with their dissolution from one another are naturally drawn
away to what is kindred and proper to them, sense perception is necessarily distressed when what has grown together with it is dissolved and cut
off; and the soul's thinking, inclined by habit to what harms it, is distressed
together with sense perception. At that time, then, the mind ceases being
vexed and distressed, when it comes to be outside the battle established by

the joining of opposite elements. For since either cold becomes less when heat prevails, or contrariwise heat flees the abundance of cold, and since the moist withdraws from the prevalence of the dry or the compactness of the dry is dissolved by the abundance of the moist, it is at the time when this war within us is destroyed by death that the mind maintains peace, having left [44] the disputed frontier of the battle, I mean the body, and coming to be outside the battle lines drawn up by the elements against one another, then it lives by itself, taking up by rest its own strength which had toiled in its intertwining with the body."

Therefore, these and such things are what my mind discusses with those who are living in the body, all but saying aloud, "My friends, you do not know accurately the situation in which you find yourselves, and you do not yet understand what it is to which you will go away." Indeed, my speech has not yet been able to discover what the present is like by nature, but it looks only at what is customary in living, since it is unable to know what the body's nature is, what the power of the senses, what the arrangement of its organic members, what the dispensation of its inner parts, what the self-moved operation of the sinews is, how of what is in us part is hardened to the nature of bone, part is given substance for the luminous ray of the eye, how from the same food and the same drink part is made thin with hairs, while part is made flat for nails at the tips of the fingers, or how the heat in the heart carried through the arteries to the entire body is kindled, or how what is drunk, since it comes to be in the liver, changes both its form and its quality when it is spontaneously turned into blood by some alteration. Knowledge of all these things is up to the present time incapable of being expressed, so that we are ignorant of the life in which we are living. And those who live together with sense perception are completely unable to contemplate life separated from sense perception. For how would anyone see by sense perception what is outside sense perception? Therefore, since both lives alike are unknown, this one because it is only at what appears [45] that we look, and that one because sense perception does not attain it, why have you suffered, my friends, by clinging to this one as though it were good even though it is unknown and by fearing and shuddering at that one as though it were hard to bear and worth fearing for no other reason than this alone, that it is not known of what sort it is? And yet we do not fear many other things that are manifest to us by sense perception and yet are unknown. For what the nature of the objects that appear in heaven is, or what turns the movement of their orbits around in opposite directions, or what supports the solidity of the earth, and how the flowing nature of waters always comes from the earth and yet the earth is not used up, and many other such things—these we neither know nor judge our ignorance worthy of fears. But as for the nature that itself surpasses thought in every respect, the nature that is divine, blessed, and incomprehensible—we have come to believe that it exists, and not yet has any understanding based on guessing been found by which its existence is comprehended. Nevertheless, we love what is unknown with all our heart and soul and strength (Deut 6:5), even though it cannot be comprehended by reasonings. Why, therefore, only in the case of the life awaiting us after this life[3] is this irrational fear established only because of our ignorance? We have come to fear what we do not know, just as happens with children who are frightened by suspicions without foundation. For whoever wishes to look at the truth of existing things first engages in deliberation about the matter, then takes account of what it is like in its nature, whether it is something good and agreeable or difficult and to be avoided. [46] How would anyone with sense judge that what is completely unseen and unknown is hard to bear simply by suspecting its departure from what is usual as though it were the assault of some fire or wild beast? And yet we are taught by life wisely not always to look at what is customary, but always to change our desires toward the good. For life for those being fashioned in embryo is not for all time, but as long as they are still in the inner parts nature makes life in the womb sweet and appropriate for them. Nor when they come forth do they remain for all time at the breast, but only as long as such a thing is good and appropriate for the immaturity of their age. After this they change to another stage of life, persuaded in no way by habit to remain at the breast. Then after the condition of infancy there are other suitable ways of life for youths, and still others for the succeeding stages of life to which the human being successively changes, altering without grief his habit in accord with his stage of life. Therefore, suppose that there were some voice addressed to the embryo being nourished in its mother's womb, and that it vexed the embryo with its banishment from the inner parts by birth, and cried aloud that it would suffer terrible things once dragged away from its agreeable way of life. (This indeed is what the infant implies at its first breath when it sheds tears at the same time as its birth, as though it were vexed and lamenting its separation from its accustomed life.) In just the same way those who are displeased by the change from the present life seem to me to experience the suffering of embryos by wanting to live their lives at all times in the place of this material odiousness. [47] For since the birth pangs of death serve as the midwife assisting the birth of humans to another life, when they go forth to that light and draw in the pure Spirit, they know by experience what a great difference there is between that life and the present one, while those left behind in this moist and flabby life,

3. Here Gregory uses βίου of the life to come, ζωήν of this life.

since they are simply embryos and not humans, call the person departing before them from the affliction that surrounds us unhappy, as though he were leaving some good. They do not know that just as for the newborn infant, an eye is opened for him when he leaves what now afflicts him. (And it is, of course, necessary to think of the soul's eye by which it sees clearly the truth of existing things.) And the sense of hearing is opened through which he hears "words that are not to be told, that no mortal is permitted to repeat," as the apostle says (2 Cor 12:4). And the mouth is opened and draws in the pure and immaterial Spirit, by which he is stretched up to the spiritual voice and the true word when he is joined with the sound of those celebrating in the chorus of the saints. Thus he is also made worthy of the divine taste, by which he recognizes according to the psalm "that the Lord is good" (Ps 33:9).[4] And by the activity of smell he grasps the fragrance of Christ (cf. 2 Cor 2:14). And the soul receives the power of touch, touching the truth and handling the Word, according to John's testimony (1 John 1:1). Therefore, if these and such things are stored up for humans after the birth through death, what is the purpose of grief, sorrow, and dejection? Now let whoever sets his sight on the nature of concrete realities give us an answer as to whether [48] he thinks that being led quite astray by the bodily senses concerning judgment of the good is more to be preferred than looking at the very truth of concrete realities with the soul's bared eye. For here a certain necessity is placed upon the soul to make it serve a foreign judgment in its opinion concerning the good. For since the perfect power of the soul is still not contained in the infantile body, while the operation of the senses is born immediately perfect together with the baby, because of this reasoning in judging of the good is prejudged by sense perception, and what already appears to the senses is also supposed to be good. And the soul accepts what has been prejudged by custom without testing it, persuaded that what sense perception by its prejudgment testifies is good, beholding the good in certain colors and flavors and such futilities. Since these things no longer manifest themselves after the departure from the body, it is entirely necessary that there should appear to the soul the truly good to which by nature it has been adapted. For neither will the sight of this eye, since it will no longer exist, be snared by what is beautifully colored, nor will the inclination of free choice be to any other of the objects that sweeten the senses, since all bodily sense perception will have been extinguished. And because the operation of the mind alone attains intelligible beauty apart from matter and the body, its nature will recover without hindrance its proper good, which is neither

---

4. NRSV of Ps 34:8: "O taste and see that the Lord is good."

color, nor shape, nor extension, nor size, but what transcends every likeness that can be guessed.

Why, then, perhaps someone will say, should we be displeased with our present life? What purpose and what function does the body serve for us, if indeed life [49] has been demonstrated by your argument to be better apart from it? We shall say to him that the profit is not small even from the present life and the body for those capable of looking at the entire dispensation of nature. Indeed, really blessed is that life of angels which has no need of bodily weight. Nevertheless, not even this life is useless by comparison with that one; for the present life becomes the path to what is hoped, just as it is possible to see in the case of shoots.[5] The fruit, beginning from the blossom progresses through it to become fruit, even though the blossom is not the fruit. Moreover, the standing crops generated from seeds do not immediately appear with ears of grain, but the shoot first becomes grass, and then from this a stalk is framed, while the grass is withered around it, and so the fruit is ripened in the head of the ear of grain. Yet the husbandman does not complain about this necessary period of time and the successive stages, saying why does the blossom come before the fruit or for what purpose does the grass shoot up first from the seed, if indeed the blossom drops off and the grass dries up in vain, contributing nothing for human food. For whoever looks at the wondrous working of nature knows that in no other way would the fruit be matured from seeds and shoots unless this artful sequence guided it to its maturation. Indeed, since the grass produced from seeds is useless for our enjoyment, what happens is not because of this superfluous and beside the point. For whoever uses food looks to his own need, but the principle of nature looks at nothing else but how it may bring forth produce by an appointed sequence to its maturity. Therefore, first [50] the plant in many different ways grows in the soil beneath it through roots by which it draws the nourishment appropriate for itself through moisture, then grass shoots up,[6] which is not the fruit, but becomes a certain assistance and way for the maturation of the fruit. First it clears out by itself the power laid up in the seed (since nature has prepared ahead of time for the grass to be some sort of refuse of the seed); then it becomes a covering for the root, protecting it from damages caused by the air through cold and heat. When the seed has now been more vigorously established through depth in the roots, and when from then on the grass is neglected because it is no longer needed as a covering for the root, the seed's entire power is given over to

---

5. Cf. *In sanct. Pasch.* (*GNO* 9:259–60).

6. *GNO* regards the following words as a gloss: "making grass a cover for the root because of harm from the air."

the sprouting up of the stalk, since nature has artfully devised by a certain resourceful wisdom the flute-like structure, the straight shoot of which is distributed in a circle to the pods one after another. For it is necessary that the stalk which is moist and slack at first should nourish them supported by bonds in the middle for the sake of safety. If its length runs up in equal measure, then the stalk grows long when the last pod of itself shows before-hand the ear of grain, which is divided like hairs into many unripe kernels and hides the grain being nourished by the husks at the base of the unripe kernels. If, therefore, the farmer is not displeased either with the roots of the seeds, or with the grass produced from the seed, [51] or the unripe kernels of the ear of grain, but in each of these things observes what is their necessary function by which nature in its artful way guides and brings forth the fruit to maturity, clearing out the generative power by putting away what is useless, then it is time also for you not to be displeased with our nature as it goes forward by necessary paths to its own end. Rather, you should consider by the analogy given by the seeds that what is always present is certainly usefully and necessarily conditioned for some purpose; this is not, however, the purpose for which we came into being. For we do not have our subsistence from the one who created us so as to be an embryo, nor does the aim of nature envisage life as a baby, nor does it direct its sight to the following stages of life, with which nature always clothes us in succession, changing our form in time, nor to the dissolution that comes to the body through death, but all these and such stages are parts of the path by which we travel. And the aim and limit of the journey through these stages is restoration to our original condition, which is no other than likeness to the divine. Compare the image based upon the ear of grain. Even the grass that first sprouted up appeared as necessary by nature's principle. Nevertheless, the farming does not take place for its sake, nor is it the pods, kernels, stalk, and undergirdings that are appointed for the pursuit of farming, but it is the nutritious fruit that progresses to maturity by these stages. In just the same way the expected limit of life is blessedness, and whatever is now discerned concerning the body—death, old age, youth, infancy, and the formation of the embryo—all these in some way like grass, kernels, and stalk, are a way and succession [52] and potentiality of the perfection that is hoped. If you delight in looking to it, you will not be in a condition to hate these things, nor will you indeed be disposed by passion and desire either to be distressed when you are separated from them or to go to death of your own accord.

If it is necessary to add this to my argument, perhaps it is not useless, even if it seems to be out of right order, to say that nature always trains us by death and that death has certainly been made to grow together with life as it passes through time. For since life is always moved from the past to the

future and never does away with what follows afterwards, death is what always accompanies the life-giving activity by being united with it. For in past
time every life-giving movement and activity certainly ceases. Since, then,
impotence and inactivity are the special property of death, and certainly this
always follows after the life-giving activity, it is not outside the truth to say
that death has been woven together with this life. And who would find such
a thought confirmed for us by truth otherwise than by experience itself,
which testifies to the teaching that the person of today is not the same as
the one of yesterday with respect to what underlies him in a material way.
Rather, something of him certainly through all time is mortified, stinks,
is corrupted, and is thrown out as though from the construction of some
house, I mean from the body, when nature carries away the bad odor of
mortification and entrusts to the earth what has already come to be outside
the life-giving power. That is why, according to the words of the great Paul,
"we die daily" (1 Cor 15:31). We do not remain constantly the same persons
in the same [53] house of the body, but from time to time we become different from something else, by addition and subtraction being constantly
changed as though to a new body. Why, then, are we astonished at death
when the life existing through the flesh has been demonstrated to be its
constant care and its training ground? Even if you were to speak of sleep and
waking, you would be talking about another form of death woven together
with life, since sense perception is completely extinguished in those who
sleep, and in turn waking by itself activates for us the rising hoped for.

But the subject placed before us has not yet been clarified by what has
been said, since the thought I have introduced has led my argument aside
to another idea. Therefore, let us take up once more what was proposed,
that not even the nature of the body is useless with respect to the hope of
good things we await. For if we were what we became in the beginning, we
would certainly not have needed the coat of skin (cf. Gen 3:21), since likeness to the divine would be shining upon us. The divine characteristic mark
that was displayed in us at the beginning was not a kind of special property
belonging to some shape or color, but the divine beauty is contemplated in
qualities such as those with which humanity was also adorned by imitating
the grace in the archetype through impassibility, blessedness, and incorruption. But through the deceit of the enemy of our life humanity willingly
had an inclination to what is bestial and irrational. To remove those under
constraint from the worse and to transfer them to the better by compulsion would perhaps seem useful to the unquestioning, but to the Former of
nature it appeared profitless and unjust to impose the loss of the greatest of
goods on our nature by such a dispensation. [54] Since, then, humanity was
made godlike and blessed because it had been honored with free autonomy

(as ruling oneself and being without a master is the specific property of divine blessedness), for humanity to be forcibly changed to something else through constraint would have been a removal of its dignity. For if God had willingly removed human nature from what pleased him because against the movement of its free autonomy it had rushed into something not right by force and constraint, it would have been the removal of the good that previously held fast what was created and the deprivation of its honor as godlike (for free autonomy is godlike). Therefore, so that this authority might remain in human nature and evil might pass away, God's wisdom found this device to permit humanity to become what he wished, so that by tasting the evils it desired and learning by experience what sort of things it had exchanged for the kinds it chose, it might return willingly by desire to its first blessedness, after shaking off from its nature like some burden passibility and irrationality, either having been purified during the present life by diligence and philosophy, or after removal from here by the purifying furnace of fire. For consider this example. Suppose there is some physician who has from his art all knowledge of what preserves and what harms, and suppose that when he counsels a youth about what is right, he is unable by his advice to hinder the immature youth because of his age and an intention governed by desire for some corrupting fruit or herb set forth. But since he has a varied preparation of antidotes, [55] suppose that the physician were to turn the boy away from partaking of what was harming him, provided he had learned by his experience of painful suffering the usefulness of the physician's fatherly advice and had become desirous of health, and suppose that by his antidotes the physician brought the boy back once more to the good condition from which he had fallen because of his foolish desire for harmful things. In just the same way the sweet and good Father of our nature, who knows both by what we are saved and by what we are destroyed, recognized what was harmful to the man [Adam] and advised him not to partake of it (Gen 2:17); and when human desire for the worse prevailed, God was not at a loss for good counter-medicines by which he might lead humanity back once more to its good condition at the beginning. For since humanity had chosen this material pleasure instead of the soul's delight, God somehow decided to concur with this impulse through the coat of skin (Gen 3:21), which he put around humanity on account of its inclination to the worse, and by which the particular properties of the irrational nature belonging to animals were mingled with humanity. This cloak for the rational nature was fashioned by the wisdom of God, who was dispensing better things by the opposing natures. For that coat of skin, bearing in itself all the particular properties, comprehending as many as held fast the irrational nature—pleasure, anger, gluttony, greediness, and the like—gives a path to human free choice that is an inclination in either direction, to virtue and to vice, since the coat means becoming material. For since in this life humanity lives it life in these two ways by its free movement, if someone were to discern what is proper to the irrational and were to pay attention to himself by a better life, he would make the present life a purification of the evil mixed into it, [56] mastering irrationality by reason. But if he were to be bent toward the irrational inclination of the passions, using the skin of irrational animals as a fellow worker for the passions, he would later wish otherwise for the better after his departure from the body, having recognized the difference between virtue and vice by being unable to participate in divinity, unless the purifying fire were to cleanse the stain mixed into his soul.

These conditions are what have made the use of the body necessary for us; by the body free autonomy is preserved, and returning again to the good is not prevented. Rather, by this recurrent succession through voluntary acts there comes to be an inclination to the better for those of us who already from here on through life in the flesh direct the spiritual life by impassibility. We hear that the patriarchs and prophets became such people, as well as those with them and after them who hastened upwards to perfection through virtue and philosophy. (I mean the disciples, apostles, and martyrs and all those who have honored the virtuous life instead of this material life, who even though they were fewer in number than the multitude of those who fall away to the worse, nevertheless bear witness to the possibility of achieving virtue through the flesh.) As for the rest, by the guidance later on given in the purifying fire they will cast away their passionate attachment to matter and will return to the grace that had been allotted to them by nature in the beginning [57] through their willing desire of good things. For the desire for things alien to nature does not last forever, because what satisfies and satiates each one is not the characteristic property which our nature shared but failed to keep at the beginning; and only what is innate and of the same kind as it remains forever longed for and loved, while of itself the nature remains unchanged. And if the nature suffers some turning aside because of wicked free choice, then there comes into free choice the desire of alien things, the enjoyment of which gives pleasure not to the nature but to the passion of the nature. But when the passion goes away, the desire of things contrary to nature goes away with it; and what is nature's own becomes again longed for and appropriate. And this is what is pure, immaterial, and incorporeal. And if one were to say that this is the special property of the divinity that transcends all things, he would not be mistaken. For as when some very sharp discharge in the bodily eyes clouds the vital force of sight, gloom becomes their special property because of the kinship of the thickness with darkness. But if what troubles the vital force is consumed by some remedy, the eye's own appropriate light comes back, mingled with what is pure and luminous in the pupil of the eye. In the same way when like some discharge wickedness by the deceit of the adversary were to flow upon the sight of the soul, the reasoning power would willingly be inclined to the darkened life, since by passion it would have been made to belong to gloom. (For everyone who does evil hates the light, as the divine Word says [John 3:20].) But when the evil has been consumed, leaving existing things and going into non-being, the nature again looks at light with pleasure, since what was troubling the purity of the soul has gone away.

[58] Therefore, what I have said has proved that the hostile hold flesh has on our nature is vain, for the cause of evils did not depend on nature. (For otherwise evil would equally have had power over all those allotted a bodily life.) But since of those remembered for virtue each one was both in the flesh and not in evil, it is thereby clear that the body is not the cause of the effects of passion, but free choice is what creates the passions. For the body is moved in a way appropriate to its own nature, motions by which it is preserved with respect to its own structure and continuance, managing itself for these by its own impulses. What sort of thing do I mean? The body needs food and drink so that what has been dissipated from its power may once more be restored to it in its lack. Appetite is moved for this purpose. Again, though it is mortal, the nature of the body is made immortal through the succession of humans that come to be. Therefore, its condition is suitable also for this impulse. Besides, in addition to these the body has been made naked of a covering from hair, which is why we need external clothing. Moreover, since we cannot withstand heat, cold, and rain, we have required the shelter of houses. Whoever has taken account of these and such things, if he looks at need, accepts each of them without trouble, making the aim of need the limit of appetite—a house, clothes, a wife, food, by each of these ministering to what is needed by nature. But whoever is the servant of pleasures has made necessary needs paths for the passions, instead of food seeking sumptuous fare, instead of a cloak preferring to choose ornamentation, instead of the need for houses [59] extravagance, instead of bearing children looking to lawless and forbidden pleasures. Because of this greed with great gates[7] has burst in upon human life, and effeminacy, luxury, frivolity, various kinds of profligacy, and such things like some withered offshoots of necessary needs have sprouted up because appetite has gone beyond the limits of need and has expanded still more for those who eagerly pursue nothing useful. For what does a silver coffered ceiling adorned with gold and precious stones have in common with the usefulness of food? Or

7. πλεονεξία πλατείαις πύλαις.

for what purpose would there be needed a garment of gold thread, flowery purple, and woven pictures by which wars and monsters and such things are portrayed on clothes and coverings on the part of the weavers, who are helped by the disease of greed that has grown up? For so that they may obtain the preparation and power for such things, people provide themselves with the materials for what is desired from greed. And greed opens an entrance for insatiate desire, which according to Solomon is "a perforated jar" (Prov 23:27), always lacking and found empty for those who try to draw water from it. Therefore, it is not the body that provides the starting points for evils, but free choice produces them by turning aside the aim of need to the desire for wicked things.

Therefore, let the body not be reproached by thoughtless people. The soul will be adorned with it in its more divine condition, when afterwards the body's elements will be changed by regeneration, when death has cleansed it of what is superfluous [60] and useless for the enjoyment of the life to come. For the condition of the body suitable for the present will not also be the same as the one useful for the life hereafter. Instead, the structure of our body will be suitable and appropriate for the enjoyment of that life, since it will have been disposed in harmony with sharing in good things. What sort of things do I mean? (For the idea is made clear to someone better by an example from what is well known.) A lump of iron is useful for a smith's art even when it is a rock not worked on by the craftsman. But when the iron needs to be fashioned into something more fine, then when the fire purifies the lump through the smith's care, everything earthly and useless is cast off, which the craftsmen of this trade call slag; and in this way what was once a rock, when refined, becomes either a breastplate or some other piece of fine equipment, since it has been purified of its superfluity by smelting, which as long as it was a rock was not supposed a superfluity regarding its usefulness at that time. For even the slag contributed something to the mass of the iron, since it was mixed into the lump. If our example has been understood, we must now return to the thought proposed, the idea envisaged by the example. What, then, is this? The nature of the body has many slag-like qualities that in the present life contribute what is useful for some purpose, but are altogether useless and alien to the blessedness expected hereafter. [61] So what happened to the iron in the fire when the smelting removed everything useless, this is accomplished for the body through death, since everything superfluous is removed through the dissolution by mortification. It is, then, completely apparent to those who have examined the question what sort of things they are of which later on the body is purified, things that would have damaged life if they had been missing in the present life.

Nevertheless, we shall say a few more words by way of clarification. Hypothetically, let appetite, which is naturally set to work for all things, correspond to the lump, and let those things toward which the appetite now has its impulses correspond to the slag—pleasures, wealth, love of reputation, offices, angers, luxuries, and such things. Death becomes the exact purification of all these and such things. When it has been trained and purified of all of them, appetite will be turned in its activity to what alone is to be longed for, desired, and loved, not by having completely quenched the impulses naturally innate in us for such things, but by transforming them for the immaterial participation in good things. For there love for true beauty is unceasing, there greed for the treasures of wisdom is praiseworthy, and the noble and good love of reputation is the one set right by fellowship in the kingdom of God, and the noble passion of insatiate desire is the longing that ascends to the good, never cut off by being satiated with what lies above. Therefore, since you know that the craftsman of the universe will at the appropriate time forge the lump of the body into a "weapon of good pleasure" (Ps 5:13), "the breastplate of righteousness," as the apostle says, and "the sword of the Spirit," and the "helmet" [62] of hope, and "the whole armor of God" (Eph 6:14, 17, 11, 13), love your own body according to the law of the apostle, who says, "no one has hated his own body" (cf. Eph 5:29).

It is the body when purified that must be loved, not the slag that is cast off. For it is true, as the divine voice says, that "if the earthly house of our tent is destroyed, then we shall find it has become a building from God, a house not made with hands, eternal in the heavens" (2 Cor 5:1), worthy of being "a dwelling place of God in the Spirit" (Eph 2:22). And let no one describe to me the characteristic mark, shape, and form of that house not made with hands according to the likeness of the characteristic marks that now appear to us and that distinguish us from one another by special properties. For since it is not only the resurrection that has been preached to us by the divine oracles, but also that those who are renewed by the resurrection pledged by divine scripture must be changed (cf. 1 Cor 15:51), it is entirely necessary that what we shall be changed to has been hidden from absolutely everyone and is unknown, because no example of what is hoped is to be seen in the life we live now. For now everything thick and hard from nature holds our motion downwards, but then the transformation of the body becomes a relation to what is aloft, since the word says that after our nature changes through the resurrection in all the ways in which we have been living, "we will be caught up in the clouds to meet the Lord in the air, and so we will be with the Lord forever" (1 Thess 4:17). Therefore, if for those who have been changed weight does not persist for the body, and if those, the elements of whose bodies have been changed to a more divine condition, will travel through the air with the incorporeal nature, certainly also the rest [63] of the body's properties—color, shape, individuality, and everything each by each—will be transformed along with weight to some aspect of more divine things. For this reason we see no necessity for envisaging in those changed by the resurrection such a difference as the nature necessarily has now through the succession of events. (Nor surely is it to be clearly asserted that this will not be, since we are ignorant of into what the change will take place.) But because there will be one kind for all when all of us become one body of Christ, having been shaped by one characteristic mark (cf. Rom 12:5; 1 Cor 12:12, 27), we do not doubt that since the divine image shines equally on all, as to what will become ours in the change of nature instead of such properties, we shall appear to be something better than any thought can guess. But lest our account of this should be left entirely unexercised, we say that since the difference between male and female functions with our nature for nothing other than the procreation of children, perhaps it is possible to adopt some guess worthy of God's promised blessing of good things by saying about this that the procreative power of nature will be changed to that service of birth in which great Isaiah participated when he said, "From fear of you, Lord, we have received in the womb, have undergone labor pangs, and have given birth; we have conceived[8] the spirit of salvation on earth" (Isa 26:18). If such a birth is good, and the procreation of children becomes the cause of salvation, as the apostle says (cf. 1 Tim 2:15), someone who has once by such a birth produced as children for himself a multitude of good things never ceases generating the spirit of salvation. But even if [64] someone should say that the characteristic mark in which we have been formed male and female will be present with us once more in the new life, our idea with respect to this cannot easily imagine a condition in this or any other way.[9] For if someone were to say that the new life will be in the same form, his account would fall into much helplessness because of the fact that a human being does not always remain the same as himself with respect to the form of his characteristic mark, since he is refashioned by the stages of life and by experiences at different times to a different form. For in different ways the infant and the youth are formed, in different ways the child, the man, the middle-aged, the person beyond his prime, the aged, the old man. None of these are the same condition as another. Moreover, consider the person turned yellow by jaundice, the one swollen by dropsy, the one dried up by consumption, the one become obese by some bad temperament, the

8. ἐκυήσαμεν, instead of the usual LXX reading, ἐποιήσαμεν.

9. Presumably, the male-female distinction might obtain with or without sexual intercourse and procreation.

bilious person, the one flushed with blood, the phlegmatic person. Since each of these is formed in relation to the ruling bad temperament, neither is it right that these conditions should be reckoned to remain after the new life, since the change refashions everything to what is more divine, nor is it easy to to give a satisfactory analogy for what sort of form will come to flower for us, since the good things set before us by hope are believed to be beyond sight, hearing, and thought. Or perhaps if someone were to say that the form making someone known will be the special property belonging to the moral character of each, he would not be entirely wrong. For just as now the variation in some respect of the elements within us works out the differences of the characteristics in each according to the excess or deficiency of the opposed elements to the special property shaped and applied according to outward form,[10] so [65] it seems to me that the things that characterize the form of each at that time are not these elements, but the special properties of vice and virtue. The sort of mixture they have with one another either in this or in some other way fashions the form to be characterized in a way similar to the sort of thing that happens in the present life when the external disposition of a person indicates the disposition in the secret part of the soul. From this we easily recognize someone overwhelmed by grief, someone roused to anger, and someone given over to desire, and on the contrary, someone cheerful, someone without anger, and someone adorned with the venerable characteristic mark of moderation. Therefore, just as in the present life the quality of the heart's disposition becomes an outward form, and the appearance of the person reflects his underlying emotion, so it seems to me that when the nature has been changed to what is more divine, the person is endowed with a form through his moral character with no difference between what this is and what he appears to be. Instead, whatever the form is, he is also known as self-controlled, just, meek, pure, affectionate, loving God; and again among these either a person has all good things or is adorned with only one, or is found with the greater number, or having less in such a one but more in another. For since the special properties are envisaged both as those according to the better and those according to the opposite, from these and such characteristics they are divided individually from one another as though into different semblances, until, when the last enemy has been destroyed (1 Cor 15:26), as [66] the apostle says, and when evil has been completely banished from all existing things, there will lighten upon all the single godlike beauty in which we were formed in the beginning. This is light, purity, incorruption, life, truth, and such things.[11] And

---

10. μορφὴν, as opposed to εἶδος.

11. The following words are a gloss: "For there is no difference in the children of day and light between what they are and what they appear to be."

no variation of difference between light, purity, and incorruption will be found with respect to their being of one kind, but a single grace will shine upon all when becoming children of light they will shine like the sun (cf. Matt 13:43) according to the Lord's word that cannot lie (cf. Eph 5:8; 1 Thess 5:5). Moreover, that all will have been made perfect in the one according to the promise of God the Word (John 17:21) has the same meaning because one and the same grace has appeared to all, so that each returns as a gift to his neighbor the same joyfulness because each also rejoices when looking at the other's beauty, and the other rejoices in return since no evil changes the form to an ugly characteristic mark.[12]

These things are what our mind has discussed with us on behalf of the departed, explaining thoughts in words as much as we could. But as for us, let us conclude our advice to those who deeply grieve with great Paul's voice, "I do not want you to be uninformed, brothers and sisters, about those who have fallen asleep, so that you may not grieve as others do who have no hope" (1 Thess 4:13).

If, then, we have learned something worth the effort about those who have fallen asleep because of whom our discourse has examined philosophically their conditions, let us no longer accept this mean and abject grief; [67] but if we must grieve, let us choose that grief which is praiseworthy and virtuous. For just as in the case of pleasure, one kind is bestial and irrational, while another is pure and immaterial, so too what is opposed to pleasure is divided between vice and virtue. Therefore, some form of mourning is blessed and not to be cast away for the acquisition of virtue, because its condition is opposed to this irrational and abject dejection. For whoever finds himself in this form of grief will thereafter be held fast by regret, since he has been carried aside from his settled condition when he became unable to resist the emotion. But blessed mourning keeps sorrow without regret and without shame for those who by it set their life on the right path to virtue. For the person truly mourns who becomes aware of those good things from which he has fallen, having compared this mortal and stained life with that undefiled blessedness which was in his power before he misused his power for evil; and the more mourning for such a life as this weighs him down, the more he urges himself forward to the acquisition of the goods for which he yearns. For an awareness of the loss of the good becomes fuel for the pursuit of what is yearned for. Therefore, since some mourning works for salvation, as my argument has demonstrated, listen, you who are easily carried aside to the passion of grief, because we are not preventing grief but

12. *GNO* places a mark indicating the end of a quotation here, but has no opening mark. But cf. p. 44, where the closing mark follows the opening of the quotation on p. 40.

are recommending good grief instead of the one condemned. Therefore, do not grieve with the world's grief which works death, as the apostle says (cf. 2 Cor 7:10), but with grief in accord with God, the end of which is the soul's salvation. For the tear shed at random and in vain for those who have fallen asleep perhaps also becomes a cause of condemnation [68] for the person who manages what is useful in an evil way. For if he who made all things in wisdom built into our nature this disposition of grief because it is a cleansing of the evil that previously gained possession and a provision for the path to participation in the good things for which we hope, perhaps the tear shed in vain and useless will be reproached by our own master according to the Gospel account of how the wicked steward uselessly scattered the wealth entrusted to him (Luke 16:1–13). For everything serviceable for the good is wealth counted up in the costly contents of the treasuries. And so, "I do not want you to be uninformed, brothers and sisters, about those who have fallen asleep"—these words which we have learned, as well as any other lesson possibly revealed in addition from the Holy Spirit to the more perfect, are "so that you may not grieve, as others do who have no hope" (1 Thess 4:13). For it belongs only to the faithless to confine the hopes of living to the present life, and that is why they make death the equivalent of a disaster, because what is believed on our part is not hoped by them. As for us, because we have believed in the great guarantor of the resurrection of the dead, the Ruler of all creation himself, who for this reason died and rose again so that by his deed he might make the assertion of the resurrection trustworthy, without doubting we hold fast the hope of good things; when hope is present, grief for the departed will not have a place. And our God and Lord, Jesus Christ, who comforts the lowly, will comfort your hearts and will establish you in his own love through his mercies—to him be glory forever and ever. Amen.

Gregory, Bishop of Nyssa

ON "THEN ALSO THE SON HIMSELF WILL BE SUBJECTED TO THE ONE WHO SUBJECTED ALL THINGS TO HIM"

(In illud: Tunc et ipse Filius, GNO 3.2)

All the Lord's sayings are both "holy sayings" and pure, as the prophet says (Ps 11:7), when the meaning of the sayings, like the purity brought about in silver by fire, possesses its own natural reflection of the truth, once it has been purified of every heretical notion. Above all, I think that for all of them there ought to be the testimony found in the teachings of Saint Paul as the confirmation of all their brilliance and purity. This is because, since he was initiated in paradise into the knowledge of ineffable things (2 Cor 12:2–4) and since he had Christ speaking in himself (2 Cor 13:3), he spoke such words as were right to speak for one taught in such a school by the Word, his guide and teacher.

[4] But when cheating dealers undertake to make the divine silver counterfeit, by mixing in heretical and base ideas, they darken the Word's brilliance and the apostle's mysterious thoughts, either because they fail to understand them or because they wickedly take them according to what seems their meaning. They drag them in for an advocacy of their wickedness, saying that the apostolic word was composed for them in order to bring down the glory of the Only Begotten God. For example, they understand the text that says, "then the Son will be subjected to the one who put

all things in subjection under him" (1 Cor 15:28) as though it indicated some kind of servile humiliation. For this reason it has appeared necessary to examine quite carefully how to explain this text so as to demonstrate how truly pure the apostolic silver is once it has been separated from all base alloy and heretical understanding, and so found unadulterated.

Accordingly, we are aware that in the usage of holy scripture such a word as "subjection" has many senses that are not always in accord, having the same meanings. Instead, subjection now signifies one thing and again indicates another. For example, scripture says, "let slaves be subjected to their own masters" (Titus 2:9). Also, concerning the irrational nature it says that it has been subjected by God to humanity, as the prophet says, "you have subjected all things beneath his feet" (Ps 8:7). And concerning those subdued by war it says, "he subjected [5] peoples to us and nations beneath our feet" (Ps 46:4). Moreover, when he mentioned as from the person of God those saved by recognizing their mistake, the prophet says, "The foreigners have become subject to me" (Ps 46:4). In some way related to this seems to be what is applied to us in Psalm 61 by the verse, "Will not my soul be subjected to God?" (Ps 61:2). In addition to all these instances there is the one presented to us by our enemies from the letter to the Corinthians, "Then the Son himself will be subjected to the one who put all things in subjection under him" (1 Cor 15:28).

Since, therefore, what this word signifies extends to many meanings, it would be right for us by distinguishing each one of them separately to decide what kind of subjection is signified—to which meaning the apostle's expression properly refers. Therefore, we say that in the case of those subdued in war by the might of those who have conquered them, what is signified by subjection points out that they have submitted both unwillingly and under compulsion to those who have been victorious. For if any power were attached to the captives that suggested the hope of prevailing over those who had conquered them, they would raise themselves up again against their conquerors, judging it an insult and shame to be subjected to their enemies. On the other hand, irrational beings are under the control of rational ones in another way, because their nature is deficient [6] of the greatest of goods, that is, reason, so that it is necessary for what is lesser to be subjected to the one who excels by the good fortune of nature. Those, however, who have been subdued by the yoke of slavery by some sort of lawful consequence, even though they have equal honor by nature, nevertheless are unable to resist the law; and they accept their subordinate rank because they are brought to subjection by irresistible necessity. But the aim of the subjection that brings us to God is salvation, as we learn from the prophecy that says, "let my soul be subject to God, for from him is my salvation" (Ps 61:6, 2).

Therefore, when our opponents introduce to us the apostle's word which says that the Son will be subjected to the Father, it would follow because of the varied significance of a word like this to ask them what significance of subjection they envisage when they suppose that this word must apply to the Only Begotten God. But it is obvious that they will say they understand the Son's subjection in none of the ways mentioned. For he does not exist as an enemy made subject in war without hope or zeal for again resisting his conqueror, nor does the Word like some one of the irrational creatures have a subjection necessary by nature because he falls short of the good, like sheep, cattle, and oxen with respect to humanity. But certainly neither is he enslaved by law like purchased slaves or captives in a household, awaiting one day becoming free of the yoke of slavery by favor or grace. [7] Yet neither would anyone say that the Only Begotten God will be subjected to the Father for the purpose of being saved, since it was by him that salvation from God was accomplished through the one in human likeness. For in the case of a mutable nature that comes to be in the good by participation, subjection to God is necessary because from it sharing in good things becomes ours. But in the power that is immutable and unchangeable subjection has no place; in it every good name and concept is contemplated—eternity, incorruptibility, blessedness, being always the same, incapable of being either better or worse. It neither progresses in the good, nor does it decline to the worse. For this power is the spring of salvation for others, and it has no need itself of a savior.

Of what sort, then, will they reasonably say they properly understand in his case what is signified by subjection? For all the meanings examined are found to be far to one side of what is properly both understood and said of the Only Begotten God. But suppose it is necessary to add as well that form of subjection which Luke's Gospel mentions in saying that when the Lord advanced to his "twelfth year," he "was subject" to his parents (Luke 2:51, 42). Not even that would be said appropriately of the Son who is before time and true with his own true Father. For in the passage from the Gospel he is taken to be "the one who in every respect has been tested, yet without sin" (Heb 4:15), and who advanced through the ages [8] of our nature. And just as when he became a little child he was acquainted with the food of infants, since he ate butter and honey (Isa 7:15), so too when he advanced to youth he did not refuse what corresponded with and was suitable for such an age, becoming a model of good order in earthly life. For since in the case of other humans the understanding is imperfect in such youths and youthfulness needs guidance toward the better from those more perfect, for this reason the twelve year old is subject to his mother in order to demonstrate that what is brought to perfection by progress rightly accepts subjection as guidance to the good before attaining perfection. But as for the one who is always perfect in every good and is able to receive in himself neither progress nor diminution because of his nature which needs nothing and is incapable of diminution—those who speak unreasonably about everything would not be able to say that he is subjected by anything. Indeed, when he sojourned through flesh with human nature in a boyish age, he gave the law by what he did that subjection belongs to youth. So it is obvious that when he advanced to the perfection of his age, he no longer regarded his mother's authority. For when she urged him at Cana of Galilee to display his power in what was lacking for the wedding banquet and to gratify the need for wine with good cheer, he did not refuse the favor to those who asked it, but he rejected his mother's advice as no longer applying to him at that time, saying, "Woman, what concern is that to you and to me? (John 2:4). Do you want to take charge of me at my present age? Is it that the hour that furnishes independence and authority to youth has not yet come?"

[9] If, therefore, in his life in the flesh the appropriate measure of age shakes off subjection to the woman who bore him, no one could say what place subjection has in the case of the one who rules in the might of eternity itself. For it belongs to the divine and blessed life always to remain in the same condition and not to admit a change that would alter it. Since, therefore, the Word, who exists in the beginning, the Only Begotten God, is foreign to all progress and alteration, how does what now negates this come about as a matter of fact hereafter? Surely the apostle does not speak of the Son as always subjected, but as being subjected at the end of the future consummation of the universe. If, indeed, subjection is good and worthily said of God, how would that good now be missing from God? For certainly, it is equally good for both, for the Son to be subjected and for the Father to receive the subjection of the Son. Such a good, therefore, is lacking in the present time both for the Father and for the Son; and what neither the Father nor the Son had before the ages, this at the consummation of times will belong both to the Father and to the Son, the one undergoing subjection and the other gaining by this, as it were, an addition and increase of his own glory, something up to the present time he does not have. Where, therefore, in this is what is unchangeable? For something that takes place after certain things but does not now exist is a property of mutable nature. Therefore, either subjection is a good and it is right to believe it is now a good for God, or such a thing is unworthy in the case of God whether now or at another time. [10] But indeed the apostle says that the Son will be subjected to God the Father "then," not that he has been subjected now. Therefore, his argument envisages some other aim, and what is signified by the name "Son" is far from the heretics' wicked understanding.

What, then, is the argument? Perhaps one may better discern its thought by means of the whole passage in this part of the letter. For when Paul presented his argument in contention with the Corinthians, they accepted faith in the Lord, but thought the teaching about the resurrection of humans to be a myth, saying, "How are the dead raised, and with what kind of body do they come? (1 Cor 15:35). In many ways and many forms their bodies turn round to destruction after death, either by decay or by being consumed by flesh-eating creatures—reptiles, fish, birds, or four-footed animals." That is why Paul presented them with many reasonable considerations, trying to persuade them not to compare God's power with their own or to suppose that whatever is impossible for humans is equally so for God, but to reckon up the greatness of divine authority on the basis of examples known to us. And so he presents to them the wondrous working concerning the bodies of seeds always renewed by divine power; and he shows how God's wisdom was not too weak to search out thousands of kinds of bodies in the universe—rational, irrational, in the air, on the ground, and [11] those appearing to us in heaven, the sun, and the rest of the stars. Each of them comes to be by divine power so that God would not be at a loss also with respect to the resurrection of our bodies . . . [this] becomes a proof for us.[1] For if all existing things were not transformed into various shapes in their appearance from some underlying matter, but the divine will became the matter and being of the creatures, it is much more able to fashion what already exists with being raised again to its own form than to fashion what did not exist in the beginning with coming into substance and essence.

Therefore, Paul first demonstrated in his words to the Corinthians that since the first human being was dissolved into earth by sin and for this reason was called "dusty" (1 Cor 15:47–49), it consequently followed after him that all those who came to be from him are "dusty," and those sprung from such a one are mortal (1 Cor 15:21). Then he necessarily continued with a second consequence by which humanity is reconstituted from mortality to immortality, saying that in a similar way the good has sprung up for human nature flowing from one to all, just as also the evil flowed from one to a multitude, extended by the succession of those who came after the one. And he used these words to construct his teaching about this: "The first [12] man was from the earth, dusty, the second from heaven. As was the man of dust, so are those who are of the dust; and as is the man of heaven, so are those who are of heaven. Just as we have borne the image of the man of dust, we will also bear the image of the man of heaven" (1 Cor 15:47–49).

---

1. The text is corrupt, and the editor supposes a lacuna, to be filled by "raising up the seeds" or something similar. As well, I have adopted the conjectural emendation reading ἡμῖν instead of ἡμᾶς.

Therefore, with these and similar reasonable considerations Paul confirmed his argument about the resurrection, and by many others he bound the heretics hand and foot with syllogisms by which he demonstrated that anyone who fails to believe the resurrection of humans neither accepts the resurrection of Christ. By the interweaving of their connection with one another he fashioned something inescapable by his conclusions, saying, "If there is no resurrection of the dead, then Christ has not been raised; and if Christ has not been raised, then faith in him is vain" (cf. 1 Cor 15:13–14, 16–17). For if the premise that Christ has been raised from the dead is true, the proposition united to this, that there is a resurrection of the dead, must certainly also be true. For by demonstrating the part, the whole is demonstrated with it. And the other way round, if anyone should say the whole is false, namely, the resurrection of the dead, certainly neither will what concerns the part be found true, namely, that Christ has been raised from the dead. For if the whole is impossible, certainly neither in any part will it be possible. [13] Moreover, for those who receive the Word it is trustworthy and undeniable that Christ has been raised from the dead; necessarily by faith in the part, Christ's resurrection, the resurrection of the whole will be believed.

Therefore, in this way by the use of syllogisms he compelled them to accept his teaching by saying "if it is not so." (For if the whole does not exist, neither can it exist in any part. But if we believe that this part has been raised, faith in this becomes proof of the general resurrection of humans.) And Paul added to his argument that by which the entire structure of his teaching about this is summed up: "For as in Adam all die, so also in Christ will all be made alive" (1 Cor 15:22). He wisely reveals the mystery about this toward which he looks in part, guiding his argument in what follows toward the limit of what is hoped by some necessary logic.

The aim of what he says is as follows. And I shall first expound the explanation of what is written in my own words; then I shall put the apostle's argument beside it in such a way as to be made congruent with the explanation I have expounded.[2]

What, then, is the aim of the argument which the divine apostle presents as his teaching in this part of the letter? It is that at some time the nature of evil will pass over to what does not exist, completely annihilated of being; [14] and divine and pure goodness will embrace in itself the entire rational nature. Not one of the things that came to be from God will fall short of the kingdom of God when the evil that had been mixed into existing things

---

2. From this point up to the full paragraph that begins on p. 25, Reinhard M. Hübner supplies a German translation of the text. See *Die Einheit*, 35–40.

has been destroyed like some kind of base matter consumed by a furnace of purifying fire. Everything that had its origin from God will become such as it was in the beginning when it had not yet received evil. Paul says that this happens in the following way. The holy and pure divinity of the Only Begotten came to exist in the mortal and perishable nature of humans. From the whole of human nature with which the divine was mixed there subsisted as a kind of first fruits of the common batch the man of Christ,[3] through whom the entire human race was assimilated to divinity. Therefore, since in him the entire nature of evil was destroyed—"he committed no sin," as the prophet says (cf. Isa 53:9), "and no deceit was found in his mouth" (1 Pet 2:22)—and since in him with sin there was also destroyed death that follows upon it (for there is no other origin of death save for sin), from him the annihilation of evil and the destruction of death took their beginning. Thereafter, as it were, [15] a sort of order was added by a certain sequence to what had taken place. For it is always according to their descent from the good that one person is further away from the first condition or is found closer to it. In this way each follows the one who went before depending upon the worth and power each has. As a result, after the man in Christ, who became the first fruits of our nature by receiving divinity in himself, who is also "the first fruits of those who have fallen asleep" (1 Cor 15:20), "the firstborn from the dead" (Col 1:18), who "loosed the pains of death" (Acts 2:24)—after this man, then, who was completely separated from sin and who in himself destroyed the power of death (Heb 2:14; 2 Tim 1:10), and put down all the devil's rule, authority, and power (1 Cor 15:24), if anyone were found like Paul, who became as far as he was able an imitator of Christ (1 Cor 11:1) by withdrawing from evil, such a person will follow after the first fruits at the time of his coming. Then again—and I am speaking by way of supposition—Timothy, who as far as possible imitated in himself his teacher, would succeed in the same way, as would any other such person. So too successively some, however many, by declining little by little from the good are always found after those preceding them until the succession of followers reaches those in whom the portion of the better is less than the expanding evil. According to the same proportion with respect to those having a lesser portion in evil, [16] the succession procures for those previously in evil the rank of those returning to the better until the progress of the good reaches the highest limit of evil, annihilating wickedness.[4] This, indeed, is the goal

3. ὁ κατὰ Χριστὸν ἄνθρωπος.

4. The argument is quite obscure. There appear to be two processions, one increasingly wicked and the other increasingly good. Apparently, when the first procession reaches the limit of wickedness or evil, the second procession will reverse the movement of the first. Sometimes Gregory seems to distinguish "evil" (τὸ κακόν) from

of hope (Col 1:5), that nothing should be left opposed to the good, but that divine life by pervading all things should completely annihilate death from existing things, with sin first destroyed by which as it is said (Rom 5:12, 14, 21) death had its reign against humans.

Therefore, when every evil authority and ruler in our midst has been destroyed, and when there is no longer any passion lording over our nature, it is entirely necessary once there is nothing else holding power against us to subject all things to the ruler over all. And subjection to God is absolute alienation from evil. When, therefore, we all come to be outside evil by imitating our first fruits, then the whole batch of our nature, mixed with the first fruits and made one in accord with the conjoined body, will receive in itself the governance of the good alone. And thus, when the entire body of our nature has been mingled with the divine and pure nature, that subjection said to be the Son's takes place through us, since the subjection successfully accomplished in his body refers to him who worked in us the grace of subjection.

This, then, is the explanation of great Paul's teachings, at least as we have understood them. But it may be time to place beside it the very words of the apostle, which read [17] as follows: "For as in Adam all die, so also will all be made alive in Christ. But each in his own order; Christ the first fruits, then at his coming those who belong to Christ. Then comes the end, when he hands over the kingdom to God the Father, after he has destroyed every ruler and authority and power. For he must reign until[5] he has put all his enemies under his feet. The last enemy to be destroyed is death. For he 'has put all things in subjection under his feet' (Ps 8:7). But when it says that he put all things in subjection,[6] it is plain that this does not include the one who put all things in subjection under him. When all things are subjected to him, then he[7] will also be subjected to the one who put all things in subjection under him, so that God may be all in all" (1 Cor 15:22–28).

Quite clearly in the last verse of the passage Paul asserts in his argument the nonexistence of evil by saying that God in becoming all things to each comes to be in all. For it is obvious that it will be true that God is in all at that time when nothing evil is discerned in existing things. Of course, it is not reasonable that God should also be in evil. Consequently, either he will not be in all when anything evil remains in existing things, or, if it is truly

"wickedness" (ἡ κακία), but in other places they appear to be synonymous. Both words are translated "evil" unless the context dictates otherwise.

5. Gregory's text reads ἕως ἂν instead of ἀχρὶ οὗ.

6. Gregory's text reads ὑπέταξεν as in Ps 8, instead of ὑποτέτακται.

7. Gregory's text reads αὐτὸς instead of αὐτὸς ὁ υἱός; but cf. p. 4, where the usual text is found.

necessary to believe that he is in all, by belief in this it is also demonstrated that nothing evil exists. For it is impossible for God to be in evil.

[18] That God is all in all existing things indicates the unmixed and uniform character of the life for which we hope. For no longer is life to be contributed to us by many and various means as it is in our present earthly life. Paul asserts this by saying that God is all things to us, as many as seem necessary for this life, since each source of life is transformed to something more divine by a kind of analogy. As a result, God is both food and drink for us, as it is proper for God to be eaten.[8] Likewise he is both clothing and shelter, air, place, wealth, enjoyment, beauty, health, strength, intelligence, glory, blessedness, and everything whatsoever judged to belong to a good portion and needed by our nature, provided the meaning of Paul's words has been elevated to what befits God, so as to learn by this that the one who comes to be in God has all things by having him. And having God is nothing other than being united to God. No one would be united to him in any other way than by becoming "members of the same body" (Eph 3:6) with him, according to Paul's word.[9] For all of us by being joined to the one body of Christ become his one body by participation.

Therefore, when the good pervades all, then his entire body will be subjected to the life-giving power, and in this way the subjection of this body is said to be the subjection of the Son himself, who has been mingled together with his own body, which is the church, as the apostle says to the Colossians. He says this in these words: "I am now rejoicing in my sufferings, [19] and in my flesh I am completing what is lacking in afflictions on behalf of Christ[10] for the sake of his body, that is, the church. I became its servant according to God's commission" (Col 1:24–25). And to the church of the Corinthians he says, "You are the body of Christ and individually members of it" (1 Cor 12:27). His teaching about this is presented more clearly to the Ephesians, where he says, "But speaking the truth in love, let us grow up in every way into him who is the head, into Christ, from whom the whole body, joined and knit together by every ligament with which it is equipped, as each part is working properly, promotes the body's growth in building itself up in love" (Eph 4:15–16). This happens since Christ builds himself up through those who are always being added to the faith. He will cease building himself up at that time when the increase and perfection of his body attains its own measure (cf. Eph 4:13), and there is no longer lacking for the body what is to be added for building it up, since all have been

---

8. The reference appears to be to the Eucharist.

9. The word in the text of Ephesians is σύσσωμα.

10. ὑπὲρ τοῦ Χριστοῦ instead of τοῦ Χριστοῦ.

built upon the foundation of the prophets and apostles (Eph 2:20) and have been added to the faith. This will be when, as the apostle says, "all of us come to the unity of the faith and of the knowledge of the Son of God, to a perfect man, to the measure of the full stature of Christ" (Eph 4:13).

Therefore, if he, existing as the head, builds up his own body by successive stages, it is through those who are always being added that he "joins and knits together" all with regard to the growth each has achieved according to the "measure of Christ's working" (cf. Eph 4:16). As a result, either hand or eye or foot or ear or [20] anything else comes to belong to what fills up the body according to the proportion of each person's faith (Rom 12:6). Since by procuring these Christ builds himself up, as has been said, it should be obvious by this that by coming to be in all he receives into himself all united to him by sharing in his body; and he makes all members of his own body so that "there are many members, yet one body" (1 Cor 12:20).

Therefore, he who united us to himself, and who was united to us, and who in all respects became one with us, makes all that is ours his own. And the chief of our goods is subjection to the divine, when the whole creation comes to itself with one voice and to him "every knee should bend, in heaven and on earth and under the earth, and every tongue should confess that Jesus Christ is Lord" (Phil 2:10–11). When the whole creation becomes one body and all people in him grow together with one another by obedience, then he offers for himself the subjection of his own body to the Father.

Let no one be surprised at what has been said. Indeed, even we by some custom reckon to the soul what happens through our body, just as that man, who in dialogue with his own soul concerning the abundant produce of his field and who said, "eat, drink, and be merry" attributes the surfeit of his flesh to his soul (Luke 12:19). So here the subjection of the church's body is attributed to the one indwelling the body.

And since everything that comes to be in him is saved, [21] salvation is interpreted by subjection, as the psalm instructs us to understand.[11] Accordingly, we learn in this passage of the apostle's letter to believe that nothing is outside what is to be saved. His argument points this out clearly by the destruction of death and by the subjection of the Son, because these things belong together with one another, namely, that death will never be and that all will come to be in life. The life is the Lord (cf. John 11:25), through whom according to the apostle's argument there is access to the Father (Eph 2:18) for his entire body, "when he hands over our kingdom to God the Father" (1 Cor 15:24). His body, as has often been said, is the entire human nature into which he has been mixed.

---

11. The reference is to Ps 61. See p. 6.

Because of this same concept the Lord is also called by Paul "the me-diator between God and humans" (1 Tim 2:5). For since he exists with the Father and came to be among humans, by this he fulfills his role as mediator by uniting all people to himself and through himself to the Father, as the Lord says in the Gospel when making his prayer to the Father: "that they may all be one, as you, Father are in me and I am in you, so that in this way they too may be one in us" (John 17:21). For this verse clearly asserts that the one who exists in the Father, having united us to himself, through himself brings to perfection our union[12] with the Father.

Moreover, the next verse in the Gospel accords with the previous one: "The glory that you have given me I have given them" (John 17:22). [22] For by "glory" here I think he means the Holy Spirit which he gave to his disciples by breathing upon them (John 20:22). For there is no other way for those who have been divided from one another to be united save by being born together in the unity of the Spirit. For "anyone who does not have the Spirit of Christ does not belong to him" (Rom 8:9). And the Spirit is glory, as Christ says elsewhere to the Father: "Glorify me with the glory that I had from the beginning in your presence before the world existed" (John 17:5). For God the Word is the one who before the world has the glory of the Father. When in the last days he became flesh (cf. Heb 1:2; John 1:14), it was also necessary for the flesh through its mixture with the Word to become what the Word is. The flesh became this by receiving what the Word had before the world, and this was the Holy Spirit. For nothing else is pre-existent except the Father, the Son, and the Holy Spirit. This is why he also says in this passage, "The glory that you have given me I have given them, so that through it they may be united to me and through me to you" (cf. John 17:22).

Let us look also at what is next put down in the Gospel: "So that they may be one as we are one, you in me and I in them, because I and you are one, so that they may be perfected in one" (John 17:22–23). Indeed, I think these words need no interpretation so as to be put in accord with the pre-ceding thought, since the text itself clearly presents the teaching concerning these matters: "So that they may be one as we are one." For it is not possible in any other way [23] for all to become one as we are one, unless those separated from all that divides them from one another should be united with us who are one, "so that they may be one as we are one." How does this happen? "Because I am in them it is impossible that I should be the only one in them; rather, it certainly includes you, since I and you are one (cf. John

---

12. συνάφειαν rather than ἕνωσις.

10:30). In this way those perfected in us will become perfected in one, since we are one."

He then indicates such a grace more clearly by the words that follow, saying thus, "You have loved them even as you have loved me" (John 17:23). For if the Father loves the Son, and if all of us who have become his body through faith in him are in the Son, it follows that the one who loves his own Son also loves his Son's body as he loves the Son himself; and we are the body. Therefore, the apostolic concept has become apparent through what is said, namely, that the Son's subjection to the Father clearly points out the knowledge of him who is and the salvation that comes to the entire human nature.

The argument may become still clearer for us on the basis of some other apostolic concepts, of which I shall mention only one, since I excuse myself from the multitude of testimonies to avoid prolonging my argument at too great a length. Somewhere Paul says in his own words, "I have been crucified with Christ; [24] and it is no longer I who live, but it is Christ who lives in me" (Gal 2:19–20). Therefore, if Paul, who was crucified to the world (Gal 6:14), no longer lives, but Christ lives in him, then everything Paul did and said is rightly attributed to Christ, who lives in him. Moreover, it says that Paul's words were spoken from Christ; Paul says, "Do you desire proof that Christ is speaking in me?" (2 Cor 13:3). He even says that his virtuous acts following the gospel are not his, but he attributes them to Christ's grace indwelling him. If, therefore, Christ living in him is said by analogy to act and speak for him, and if Paul, after he took his stand against all that previously ruled him when he was a blasphemer, a persecutor, and a violent man (cf. 1 Tim 1:13), looks to the true good alone and makes himself compliant and obedient to it, therefore, Paul's subjection which took place to God has reference to the one living in him, who both speaks good words and does good works in him. The chief of all goods is subjection to God.

What the argument has found in the case of one will reasonably be in accord with the entire human creation, when, as the Lord says, the gospel reaches the whole world (cf. Mark 13:10; 16:15). For when all have stripped off the old self with its practices and lusts (Col 3:9; Eph 4:22) and have received the Lord in themselves, it is necessarily the one living in them that accomplishes the good things that come to be from them. [25] The highest point of all goods is salvation, which takes place for us by alienation from evil. Moreover, there is no other way of being separated from evil than to have been mingled with God by subjection. Therefore, as well, subjection to God is itself analogous to Christ living in us. For if there is anything noble, it is his; and if there is anything good, it comes from him, as says one of the prophets (cf. Jas 1:17). Since, then, his subjection has been demonstrated to be something noble and good, its good is certainly from the one from whom the nature of every good comes, as the prophet's word says.

Let no one, then, by looking at the common usage of the word subjection reject the word. For the wisdom of great Paul knows that he has used words as he sees fit authoritatively; and he brings the connotations of the words into harmony with the particular connection of his thought, even though custom refers his peculiar usage of the lections to some other meanings. Or where did he get his usage of "he emptied himself" (Phil 2:7) and "no one will empty my boast" (1 Cor 9:15) and "faith has been emptied" (Rom 4:14) and "so that the cross of Christ might not be emptied" (1 Cor 1:17)? From what use did he receive these into his own speech? And who will condemn him when he said "desiring you" (1 Thess 2:8), by which expression he indicates a loving relationship? From what source did he point out the absence of arrogance in love by the expression "not to boast" (1 Cor 13:4)? How are contentions and defensive rivalries signified by his use of the word "wool-working" (Phil 1:17; 2 Cor 12:20), since it is clear to everyone that [26] outside scripture this is the word for a female laborer in wool work, and we are accustomed to signify an occupation concerning wool by the word wool-working?[13] But for all that, Paul, after bidding farewell to all cold etymologies, asserts the thought he wishes by the expressions he wishes. Moreover, for those who examine them carefully there are many other places found in the apostle's writings that do not observe the customary usage, but are presented according to some idiosyncratic meaning on the authority of one who pays no attention to custom.

So then, here too what is signified by subjection is understood by Paul as something other than its common meanings. A proof of the argument is that not even the subjection of the enemies Paul mentions in this passage has the character of something compelled and involuntary, as those observing the customary sense would say. Instead, by the word subjection salvation is interpreted to be upon them. The proof is that in this passage the word enemy is defined by Paul to have a double significance. For of enemies he says that some will be subjected (1 Cor 15:27), while others will be destroyed (1 Cor 15:26). Therefore, the enemy by nature, that is, death, is destroyed, as well as the rule, authority, and power of sin that is concerned with it. But those said to be God's enemies in another sense will be subjected.

---

13. Presumably these words are rare or have different connotations for Theodore than what we can find in the lexicons. The NRSV translates the Greek words as follows: 1 Thess 2:8, ὁμειρόμενοι is "longing for [you]"; 1 Cor 14:4, περπερεύεσθαι is "[not] to boast"; Gregory takes ἐριθεία to be a synonym of ἐριουργία ("wool-working"); as well, ἡ ἔριθος means "a female worker in wool." NRSV translates "selfish ambition" in Phil 1:17 and "selfishness" in 2 Cor 12:20.

These are those [27] who have deserted from his kingdom to sin, of whom Paul also makes mention in his letter to the Romans, where he said, "For if while we were enemies, we were reconciled to God" (Rom 5:10). For what he calls here subjection he calls there reconciliation, indicating by each of the two words a single concept, salvation. For just as being saved happens by subjection, so too in the other place he says, "having been reconciled, we will be saved by his life" (Rom 5:10). Therefore, he says that such enemies will be subjected to God the Father, but that death and the rule associated with it will no longer exist. For he indicates this by the expression "will be destroyed" (cf. 1 Cor 15:26), so that by this it becomes clear that the dominating power of evils will be completely laid to rest. But those called God's enemies because of their disobedience, these by subjection will become the Lord's friends when they obey the one who says, "We are ambassadors for Christ, since God is making his appeal through us; we entreat you on behalf of Christ, be reconciled to God" (2 Cor 5:20). And according to the promise found in the Gospel, having been reconciled, they will be numbered by the Lord no longer as among his servants, but as among his friends (John 15:14–15).

We shall then, as I think, accept in its true religious sense the verse "he must reign until he has put his enemies under his feet" (1 Cor 15:25), if we have understood that through his reigning he is valorous. For he who is "mighty in battle" (Ps 23:8) ceases from valor when everything opposed to the good has been annihilated and when, having gathered together all his kingdom, he offers it to God the Father after uniting all things to himself. For his handing over the kingdom to the Father (1 Cor 15:24) [28] has the same meaning as bringing all people to God, by which we have "access in one Spirit to the Father" (Eph 2:18).[14] Therefore, at the time when all enemies are under God's feet by having received the divine footprint in themselves, and when death has been destroyed (for when there are no people dying, certainly neither will death exist), then by the subjection of all of us—not understood as slavish humiliation but as kingship, incorruption, and blessedness—the one who lives in us is said by Paul to be subjected to God. He is the one who perfects our good through himself and does what is well pleasing to himself in us.

This is what we have apprehended in this passage according to the measure of our understanding of great Paul's wisdom, as far as we were capable. We wished to show that the champions of heretical teachings have not examined the aim which the apostle envisaged when he made his

---

14. The translation cannot express the relation of "offers" (προσαγαγεῖν) and "access" (προσαγωγὴν).

present argument. If, then, the assurance given by what has been said in this inquiry is sufficient for you, refer your gratitude to God. But if something should seem to you lacking, we shall gladly accept the completion of what is lacking if it should be made known to us by you through a letter, and if the revelation of hidden things should be revealed from the Holy Spirit through our prayers.

PART TWO

Essays

1

The Promises and Baptism

It is a commonplace that human life for the individual and for the entire race is metaphorically a journey. Scripture treats the journey as one that begins in a garden and ends in a city, and Gregory partly agrees, since he can think of the end as a return to the beginning.[1] Yet there is a difference between paradise before the fall and the destiny that awaits humans after this age. I am reminded of "Little Gidding," the last of T. S. Eliot's *Four Quartets*. In section 5 he says,

> What we call the beginning is often the end,
> And to make an end is to make a beginning.
> The end is where we start from. . . .
> We shall not cease from exploration,
> And the end of all our exploring
> Will be to arrive where we started
> And know the place for the first time.[2]

---

1. See, e.g, *Prof.* 136; *Perf.* 195, 208. Cf. *Mort.* 51: The changing forms of the body, including death, "are parts of the path by which we travel. And the aim and limit of the journey through these stages is restoration to our original condition, which is no other than likeness to the divine." Presumably this restoration includes the resurrection of the body. According to *De hom. op.* 17.2 (PG 44:187d) it also means a condition like that of the angels, as Luke 20:36 shows. Being *like* the angels need not mean being the same as they, any more than being *like* God identifies humans with God. It may not be possible, however, to find any clear account in Gregory's writings of humanity's original condition. See my attempt to worry with the question in essay 4, and see Ludlow, *Universal Salvation*, 74–94; Smith, *Passion and Paradise*, 28–47, 116; Zachhuber, *Human Nature*, 154–74, 200–204.

2. Eliot, *Four Quartets*, ll. 214–16, 239–42.

For Gregory the end will differ from the beginning because it completes and stabilizes the beginning. While it goes beyond what he actually says, the return is as much to God's intention in creating humanity as to an actual original state he specifies. His concern, however, is with another journey, one that is caught up into the longer story from creation to the new age that will come about after the consummation of this one.

BAPTISM

This second journey, of course, is the one that Christians must take. Speaking of "those who love virtue" Gregory says that "the one path to a life both pure and divine is to know what the name of Christ means" (*Perf.* 181). In his second homily *In Praise of Stephen* he calls attention to those who in a special way have walked along this path. Christ is the Savior and "the martyr of truth," who came into this world "to shed light." His disciples, the martyrs of whom Stephen is the first, "traveling in the Lord's footsteps, followed their teacher—those bearing Christ after Christ, the lights of the world (Phil 2:15) after the sun of righteousness (Mal 3:20)" (*St.* 2 97). Neither the text from Philippians nor Gregory's allusion to it need to refer to baptism, but the connotation may be present for the simple reason that a common name for baptism in the early church was "illumination or enlightenment" (φωτίσμος). Despite the fact that Gregory usually speaks of "baptism" or of "the bath or washing," he recognizes the term *illumination*.[3] In his second homily on Song of Songs he is interpreting the bride's statement that she is "black and beautiful" (Song 1:5). The blackness represents the bride's sin, while her beauty has been given her by the bridegroom's love. So too Paul "became radiant from darkness," and he says that "Christ came into the world to make the black bright, not calling the righteous to himself but sinners to repentance, those whom he made to shine like stars (Phil 2:15) by the washing of regeneration" (Titus 3:5).[4]

---

3. Baptism is called "illumination" as early as in Justin Martyr's *First Apology* 61.14. See Ferguson, *Baptism*, 109, and the other references in his index of subjects under "enlightenment." By the fourth century those catechumens enrolled for baptism were called "the ones to be enlightened." Gregory certainly accepts the term *illumination* (see *Or. cat.* 32 [*GNO* 3.4:82] and *In diem lum.* [*GNO* 9:227]). Ferguson claims that it is a "key aspect of Gregory's baptismal theology, although not developed as much as might be expected in his sermon *On the Day of Lights*." Ferguson, *Baptism*, 613.

4. *In cant.* 2 (*GNO* 6:48–49). Cf. Origen, *Commentary on Song of Songs* 2.1 (GCS 33:113–14), where the bride represents the church from the Gentiles and has become beautiful by receiving the Word made flesh, who is "the radiance of [God's] glory and the imprint of his being" (Heb 1:3).

It can be no surprise that Gregory treats baptism as the entrance to the Christian path.[5] Nevertheless, his only full treatments of baptism are found in the *Catechetical Oration* and in his homily *On the Day of Lights*.[6] Even here it is not possible to ascertain the rite with which he was familiar save for references to the enrollment of candidates, the invocation of grace or blessing of the water, and the three immersions.[7] Nevertheless, it seems reasonable to argue that the structure of Gregory's rite was similar to what we know of the Eastern rite from Cyril of Jerusalem, Theodore of Mopsuestia, and John Chrysostom. John Baldovin persuasively concludes that "an original diversity began to come together in remarkably similar ritual patterns in the fourth century only to diversify subsequently into the major rites still known in the early twenty-first century."[8] Gregory, then, presupposed a period of preparation for catechumens who had enrolled themselves as "those to be enlightened." While this period need not have been the forty days before Easter, baptism at the Christian Pasch seems the likely norm. The candidates for baptism would have received not only instruction and the handing down of the baptismal creed, but also regular exorcisms. The rite itself probably began with the renunciation of Satan and the *synaxis* with Christ, followed by the anointing of the head. The candidates were then stripped of their clothing and anointed over their entire bodies like athletes. They then repeated the creed in response to interrogations. This must have been followed by the blessing of the water and certainly by the triple immersion of the candidates and their being sealed with the oil of chrism. They were then clothed in the white robe called the chrysom, and the eucharist followed.

While we learn little from Gregory's writings about the rite of baptism, he does give us a fairly extended account of its meaning in the *Catechetical Oration*. We can call "the dispensation by washing" baptism or illumination or rebirth (Titus 3:5).[9] This rebirth, in contrast to our mortal birth, takes

---

5. See Cortesi, *Le Omelie sul Cantico dei Cantici*. His study locates references to baptism in the homilies and persuasively shows how they are tied to the central themes of light, odor, and nourishment, as well as water. He is less concerned with the relationship of his evidence to the text of Song of Songs and to Gregory's attempts to provide a narrative understanding of them.

6. The homily, also known as *In baptismum Christi oratio*, was preached in Cappadocia ca. 383. See Ferguson, "Preaching at Epiphany," 1–17.

7. See Ferguson, *Baptism*, 603–8.

8. Baldovin, "Empire Baptized," 77–130. The citation is on 77, and what follows depends largely on Baldovin.

9. The verse from Titus refers to "washing" and for "rebirth" uses the word παλιγγενεσία. Ferguson, *Baptism*, 608–9, points out that he frequently uses the term "washing," prefers to speak of "rebirth" as ἀμαγέννησις, as found in 1 Pet 1:3, 23 and

place so that we may "become better than the corruption that comes from death." It is effected by "prayer to God and the invocation of heavenly grace, as well as by water and faith."[10] Those who doubt this may be persuaded by the argument that the regeneration made possible through water is no more incredible than our first birth from "a certain moist quality."[11] Positively, then, the new birth of baptism consists in the imitation of Christ's death and resurrection, an imitation only partially possible now, with the rest "stored up"[12] for what will come about after this life. It is the triple immersion of the baptized that points to this understanding, since "three" conjures up Christ's "death for three days and his return once more to life." Those who follow this pattern travel "through similar ways." Human life is like a labyrinth in which people inevitably lose their way, and it is also like "an inescapable prison of death." But those who follow Christ's footsteps will find their way out of both through death as the gateway to resurrection.[13] Participation in Christ's death and resurrection in baptism must be followed by imitating him in order to lead to this destiny.[14] As well, the present meaning of death and resurrection involves "a certain break in the continuity of evil." This is represented by repentance as a dying to sin, and Gregory cites Rom 6:10, "he died to sin once for all."[15] Baptism is only the beginning, and the destruction of evil involves penitence and the spiritual imitation of Christ's death by which evil will finally be destroyed.[16]

Gregory rightly understands Paul's explanation of baptism in Rom 6. It is both a guarantee and promise of the Christian's actual death and resurrection with Christ, and a present death to an old way of life and new birth to the Christian life. What is done in baptism is "brought to effect by God," for "his grace is present to those who are born again through the

---

implied by John 3:3–7. See also his "Preaching at Epiphany," 3 n. 10.

10. *Or. cat.* 33 (LCC 3:312; *GNO* 3.4:82).

11. *Or. cat.* 33 (LCC 3:313; *GNO* 3.4:83). Cf. *In diem lum.* (*GNO* 9:227), where Gregory makes the same argument.

12. *Or. cat.* 35 (LCC 3:316; *GNO* 3.4:89).

13. *Or. cat.* 35 (LCC 3:315; *GNO* 3.4:87).

14. See Bouchet, "La vision de l'économie du salut," 613–44; Hübner, *Die Einheit*, 168–75; Kees, *Die Lehre*, 162–78. All three agree in emphasizing the imitation of Christ; but Bouchet focuses on the incarnation, while the others refer to dying and rising with Christ. There need be no contradiction, since the incarnation refers to the whole of Christ's human life which culminates in his death and resurrection.

15. *Or. cat.* 35 (LCC 3:316; *GNO* 3.4:89).

16. See Ferguson, "Doctrine of Baptism," 228–29.

sacramental act."[17] This grace is "the gift of the Holy Spirit,"[18] but it is important to recognize that a gift must be rightly used to have its proper effect. "What happens in the sacrament of Baptism depends upon the disposition of the heart of him who approaches it." Since Christians are baptized in the name of the Trinity (Matt 28:19), anyone with a false understanding by supposing the Son or the Spirit to be created has made himself the child of "a defective nature."[19] Equally important, baptism does not change our nature, but it should result in a changed character. If "the stains of passion" are not washed off, Gregory is bold enough to say, "the water is only water, and the gift of the Holy Spirit is nowhere evident in the action."[20] The gift must be rightly used.[21]

In his homily *On the Day of Lights* Gregory repeats a number of the themes already mentioned. The "grace of the washing" is "a great gift," but he describes the gift somewhat differently. It is "the loosing of punishments, the breaking of bonds, intimacy with God, free boldness instead of humiliation, equal honor with the angels."[22] The water "serves as a sign of the cleansing," which is effected "by God's command and the Spirit's coming upon us."[23] The three immersions are again an imitation of Christ's three days in death, for we are buried in water as he was in earth; and so this is "made an image for ourselves of the third day grace of the resurrection."[24] Several themes, however, are new and elaborate those of the *Catechetical Oration*. Gregory appeals to Zech 3:3-5, where the priest Joshua (Jesus) is ordered to take off his "filthy clothes" and is dressed in "festal apparel." So "in the baptism of Jesus all of us by stripping off our sins like a poor and much patched tunic, are clothed with the sacred and most beautiful garment of rebirth."[25]

17. *Or.cat.* 34 (LCC 3:314; GNO 3.4:85). διὰ τῆς μυστικῆς ταύτης οἰκονομίας, which could also refer to the "economy" of the incarnation. See Kees, *Die Lehre*, 64–66, 318–22.

18. *Or. cat.* 40 (LCC 3:324; GNO 3.4:103).

19. *Or. cat.* 39 (LCC 3:322; GNO 3.4:98–101).

20. *Or. cat.* 40 (LCC 3:324; GNO 3.4:103).

21. Cf. *Vit. Mos.* 125–29 (CWS 83–85; GNO 7.1:72–74), where anyone who has crossed the Red Sea of baptism and discovers the passions (Pharaoh's army) still in pursuit, has not used baptism rightly nor profited by it. Martin Laird in *Grasp of Faith* provides a fine account of "the grasp of faith" (*Hom. 6 in cant.*, GNO 6:183) in the context of the mind's ascent to union with God and its result in what he usefully calls *logophasis*. He refers at several points to baptism, arguing for its gracious role (see index), but he bases his account of "'The Grace of Baptism" (46–49) largely upon this passage from the *Vit. Mos.* without noting that here grace is effective only when rightly used.

22. *In diem lum.* (GNO 9:222–23).

23. *In diem lum.* (GNO 9:224).

24. *In diem lum.* (GNO 9:228).

25. *In diem lum.* (GNO 9:236).

It is impossible not to understand this as an allusion to the white robe, the chrysom, with which the newly baptized were clothed. Perhaps more important, Christ's baptism and that of Christians are associated with Christ's undoing of the fall by his conquest of Satan. Christ was baptized "so that the one who fell away may be raised up, and the one who overthrew him may be put to shame."[26] Gregory warns his hearers that "after the dignity of adoption as children the devil plots against us more violently, sharpening himself with his malevolent eye when he sees the beauty of the new born person who is hastening to the heavenly citizenship from which he fell."[27]

The homily ends with an address to "the generous benefactor who has given such a great gift, contributing in return to him a small word as a repayment for large matters." The address reads as follows:[28]

> For you truly exist as the pure Ruler and eternal spring of goodness. You righteously turned away from us and graciously had pity. You hated us, and you reconciled us; you cursed, and you blessed. You cast us out of paradise and summoned us back again. You stripped off the fig leaves that covered our shame, and you put around us a costly robe. You opened the prison and released those who had been condemned. You sprinkled us with pure water and washed away our stains. No longer will Adam be ashamed when you summon him, nor will the flaming sword circle paradise, blocking the entrance to those who draw near. And everything for us as heirs has been transformed from sin to joy; both paradise and heaven itself are accessible to humanity. The creation in this world and above this world, of old in conflict with itself, has been brought into friendly accord; and we humans have become harmonious with the angels, reverently offering the same praise of God with them.

In this way Gregory locates baptism within the longer journey and the story that encompasses the whole of this age and is to be consummated in the age to come.[29]

Keeping this discussion of baptism in mind, let me now turn to the works translated in Part One, primarily *On the Christian's Profession* and *On Perfection*, in order to describe how these works understand the Christian

---

26. *In diem lum.* (GNO 9:223).

27. *In diem lum.* (GNO 9:234).

28. *In diem lum.* (GNO 9:241).

29. For a fuller discussion of Gregory's view of baptism, see Ferguson, *Baptism*, 603–16.

path in ways that can be associated with baptism both as the entrance into the path and as an ideal paradigm of the journey that lies ahead.

PROFESSION AND PERFECTION

From the preceding discussion it is possible to argue that Gregory understands imitating Christ as primarily the Christian's task in renouncing an old way of life and embracing the great gift of the new life exemplified in and given by Christ. Christians make their promise, but it is caught up in the better promise of Christ. The profession of Christians is meant to receive the perfection in which they will fully participate only after death and in the age to come. Renouncing Satan, defeating the passions, and being purified from sin are the necessary steps that lead to the acquisition of virtue. Put together, we can speak of this as a dying to sin and a rising to the new life of virtue. Dying and rising with Christ also involves the incorporation of the baptized into the church, Christ's body. Christ's death and resurrection, the climax of his incarnate life, makes all this possible, and in a real sense this takes us beyond imitation to worship and to the reception of Christ's promises in contemplating the glory of his divinity and of the holy Trinity. All this and more is implicit in baptism as a foreshadowing, an anticipation, and a challenge for what Christians should become and may become by grace.

What is it that people profess when they call themselves Christians? In formulating the question I am, of course, thinking of Gregory's letter to Harmonius and the "question" (πρόβλημα; *Prof.* 130) he seeks to answer. The careful reader, however, will notice that I have posed the question by speaking of Christians in the plural. The manuscript tradition of the letter's title agrees in part with this, even though Jaeger's critical edition uses the singular, following not only the chief manuscripts but also Gregory's own articulation of the topic. This need be no special difficulty, because throughout the letter it is obvious that Gregory is thinking not merely of the individual, but of "us." The profession of the Christian is what defines Christianity as a whole. If we are able to apprehend the many concepts implied by "the name of Christ," then we are able to have "some means for understanding how to interpret Christianity" (*Prof.* 135). The Christian profession, then, is one common to all Christians and refers to the "one path" they must tread (*Perf.* 181). What does the term "profession" (ἐπάγγελμα) mean? The dictionaries give several other possible meanings of the Greek word: promise, undertaking, art, proclamation. Even if we grant the usual translation, profession, it is reasonably clear that Gregory supposes that the profession is also a promise and an undertaking. He thinks that it is "obvious to everyone" that "promising to assume the name Christian professes the imitation of God" (*Prof.* 137).[30] When people call themselves Christians, they are making both a profession of their faith and a promise.[31]

One puzzling fact about Gregory's *On the Christian's Profession* is that he makes no explicit reference to baptism. Nevertheless, this must surely be what he has in mind. He speaks of "participating in Christ" and of "assuming" or putting on "the name of Christ" (*Prof.* 135). Could it be that this "assuming" can be understood as an allusion to the "clothing" of the newly baptized with the white robe or chrysom, something in all likelihood familiar to Gregory? The cognates of the verb Gregory uses refer in the New Testament to shoes, but a similar verb found in Gal 3:27 is associated with baptism: "As many of you as were baptized into Christ have clothed yourselves with Christ."[32] We need not assume that Paul is speaking specifically of the chrysom, but it does appear that the metaphor of clothing is indeed associated with baptism. Three other references in Gregory's letter, however, have a clearer association with baptism. At one point he cites Christ's command to "be perfect, as also your heavenly Father is perfect" (Matt 5:45). He then goes on to say: "For when he [Christ] called the true Father the father of those who believed, he wanted also those born through him to be like the perfection of good contemplated in him" (*Prof.* 138). What Gregory means is that those "born" through Christ are to imitate God's virtues and actions. It is impossible not to think of Christ's words to Nicodemus: "no one can enter the kingdom of God without being born of water and Spirit" (John 3:5). In another place Gregory refers to "the person who has not yet accepted the account of the mystery" (*Prof.* 137). He is speaking of someone who is not a Christian and will form his idea of the Christian God by observing "the behavior of those professing Christianity." To say that someone has not accepted the "mystery" need not define the person as unbaptized, but the connotation is far from impossible.

The third passage I have in mind occurs as part of the moral Gregory draws from the story of the trained monkey that betrays its true character when enticed by the almonds some wit throws to it and is thereby seduced from its dancing. Just as the monkey was a false dancer, so we must beware of being false Christians, betraying our profession by failing to conform our lives to it. We should become what our name, Christ's, means, "lest, if we are formed by the bare confession [ὁμολογία] and the pretext of the name alone,

30. ἡ ὑπόσχεσις τοῦ ὀνόματος μίμησιν θεοῦ ἐπαγγέλλεται. Cf. *Prof.* 136: "promising to assume the appellation [Christian]."

31. The double meaning of ἐπάγγελμα is reflected in Gregory's view of imitation. See McCambley, "On the Profession of a Christian," 434–35.

32. The verb Gregory uses is ὑποδύομαι, while that in Galatians is ἐνδύομαι.

we should be exposed to the one who perceives what is hidden to be other than what we appear" (*Prof.* 133). Like the monkey "those who fail truly to form their own nature itself by faith will be exposed by the greeds of the devil to be other than what they profess." The dainties offered by the devil are "vainglory, ambition, love of gain, love of pleasure, and whatever such things the evil market of the devil proffers for sale" (*Prof.* 133). To be sure, "confession" need not always refer to the baptismal confession; but this is certainly a possible meaning. And we can think of texts from the New Testament: Rom 10:9–10; 1 John 2:23; 4:2–3, 15; 2 John 7. If I am correct that Gregory implicitly links the Christian profession to baptism, the question remains why he makes no explicit reference to it. The simple answer that occurs to me is that he wishes to emphasize the life that must follow baptism. Baptism is no more than the beginning of the Christian life; and its gift must be used wisely and conscientiously. It could be, as well, that Gregory does not wish to exclude those enrolled as catechumens from consideration. He and others recognized the custom of delaying baptism to a time beyond the storms of adolescence, even though they argued against what seems to have been a common attitude.[33] Despite complications, then, I want to conclude that Gregory does think of baptism as, in principle, the beginning of the Christian life and the point of departure for the path leading to its goals. Both the path and its beginning are common to all Christians, despite differences of age, sex, nationality, race, social position, or any other difference that in this world tends to divide humans from one another.

Turning from *On the Christian's Profession* to *On Perfection* is to discover what seems a shift in genre. The letter to Harmonius has been reworked and elaborated as a treatise sent to Olympius. As well, *On Perfection* resolves and clarifies a puzzling tension that can be discerned in the earlier letter to Harmonius.[34] In it the Christian profession has to do with what the name "Christ" means, and I have assumed that the allusion is to the baptismal confession of Christ. But Gregory concludes that "Christianity is the imitation of the divine nature" (*Prof.* 136). It is by no means clear how we

---

33. The practice of delaying baptism until after adolescence or until death is near is attested in the fourth century and earlier. See the *Pseudo-Clementine Homilies* (11.26–27) and *Apostlic Constitutions* (6.15.6). The term ἀναβολή ("delay") acquired the technical meaning of postponing baptism. See Hammerich, "Taufe und Askese," 85. Ferguson, *Baptism*, 364 n. 5, cites Tertullian's warning in *On Repentance* 6 against either hasty entrance into baptism or delaying it as evidence that the fear of post-baptismal sin caused the practice. Gregory addressed the issue in *Adv. eos qui baptismum differunt* (*GNO* 10.2:357–70).

34. See Jaeger, *Two Rediscovered Works*, 27–31, 86, 119–20. He gives a late date to both works, and regards the *De instituto* as following them, probably after 390. See, however, May, "Die Chronologie des Lebens," 52–56, 61–62.

are to correlate these two themes. We could understand the problem as one related to Gregory's use of Platonizing themes to explain Christian claims, and it is obvious that the "imitation of the divine nature" is a phrase alluding to the passage in the *Theaetetus* (176b) where Plato defines the goal of human life as "likeness to God as far as possible." Of equal or more importance are scriptural texts such as Gen 1:26 (image and likeness of God) and 2 Pet 1:4 (participants of the divine nature). Without denying this aspect of the problem, I wish to argue that resolving it depends upon clarifying the identity of Christ in his twofold relationship to the Godhead and to human nature. This is precisely what Gregory has done in *On Perfection*, at least in a partial way. The treatise finds its organization in the Pauline texts that identify Christ and give us the various concepts and characteristic marks that constitute the Christian confession and the Christian life. "As many of them as we grasp we imitate, but as many as our nature does not grasp for imitation we both venerate and worship" (*Perf.* 178).

This ideal finds its contrast in anyone "maiming his soundness by wickedness." Gregory elaborates his point by appealing to "those who fashion mythic marvels either by words or by the art of painting, when they construct out of different species people with the heads of bulls or centaurs or people with snakes for feet." These fabulous monsters are only half human. No one can be a Christian with the bull's head of idolatry instead of having Christ as his head. Nor can true Christians be bestial by having "the anger of snakes" or "the madness for women" of horses. In varying ways these false Christians really have two natures, rational and irrational. This means that they will find in themselves "a civil strife between virtue and vice." There can be no fellowship between light and darkness (2 Cor 6:14), for "the mixed life" with its "intestine battle" falls short of the ideal Gregory seeks to articulate (*Perf.* 178–81).

The imitation of Christ has replaced that of the divine nature, or at least so it seems at first. For example, since Christ is called a "rock" (1 Cor 10:4), we should also become a rock, "imitating as far as possible in a changeable nature the changelessness and immutability of the Master" (*Perf.* 192). I suppose that the obvious understanding of what Gregory means is to conclude that Christians must imitate the human Christ, following the "Master" and modeling their lives on what we find in him that represents a likeness to our own human experience. The "Master" must surely refer to the incarnate Lord. But how are we to explain "the changelessness and immutability" of this Master, this incarnate Lord, without appealing to his divinity? Gregory does not fully explain what he means, but I think it does not go too far to say that his implication is that somehow to imitate the human Christ is, in fact, to imitate the divine nature so far as that is possible for human beings. In this way humans are to be "made divine" (θέωσις). Qualifying and limiting the imitation of God by restricting it to the imitation of Christ makes room for Gregory's insistence upon the incomprehensibility of God and for his understanding of humanity as created in the image of God. As I shall argue, imitating the human Christ leads not to a comprehension of his divinity, but to its apprehension in worship, and this in turn leads to an apprehension of God, the Trinity, that does not compromise divine incomprehensibility.

Here let me raise the question of baptism in *On Perfection*. Just as in *On the Christian's Profession* it is possible to find a number of implicit allusions to baptism, so the same possibility attaches to a number of passages in *On Perfection*. "Our good Master Jesus Christ has granted us a share in the name that is worshipped" (*Perf.* 173–74). The name "Christian" is what represents our participation in Christ, the immediate object of Christian worship. We have been "honored with the title of Christ" (*Perf.* 177). It would seem a reasonable inference to associate this honor with baptism. One aspect of this honor is immortality. By giving himself "as a ransom for us" Christ became "redemption" (1 Cor 1:30). In this way "he made his own possession those whom he ransomed from death by the life that came from him" (*Perf.* 185). "And the beginning of this lofty tower of life (cf. Luke 14:28) comes about as faith in him, on which as a kind of foundation we lay down the beginnings of our life. . . . Thus, the head of the universe becomes our head" (*Perf.* 193). Christ, then, is "the head of the body of the church" (Col 1:18). And by becoming "the image of the invisible God (Col 1:15) because of his love for humanity" Christ "has been formed in you in the form he assumed and made his own" (*Perf.* 195).

While none of these passages or others that could be adduced mention baptism, it is difficult to read them without making that association. Still more striking is Gregory's metaphor of Christ as "a pure and incorruptible spring." Drawing to ourselves "the thoughts taken from Christ's name" is like drawing water from him and so "transferring the beauty of the concepts" to our own lives (*Perf.* 212). Can we not think of the water of baptism? Slightly earlier in his argument Gregory considers Christ as "the king of both righteousness and peace." It is Melchizedek who has these titles, but the argument of Hebrews implies that they may properly be referred to the Son of God (Heb 7:2–3). Those ranked in this king's army are equipped with the armor of God Paul describes in Eph 6; they must embrace righteousness and peace, that is, "all the virtues." "How blessed is that person who has taken his rank in the divine army and has been enrolled in ranks numbered by ten thousand times ten thousand and has armed himself against wickedness with the virtues that signify the image of the king for the one who puts them on!" (*Perf.* 209). Gregory also speaks of those who desert this army and become soldiers "of the one who invented evil." His discussion echoes the opening part of the baptismal liturgy, when those to be baptized renounce Satan and his army and enroll themselves in Christ's army.

What persuades me that the references from *On Perfection* that I have assembled represent implicit allusions to baptism is Gregory's discussion of the Pauline passages identifying Christ as "firstborn." He is "the firstborn of creation" (Col 1:15), "the firstborn of the dead" (Col 1:18), and "the first-born among many brothers" (Rom 8:29). The difficult text is the first, since the so-called Arians understood the phrase to mean that Christ was the first created being, who then acted as God's created agent in bringing the universe into being.[35] I shall want to return to this point later. For my present purpose, however, it is the third of the passages that demands attention. Gregory interprets the text as follows (*Perf.* 202):

> And when he [Christ] was going to make us, who were previously by nature children of wrath (Eph 2:3), sons of day and sons of light (1 Thess 5:5) by the new birth through water and the Spirit (John 3:3, 5), he led the way to such a birth himself in the stream of Jordan, drawing the grace of the Spirit upon the first fruits of our nature so as to give the title of brothers to all born to life from spiritual rebirth, since he was born as the first by water and the Spirit.

Gregory continues by arguing that we must understand "the firstborn of creation" in just the same way. "Creation" in the text does not refer to the "old creation," which "has passed away because it was rendered useless by sin." Consequently, Christ in his incarnation became the firstborn of the *new* creation; and earlier in the treatise Gregory actually cites the text from Col 1:15 with the addition of the qualifying adjective "new" (*Perf.* 176). This new creation "consists of rebirth and the resurrection of the dead." Baptism (Rom 8:29) points beyond itself to the general resurrection (Col 1:18). In a

---

35. Origen understood Col 1:15 to be a reference to the mediatorial Logos (*Comm. Jn.* 1.5.28, 1.38.283, 2.2.17, 2.14.104, and 2.31.187). By exploiting the subordinationist implication of this idea the Arians employed the text from Colossians to argue for Christ's creaturely status. In his earlier writings Athanasius retained Origen's understanding of Gen 1:26, retaining the old image theology that treated humanity as created "according to the image of God," that is, modeled after Christ (e.g., *De inc.* 11). He also reworked Origen's view of Col 1:15 by replacing the mediatorial Logos with the consubstantial Son (e.g., *C. Gent.* 1.41; *C. Ar.* 1.39, 2.45, and 2.62). Even Gregory Nazianzen accepted the Dedication Creed's reference of Col 1:15 to the divine Christ. (See Beeley, *Trinity and the Knowledge of God*, 315; also Kelly, *Early Christian Creeds*, 268–71.) Gregory's interpretation differs and succeeds in reconciling Col 1:15 with Gen 1:26 (see *C. Eun. GNO* 1:75–85 and *GNO* 2:67–71). See Mateo-Seco, "Imágenes de la imagen," 677–93.

sense baptism becomes the key to all three of the texts naming Christ in his humanity as "firstborn." If baptism is a spiritual dying and rising with Christ (Col 2:12; Rom 6), it is a pledge of the general resurrection; and the term "new creation" holds together both the pledge and its fulfillment. Gregory continues his argument by claiming that taking "the title brothers of the one who led the way to our birth" involves giving proof of our kinship with Christ by seeking sinlessness and embracing the other titles of Christ so as to "present clear tokens of our noble birth" (*Perf.* 203–4). Baptism, then, becomes the key to what it means to imitate and worship the titles of Christ. But it is only the beginning of the Christian journey, and Christians are called to become what they already profess to be in baptism.

Since I suspect we are tempted to understand baptism in individualistic terms, I think it important to add that Gregory's emphasis is upon the incorporation of the individual into the church as the body of Christ. His text is Col 1:18: "He is the head of the body, the church." And he begins his interpretation of the phrase by employing language commonly used in medical treatises.[36] We must recognize that "every head is of the same nature [ὁμοφυής] and being [ὁμοούσιος] as the body placed under it, and that there is a certain single natural union [συμφυία] of the individual members with the whole, a union that by a single agreement [σύμπνοια] achieves for the members a sympathetic affection [συμπάθεια] for the entire body" (*Perf.* 198). Just as in the analogy there is an identity of nature and being for both the head and the body, so Christ is the head of the body of the church through his humanity, which is the same as ours in nature and being. But the relationship of the members to the head of the church transcends any natural union; instead it is moral and spiritual, depending upon the members' conformity to Christ and to the concepts by which he is known. In another respect, in the case of animals, the analogy treats the head as giving "the signal for the body's activities." Similarly, "for us the body must be moved to every impulse and activity in correspondence with its true head. . . . And since the head looks up, the members must in all respects follow what is suitable to the head by the head's guidance, and must keep their inclination directed to what is on high" (*Perf.* 199–200).

Gregory also notes that Christ is called "peace" (Eph 2:14). Although he does not speak here of the body of Christ, he understands this title as one requiring us to "display Christ in our life by peace among us." Christ put "hostility" to death (Eph 2:16), and so we must leave "anger and malice" behind. "For just as Christ, having broken down the dividing wall, created two in himself into one new humanity, making peace (cf. Eph 2:14–15), so

36. See Daniélou, *L'être et le temps*, 52, 59.

let us also lead to reconciliation not only those who fight against us from outside, but also those who sow discord among ourselves" (*Perf.* 184). The emphasis is no longer, as for Ephesians, the union of Jews and Gentiles, but instead the attainment of concord in the church. The passage treats peace and what could be called the concord and harmony of the body of Christ as an ideal to be pursued rather than a condition that presently obtains. Similarly, it is arguable that Gregory understands the ideal of baptism the same way. Christians must become in fact what they are by their profession.

It is already possible to see how Gregory treats the imitation of Christ's titles. A few more examples will suffice. If Christ is "light" (1 Tim 6:16), we must "be illumined by the rays of the true light." These rays of "the sun of righteousness" (Mal 4:2) are the virtues by which we remove "the works of darkness" and let our light "shine before others" (Rom 13:12–13; Matt 5:15–16). These virtues are not here specified (*Perf.* 184–85). Similarly, Christ as "sanctification" (1 Cor 1:30) requires us to remove ourselves "from every profane and unclean action and thought" (*Perf.* 185). The titles "foundation of faith" (1 Cor 3:10–11) and "head of the corner" (Luke 20:17) mean that we must begin "the lofty tower" of our lives by "faith in him, on which as on a kind of foundation we lay down the beginning of our life and frame as laws pure thoughts and actions by daily good deeds." As the cornerstone Christ fits together "the two walls of our life, those of both body and soul." Therefore, we must build our life with "purity of soul," and with "the soul's virtue" corresponding to "outward appearance." Failure to bring into harmony our intentions and actions results in a "half finished" life, of which Christ cannot be the head. For this task we require "the plumb line of the virtues" (*Perf.* 193–94). Christ is also "the king of righteousness and peace" (Heb 7:2), and whoever prays that the kingdom may come to him (Matt 16:10) "will in all respects accomplish righteousness and peace in his own life." Indeed, "the whole of virtue is understood as an army for the king, for I think that it is by righteousness and peace that we must understand all the virtues" (*Perf.* 208).

It is already apparent that imitation and worship of the titles are inextricably bound together in the intertwining of free choice and grace by which our choices are placed in the larger context of Christ's love.[37] Indeed, the more we understand the titles, "the more they point out to us his ineffable greatness" (*Perf.* 176). As already noted, worship attaches to Christ's redeeming work accomplished in his incarnate life and its culmination in his death and resurrection. Central to this idea and to Gregory's

---

37. And this gracious context can be identified with baptism, which makes Christians members of the body of Christ. Cf. Daniélou, *Platonisme*, "La mystique du baptême," 23–35, esp. 23–26.

understanding of the imitation of Christ is his account of Christ's humanity as the instrument by which God's saving purpose has been accomplished.[38] At one point Gregory observes that John in his Gospel contrasts a resurrection of life with one of condemnation (cf. John 5:29), and he goes on to say that "the 'mediator between God and humans' (1 Tim 2:5), who through himself joined humanity with God, joins only that person who may be worthy of union with God." Gregory clearly supposes that the divine Christ, the Word of God, appropriated humanity in order to become the mediator. By Gregory's time Origen's doctrine of the mediatorial Word had been discredited, and mediation restricted to the incarnation. Gregory puts his point this way: "For just as by the power of divinity he appropriated to himself his own man, who was part of the common nature but did not in truth succumb to the passions of the nature that are provoked for sin (for it says, 'he committed no sin, and no deceit was found in his mouth' [1 Pet 2:22]), so too he will bring individuals to union with divinity provided they have brought forth nothing unworthy of unity with the divine" (*Perf.* 204–5).

The man of Christ as an individual human being is not, however, the whole story. The divine Christ "by assuming the first fruits of the common nature through both body and soul" made the first fruits, that is, the individual man, "holy, having preserved it [the first fruits] in himself pure and incapable of admitting any wickedness." The purpose of this was to dedicate the first fruits "by incorruption to the Father of incorruption," so that "he might through it draw everything akin to it by nature and of the same kind, and might welcome the disinherited into the adoption of sons and the enemies of God into participation in his divinity." It is, then, the divine Christ who purifies the man so as to be sinless and who remains the subject of Christ's human deeds and words. As well, the appropriation finds its completion in Christ's dedication of the first fruits to the Father; the resurrection and the ascension complete the mission of the incarnation. The ultimate purpose of this mission, despite Gregory's recognition of a resurrection to condemnation, is to draw all humans into union with the man and so with the divine Christ and the Trinity.[39] Gregory employs the metaphor of yeast

38. Gregory can speak of Christ's person both in a highly unitive and in a divisive way. See an excellent account of ways in which scholars have addressed the problem in Ludlow, *Gregory of Nyssa*, ch. 5, 97–107. My own attempt to understand Gregory's Christology may be found in "The Man from Heaven," 165–82. See also Daley, "'Heavenly Man' and 'Eternal Christ,'" 469–88.

39. Cf. *In cant.* 13 (*GNO* 6:381). Distinguishing between Christ as uncreated and as created, Gregory identifies the "manifested glory" of Christ with "the Word made flesh" (John 1:14). "We have seen his glory . . . even though what appeared was a man. But what was made known through him, he says, was 'the glory as of the Only Begotten from the Father, full of grace and truth.'" See also *GNO* 6:387: "your understanding will

leavening a batch of dough; just as "the first fruits of the batch has been made his own for the true Father and God, so we too as the batch through similar paths will be made fast to the Father of incorruption,"[40] Indeed, "we shall become the Only Begotten's crown of precious stones" (*Perf.* 206).[41] When the leaven has completed its work there will be no division between the leaven and the batch of dough, and the individual man of Christ will be transformed into the corporate humanity of the new creation in its consummation after this age.

The mediation effected by the divine Christ's assumption of the man has two functions. The man provides humans with the perfect example of what they are meant to be, and in this way he is to be imitated. The work of redemption accomplished through the man teaches us "to live no longer to ourselves, but to the one who bought us by giving his life in exchange" (cf. 2 Cor 5:15). As the high priest who offered himself as the paschal lamb he will persuade the Christian in accord with Rom 12:1–2 to "present himself to God as a living sacrifice . . . and not to be conformed to this age, but to be transformed by the renewing of his mind" (*Perf.* 185–86). The second function of the man, as noted, is to draw Christians to union with God. The same double function finds expression in the title "firstborn," already mentioned. The New Testament passages involved "contribute to the virtuous life" because if Christians are to be firstborn, they must "take the title brothers of the one who led the way to their birth" and must characterize their lives by "righteousness and sanctification, as well as love and redemption and such titles" (*Perf.* 203). On the other hand, the man is the means through whom God made the new creation, and as "the firstborn of the dead" (Col 1:18) and "the first fruits of those who have fallen asleep" (1 Cor 15:20) he made "a path to the resurrection for all flesh" (*Perf.* 202).

Paul also calls Christ "the image of the invisible God" (Col 1:15). Of course, since Christ is "God over all" (Rom 9:5) and "great God" (Titus 2:13), we might understand the title as a reference to the divine Christ. But Gregory clearly understands the text as a reference to the human Christ. By his incarnation "in order to make you once more the image of God (Gen 1:26), because of his love for humanity, [he] also himself became the image of the invisible God. As a result, he has been formed in you in the form he assumed and made his own; and through himself you have again been

---

not first be drawn up to what is incomprehensible and invisible before it grasps by faith what is seen."

40. For the metaphor of leaven, see also *In cant.* 14 (*GNO* 6:427–428). Gregory interprets the parable of the Good Samaritan, whom he identifies with Christ, whose humanity includes all peoples.

41. Cf. *In cant.* 7 (*GNO* 6:214) and the discussion of Christ's body that follows.

conformed to the exact imprint of the archetypal beauty so as to become what you were from the beginning." Since, as we shall see, "exact imprint" (Heb 1:3) refers to the divine Christ, Gregory's idea appears to be that through conformity to the man we are conformed to the Word of God and are drawn toward union with God. The moral meaning of the title depends upon the fact that "the image of the invisible God, who came by means of the Virgin, was tested in all respects in the likeness of human nature, but did not admit the experience of a single sin" (Heb 4:15; 1 Pet 2:22). Imitating him is like painting his picture in ourselves with our free choice as the artistic ability and the virtues as the colors used. Two of these colors are humility and forbearance, and Gregory gives a brief rhetorical recital of Christ's passion, concluding with his words from the cross, "Father, forgive them, for they do not know what they are doing" (Luke 23:39; *Perf.* 194–97).

In principle it is possible to construe what Gregory affirms in *On Perfection* as a series of steps, all of which can be related to baptism and its meaning. Renouncing Satan and confessing Christ means the overcoming of the passions and the acquisition of moral virtue. These steps appear to culminate in purity of heart, which is the precondition for "seeing" God (Matt 5:8). In the context of his discussion of "firstborn" Gregory specifies that someone "will be accepted by the mediator for participation in the divinity" once he has become "pure for the reception of his mediator's purity." Whoever is "pure in heart" will not "see anything in himself apart from God, since, firmly fastened to him by incorruption, he has received within himself the entire good kingly rule" (*Perf.* 205). What can this possibly mean? Is what Gregory says a reference to what will not in fact be the case until the age to come, or is there some sense in which it can at least in part be true in this life? When Paul calls Christ "the reflection of glory" and "the exact image of being" (Heb 1:3), "we take the notions expressed by these words to refer to his [Christ's] greatness, which is worshipped" (*Perf.* 187). Paul, according to Gregory, knows full well that God is incomprehensible.[42] God has never been seen, nor will he be seen (cf. John 1:18). Indeed, Paul "says that no one among humans has seen him or is able to see him" (cf. 1 Tim 6:16). Yet Paul tells of his being caught up to the third heaven (2 Cor 12:2–4), and he "searched out the unseen and hidden things

42. See *Prof.* 134–35, 141–42; *Perf.* 176. For Gregory's arguments for God's incomprehensibility it would be necessary to examine his works against Eunomius. In sum, he argues that what is created "is coextensive with a kind of extension characterized by intervals (*diastēmata*), and it is enclosed by time and space" (*C. Eun.* 1; *GNO* 1:246). God as creator is outside the intervals of time and space and so beyond our comprehension. For the role Gregory gives Paul in his *Homilies on Song of Songs*, see Laird, *Grasp of Faith*, 155–64, and his index.

of divine mysteries in the depth of God's riches, wisdom, and knowledge. The illuminations concerning the apprehension of things unsearchable and invisible came to him from God" (cf. Rom 11:33). Realizing that his visionary apprehensions (which are really auditions rather than visions) did not comprehend the divine nature, and recognizing that his tongue was "too weak to express thought," he "marked out his understanding in the mystery by certain glimmers" (*Perf.* 187–88). Gregory understands Heb 1:3 as an example of such glimmers.

Paul "failed to find a name to express and interpret what is incomprehensible; for this reason he called what transcends every good, what can neither be thought nor spoken of worthily, 'glory' and 'being.' Therefore, he left the 'being' that transcends all existing things unnamed," but he did use the two expressions of Heb 1:3 to affirm the relation of the Son to the Father. "The reflection of glory" indicates their sameness of nature, since the reflection of light cannot be separated from the glory or radiance from which it comes.[43] The "exact imprint" distinguishes the imprint from its archetype without "any diminishment." Similarly, Paul calls the Lord "the form of God" (Phil 2:6), not belittling the Lord by the idea of form, but indicating the greatness of God by the form in which there is discerned the Father's majesty" (*Perf.* 188–89).

None of this is very satisfactory, and it would be necessary to examine Gregory's Trinitarian theology to make sense of what he says here.[44] For example, in his answer *To Ablabius* Gregory begins by pointing out that a right approach to the Trinity must avoid the "blasphemy" of saying that there are three Gods and the "irreligious and absurd" denial of the divinity of the Son and the Spirit.[45] Since we cannot name God's nature, all the terms used by custom or "handed down in the Scriptures" refer to our conceptions and not to the divine nature itself.[46] What we do perceive, however, is "the varied operations of the transcendent power";[47] and unlike the case with humans where those who share the same activity of, say, philosophy

43. On the significance of glory in Gregory's Trinitarian thought and soteriology, see Maspero, *Trinity and Man*, 305–8, and Mateo-Seco, "La unidad y la gloria," 179–200.

44. Nevertheless, the soteriological function of the Trinity may be discerned. Cf. *FM. 1b* 151: "For when faith in the Trinity is confessed, for this reason grace has also in turn been measured out for them from the Trinity. What was the grace? The very fact that they were proved to be loftier than the first contestants, I mean Adam and Eve." For an excellent account of scholarly assessments of and debates about Gregory's Trinitarian theology, see Ludlow, *Gregory of Nyssa*, chs. 2–3, 51–94.

45. See the translation in *Christology of the Later Fathers*, 256 (*GNO* 3.1:38).

46. *To Ablabius* (LCC 3:259; *GNO* 3.1:42–43).

47. *To Ablabius* (LCC 3:260; *GNO* 3.1:44).

or oratory, "every operation which extends from God to creation and is designated according to our differing conceptions of it [has] its origin in the Father, proceeds through the Son, and reaches its completion by the Holy Spirit."[48] Thus, all divine operations are triune and do not divide the three persons. With this in mind it would be possible to argue that Gregory believes that the Christian experience of God's triune activity is somehow a true apprehension of God but by no means a comprehension of his being. The vision of God, then, is not really the sight of God, but a union with his triune glory. It is not that God is one and yet somehow also three, or three and yet also somehow one, but that he is both one and three in such a way as in the end to defy our understanding. Indeed, even God's promises delivered by Christ cannot "be grasped by the understanding nor brought to explanation in speech . . . the inspired scripture teaches about them by saying that 'neither eye has seen, nor ear has heard, nor has it gone up to the human heart what things God has prepared for those who love him'" (cf. 1 Cor 2:9; *Perf.* 141–42).

Gregory concludes *On Perfection* by recognizing that attaining the ideal he has described is "hard to achieve" because it requires a struggle and a contest not only against the devil and the passions, but also "against the mutability of our nature itself." This does not mean that we can or should overthrow our nature, but that we must prevent it from falling by using the changes in our lives for "growth in good things." And, as for the Christian, "by always being altered toward the better and being transformed from glory to glory (2 Cor 3:8), let him be changed this way, at all times becoming better by daily growth and always being perfected and never attaining the limit of perfection" (*Perf.* 213–14). The themes Gregory associates with baptism articulate the full scope of the Christian path, and I should argue that in this way baptism becomes paradigmatic of the Christian life as a whole. But Gregory recognizes that the promises in baptism, those Christians make and those given them by Christ, must find their actualization in their changing lives, especially in the contest of faith.[49] It is to this I wish to turn in the next essay.

48. *To Ablabius* (LCC 3:262; GNO 3.1:47–48). Cf. 1 Cor 8:6 ("Father from whom . . . Christ through whom") and 12:4–7 ("varieties of gifts, but same Lord, God, Spirit").

49. Cf. Völker, "Die Taufe als Grundlage für den Kampf gegen die Sünde," in *Gregor von Nyssa als Mystiker,* 94–99.

2

THE CONTEST

In *On Perfection* Gregory laments the fact that his life does not match his words. He continues to pray that he may attain the ideal he expounds, but says that he does not yet see himself as "such a person as could present his life instead of a word" (*Perf.* 173). Does this imply that *On Perfection* is an early work and that later Gregory did attain the perfection he describes as far as that is possible in this life?[1] Perhaps. But in the prologue to his *Life of Moses*, generally agreed to be a late work, he says much the same thing. He begins by appealing to the analogy of a horse race. As a spectator he is merely urging "the charioteers to keener effort." As an old man and the "father of many souls," whether as a bishop or as a spiritual director, he has the obligation "to accept a commission from youth." He has been requested to give an outline of the perfect life so that the grace of his words may inform the lives of those who hear him. But he says: "It is beyond my power to encompass perfection in my treatise or to show in my life the insights of the treatise." This should come as no surprise, since many "who excel in virtue will admit that for them such an accomplishment as this is unattainable."[2] Even though Christ's grace and promise will always help those who strive to keep their promise in baptism, it is not easy to put the ideal they have embraced into practice.[3] The attempt to do so involves what will probably be a lifelong contest.

1. See, e.g., May, "Die Chronologie des Lebens," 56: "*De perfectione* dürfte ebenfalls in einer verhältnismässig frühen Lebensperiode Gregors entstanden sein." He appeals to the passage here cited and says, "So spricht man nicht als alter Mann!"

2. See the translation by Malherbe and Ferguson, *Gregory of Nyssa: The Life of Moses*, Prologue 1–3, 29–30 (*GNO* 7.1:1–3).

3. See Smith, *Passion and Paradise*, 154: "Yet he [Nyssen] never suggests that the

The Christian life, then, is a continuous struggle designed to actualize what is meant by the profession of Christ in baptism. My argument in the first essay was that the themes associated with baptism encompass the whole of the Christian life and find their location in Christ. Imitating him by dying and rising with him becomes an honoring of the baptismal promises in the ongoing interaction of the Christian's free efforts and the continuing assistance of divine grace. The challenge of the contest demands that Christians should become in fact what they already are by promise. It is not clear to me that Gregory appeals to himself or to anyone else as an example of total victory in this contest.[4] To be sure, Moses seems to be such an example, but it is not so much Moses as the allegorical meaning of his story that supplies the model. It would be possible to argue that victory in the contest belongs primarily to the martyrs. With this in mind I want to begin with Gregory's account of the first martyr, Stephen, to show how he thinks the promises of baptism are fulfilled in a life. Then I wish to turn to ways in which he understands the contest for ordinary followers of Christ, as well as those like Paul, the other apostles, and the martyrs who have successfully walked in Christ's footsteps.

STEPHEN: VIRTUE THE GATEWAY TO VISION

At the beginning of his first homily *In Praise of Stephen* Gregory comes close to asking his hearers to imagine that they are present to witness Stephen's contest.[5] They are to think of "the great athlete stripped for action in the arena of his confession" and competing "with the evil rival of human life." The contest is a life-and-death one with the devil himself. The arena is also a theater, and the spectators are not only humans but also the angels (*St. 1* 96; cf. 1 Cor 4:9). Gregory employs the same metaphor in one of his encomiums of the Forty Martyrs, adding the demons to the crowd of spectators. The

soul must be totally purified before there is illumination." I am indebted to Smith because he has persuaded me of the importance Gregory attaches to the age to come as the locus for true perfection. In what follows I may well be exaggerating his point, but much of what I shall say has been learned from him.

4. I am reminded of John Wesley's doctrine of Christian perfection. He distinguishes perfection in this life from that in the life to come, and he appears to conclude that we should expect perfection in this life without claiming it. Only once that I can find does he refer to anyone in this life as perfect, and in that case it was to a woman on her deathbed. For the development of Wesley's doctrine of Christian perfection, see Maddox, *Responsible Grace*, 179–90. For further comparison of Gregory and Wesley, see Plant and Plested, "Macarius, St. Gregory of Nyssa, and the Wesleys," 22–30.

5. See Leemans, "Reading Acts 6–7," 9–19; Bovon, "Dossier on Stephen," 279–315; Trudinger, "Stephen and the Life of the Primitive Church," 18–22.

angels were watching for the time when they could convey the martyrs "to their allotted place"; humans waited for the end, wondering whether they would be strong enough to follow the martyrs' example; demons looked on, hoping for the defeat of the contestants (*FM.* 2 163). We can suppose that Gregory has a similar idea in his homilies on Stephen. In them he is, of course, obliged to rely on the account given in Acts 6–7, and he places the story of Stephen in the context of all the opening chapters of Acts, obviously treating them as evidence for the golden age of the earliest church, an ideal to which Christians should aspire to return. The homilies describe Stephen's virtues as well as the vision he has immediately before his death, and it seems reasonable to suppose that it is his virtues that prepare the way for his vision.

Even before his victory in the contest Stephen, whose name in Greek means "crown," wore a crown "truly put together out of many and various virtues." He was entrusted with the care of widows, was filled with the Holy Spirit, and "great wonders of divine working also coincided with his teachings" (cf. Acts 6:5–8). Both his work in distributing food to the widows and his preaching "guided souls, feeding some with bread, teaching others with the word, and setting a bodily table for some, while holding a spiritual feast for others." As well, "by the boldness of speech and by the power of the Spirit he stopped the mouths of truth's enemies" (*St.* 2 97–98). As a deacon he by no means "fell short of apostolic worth." In fact his diaconate followed Paul's, since Paul called himself "a deacon of Christ's mysteries" (cf. 1 Cor 4:1); and still more Christ himself, "the Lord of the universe, who through his flesh dispensed human salvation . . . was not ashamed to be called a deacon, since he said that he was in the midst as one who is a deacon" (Luke 22:27). Stephen's virtues, then, were acquired by his imitation of Paul, who himself imitated Christ (1 Cor 11:1; *St.* 1 78–79).

In the events leading up to his martyrdom Stephen "resisted anger with forbearance, threats with disdain, the fear of death with the contempt of life, enmity with beneficence, slander with disclosure of the truth." He prevailed in no single way, but "by resolving himself into various kinds of virtue against every form of evil worked by the Jews at that time, he both combined them all and prevailed over everything" (*St.* 1 85). At length Stephen is surrounded in a circle by those stoning him to death; and in this way "he accepted what was happening like a crown of victory woven by the hands of his opponents." Stephen's virtues prepare the way for his vision, yet in one respect the vision leads to a new expression of virtue. Looking to Christ, "he saw the lawgiver of forbearance [and] remembered the laws commanding us to love our enemies, to do good to those who hate us, and pray for those who fight against us" (Matt 5:44; *St.* 1 88). Finally, Stephen's last words imitated Christ's, who said from the cross, "Father, into your hands I commend my spirit" (Luke 23:46). So Stephen, "reaching up to the Master, said, 'Lord Jesus, receive my spirit'" (Acts 7:59). The angels then took away "their own devoted follower" (*St.* 2 100).

On the whole Stephen's virtues lead to and culminate in his vision: "I see the heavens opened and the Son of Man standing at the right hand of God" (Acts 7:56). But the preceding verse describes the vision somewhat differently; here Stephen sees "the glory of God and Jesus standing at the right hand of God" (Acts 7:55). While it is not entirely clear, Gregory appears to identify "glory of God" with "the reflection of God's glory" in Heb 1:3, understanding as the glory itself the God at whose right hand "the Son of Man" or "Jesus" is standing. Conflating the two verses he finds the Father, who is the glory, the Son, who is the reflection of his glory, and the man of Christ now glorified in heaven. What Gregory actually says is that Stephen, "having left his nature and before leaving his body, looked with pure eyes at the heavenly gates opened to him (verse 56) and at what appeared within the inner sanctuary, the divine glory itself ('God' in verses 55–56) and the reflection of God's glory ('glory of God' in verse 55). No one can describe in words the exact imprint (Heb 1:3) of the Father's glory, but its reflection in the form that appeared to humans (Jesus and Son of Man) was clearly seen by the athlete, since it appeared so as to be grasped by human nature" (*St.* 1 87).[6]

The vision is not a direct one either of the Father or of "the reflection of his glory." Moreover, it is given to Stephen when he had "come to be outside human nature and had been transformed to angelic grace" (cf. Acts 6:15). It came only as he entered the borderland between this life and the next. As well, the vision may not be an end in itself. As noted, it is what enables Stephen by seeing "the lawgiver of forbearance" to forgive his enemies. More broadly, Stephen's martyrdom has two lasting effects. Just as athletes who "have retired from contests train the young by athletic exercises . . . I think we also must be trained by great Stephen." This includes opposing those who "fight against the Spirit" (*St.* 1 89).[7] Gregory returns to this theme

6. Cf. *In cant.* 13 (*GNO* 6:381). Distinguishing between Christ as uncreated and as created, Gregory identifies the "manifested glory" of Christ with "the Word made flesh" (John 1:14). "We have seen his glory—even though what appeared was a man. But what was made known through him, he says, was 'the glory as of the Only Begotten from the Father, full of grace and truth.'" See also a little later (*GNO* 6:387): "Your understanding will not first be drawn up to what is incomprehensible and invisible before it grasps by faith what is seen."

7. For the polemical context of Gregory's discussion of the Spirit and the vision of glory, see Maspero, "Fire, the Kingdom, and the Glory," 226–76; Cassin, "*De deitate filii et spiritus sancto et In Abraham*," 277–311; Radde-Gallwitz, "*Ad Eustathium de sancta*

at the end of the homily. Next, Stephen was not only "the first to make a path as an entrance for the chorus of martyrs" (*St. 1* 76), it was also from the persecution following his defeat of the devil "that the course raced by the apostles into the whole world took place." Gregory follows the text of Acts (8:4—9:15) and ends by speaking of Paul's conversion and mission that "brought nations everywhere to faith" (*St. 1* 81).

Toward the end of the first homily Gregory addresses two problematic interpretations of Stephen's vision. Those who deny the divinity of the Holy Spirit point out that Stephen sees the Father and the Son, but not the Spirit, while those who think the Son to be inferior to the Father draw their conclusion from the fact that the Son stands and is, therefore, "subject to the Father's authority." Gregory disposes of the second difficulty by a careful examination of scriptural texts, concluding that "standing" and "sitting" are no more than bodily terms applied metaphorically to God in order to show that "the divine has walked without moving, while being seated immutably in the good" (*St. 1* 93). The first of the rejected interpretations is the one that has to do with the apparent absence of the Holy Spirit. Gregory points out that it is only when Stephen was "filled with the Holy Spirit" that he "saw the glory of God and the Only Begotten Son of God" (*St. 1* 90; cf. Acts 7:5). It was "when Stephen was first illuminated by the glory of the Spirit that he apprehended[8] the glory of the Father and the Son" (*St. 1* 90). Thus, the focus of Stephen's vision is the risen and glorified Lord, and yet there are at least glimmers of a vision of the Trinity.

VISION AND VIRTUE

Gregory is almost certainly aware of Origen's explanation of the soul's three stages of ascent found in his prologue to the *Commentary on Song of Songs*.[9] These three stages correspond to the three books of Solomon (Proverbs, Ecclesiastes, and Song of Songs), as well as to the division of Greek philosophy into ethics, physics, and "enoptics," and Origen treats them as "moral, natural, and contemplative" stages. Proverbs supplies moral instruction for the life of virtue in its narrower sense; Ecclesiastes surveys the visible world, pronouncing it "vanity" and encouraging the reader to renounce what is "transitory and weak" in this corporeal realm. This becomes guidance to "fellowship with God by the paths of loving affection and of love" repre-

---

trinitate," 89–109; Radde-Gallwitz, "Gregory of Nyssa's Pneumatology in Context," 259–85.

8. ἐν περινοίᾳ . . . ἐγένετο.

9. See my translation of the Prologue in *Origen* (CWS) 217–44, especially 231–34.

sented by Song of Songs. Gregory alludes to the pattern Origen establishes in the first chapter of his treatise *On the Titles of the Psalms*. The first psalm provides "some understanding of what lies ahead" in the psalter as a whole, and each of the five divisions of the book "by some suitable correspondence bears witness to what is blessed," since "blessed" is the first word of Ps 1. The psalter, then, "divides virtue into three parts." Here virtue takes us beyond the moral life to the entire Christian path. The first of the three blessings is "alienation from evil," which is presumably the movement from vice to moral virtue and is "the beginning of an inclination to the better." Next there is a blessing upon "meditation on what is lofty and more divine." Here the stage represented by Ecclesiastes has a more positive definition. The emphasis is not upon the vanity of the phenomenal world, but upon how that realization presses the Christian beyond this world. Gregory can elsewhere treat this "stage" as one in which we discern God's presence in the world by noting how it is contingent upon his power and providence. Finally, the psalter "blesses likeness to the divine, achieved by these stages and because of which the preceding blessings are pronounced."[10] The treatise itself respects the five divisions of the psalter found both in the Septuagint and in the Masoretic text, and presumably we are supposed to find the threefold pattern within each of the five sections. This is not in fact easily done.

Despite the fact that it is possible to discern in Gregory's writings Origen's threefold pattern, there are at least two complications. First, Gregory allows the scriptural text he is following to eclipse the bare bones of the pattern.[11] Next, and more important, is the fact already noted that he insists that the stages are not really successive for Christians in this life, but are intertwined aspects of the path they must take. To be sure, looking at the pattern in terms of its eschatological aim tends to construe it in a linear fashion. But in this life the aspects are reciprocal, and it even seems often the case that we should speak of two rather than three aspects. Moral virtue is from one perspective the prerequisite for vision, but it is equally true that vision is what enables moral progress.[12] Toward the end of *Homily 13 on Song of Songs* Gregory is speaking of the church as the body of Christ

10. *In inscr. ps.* (*GNO* 5:26).

11. Cf. Heine, *Perfection in the Virtuous Life*, 107: "First, there is no basis in the treatise for the three clear-cut stages of the ascent of the soul which Daniélou proposes. . . . The stages Gregory sets forth are based on the chronology of Moses' life, and what he discusses in each stage is controlled by what the imagery of the Biblical text suggests." I should agree, though with some qualification.

12. In *De hom. op.* 5.1–2 (PG 44:13a–c), Gregory compares the image of God to a portrait God makes of himself. The colors of the painting are the moral virtues, but the portrait includes "mind and word" and, finally, "love." There seems to be an allusion to the three aspects of the Christian life, which are built into human nature.

and is interpreting Song 5:2, the bridegroom's "eyes are like doves at the abundance of waters, washed in milk, seated at the abundance of waters." What this means defies comprehension, but Gregory tentatively offers his interpretation. Citing 1 Cor 12:21 ("the eye cannot say to the hand, I have no need of you"), he argues that the church needs both eyes and hands. He concludes by saying, "It is proper for the church to flourish when discernment of truth is united with what is active, since neither does contemplation by itself perfect the soul apart from the presence of works rightly directing the moral life, nor does an active way of life furnish sufficient help unless true religion presides over what takes place."[13] Here Gregory thinks of the "eyes of the church" as those entrusted with guiding the whole body, and so the bride's perfection remains incomplete apart from her guidance of the daughters of Jerusalem.[14]

A similar pattern informs the *Life of Moses*. It is certainly possible to discern Origen's outline of what will come to be called the purgative, illuminative, and unitive ways, and it is probably easier to find aspects of the moral dimension when Gregory turns attention to the children of Israel.[15] Crossing the Red Sea stands not only for baptism but also for leaving behind the pleasures of evil. The initial bitterness of renunciation finds sweetening in the cross just as the wood sweetened the bitter waters of Marah (Exod 15:25). "The campsites, where the person following the pillar of cloud is refreshed as he presses on, would be the virtues."[16] It is also possible to discern what Origen defines as the stage represented by Ecclesiastes. The theophany of the burning bush teaches Moses that nothing "apprehended by sense perception and contemplated by the understanding really subsists"; only "the transcendent essence and cause of the universe" truly subsists.[17] Later Gregory gives another but complementary account of illumination. The trumpets sounding from Mount Sinai (Exod 19:16–19) refer to "the wonderful harmony of the heavens [which] proclaims the wisdom which shines forth in the creation and sets forth the great glory of God through the things which are seen."[18] To learn that creation is vanity is also to recognize that it is contingent upon God; and this enables one to discern the divine presence in what God has made and directs by his providence.

13. *In cant.* 13 (*GNO* 6:393–94). Laird, *Grasp of Faith*, does not appeal to this passage, but it certainly coheres with his fine discussion of *logophasis*, especially in ch. 6, 154–73.

14. Cf. *In cant.* 13 (*GNO* 6:377–80).

15. See O'Connell, "Double Journey," 301–24.

16. *Vit. Mos.* 2.135 (CWS 86–87; *GNO* 7.1:76). See the whole of 2.132–36.

17. *Vit. Mos.* 2.24 (CWS 60; *GNO* 7.1:40).

18. *Vit. Mos.* 2.168 (CWS 96; *GNO* 7.1:88–89).

The transition to what Origen regards as the final stage is one that Gregory treats as indicated by the contrast between the illumination of the burning bush and the darkness of Mount Sinai.[19] But this highest level of Moses' progress has multiple and confusing meanings and includes the description of the heavenly tabernacle which he sees (Exod 26:30) and enters, as well as the vision of God's back while standing on the rock (Exod 33:18–23). What Moses sees upon climbing the mountain of divine knowledge and entering the dark cloud is paradoxically "a seeing that consists in not seeing" and a knowledge that is ignorance. Yet somehow it is an "access to the invisible and incomprehensible," and Gregory describes it as slipping "into the inner sanctuary of divine knowledge."[20] But Moses continues to advance and "passes on to the tabernacle not made with hands" (cf. Heb 9:11). This is Christ himself with the "veil of his flesh" (Heb 10:20) hiding in the Holy of Holies the Only Begotten Son of God. Here Gregory observes that whoever "loves Christ" should not be disturbed by supposing that naming God a tabernacle in any way "diminishes the magnificence of the nature of God."[21] It is tempting to conclude that the highest knowledge of God is the love of Christ. Should we then suppose that all of this—and more—represents Moses' perfection?[22] Not at all. Let me call attention to Warren Smith's fine examination of Moses' progress in terms of "cycles of purgation and illumination."[23] To put his argument in a slightly different way, Gregory tends to collapse Origen's three stages into two reciprocal aspects of the Christian life—vision and virtue interacting with one another.

In what looks like a side observation in his discussion of the dark cloud Gregory states that "religious virtue is divided into two parts, into that which pertains to the Divine and that which pertains to right conduct."[24] The order in which the two parts are mentioned implies that vision empowers virtue and not that virtue qualifies someone for vision. Moreover, in this same place Gregory goes on to say that Moses first learns "the things

19. *Vit. Mos.* 2.162 (CWS 94–95; GNO 7.1:86). One complication derives from the scriptural texts. Immediately after God speaks the Decalogue, Moses "entered the thick darkness" (Exod 20:21; γνόφον). Then he goes up again to receive the tablets of stone, and "entered into the midst of the cloud" (Exod 24:18; νεφέλη). Gregory appears to conflate the two passages, identifying the cloud with the thick darkness, perhaps because Exod 19:16 speaks of "the dark cloud" (νεφέλη γνοφώδης).

20. *Vit. Mos.* 2.163 (CWS 95; GNO 7.1:87).

21. *Vit. Mos.* 2.176 (CWS 99; GNO 7.1:92).

22. Nor is it necessary to suppose Gregory always uses the metaphor of darkness for the highest contemplation. See Laird, *Grasp of Faith*, ch.7, 174–204, where he argues persuasively that Gregory can also use the metaphor of light for the same purpose.

23. Smith, *Passion and Paradise*, ch. 6, 148–82.

24. *Vit. Mos.* 2.166 (CWS 96; GNO 7.1:88).

which must be known about God," namely that "none of the things known by human comprehension is to be ascribed to him." Only then does he learn "the other side of virtue," that is, learning by what pursuits the virtuous life is perfected." This corresponds to what he says in Book One about the consequence of Moses' experience of the burning bush. "After he was empowered by the theophany which he had seen, he was commanded to release his countrymen from Egyptian bondage."[25] Similarly, in Book Two he argues that what Moses saw in the light from the bush was "the Radiance which shines upon us through the thorny flesh and what is (as the Gospel says) the true light and the truth itself" (John 1:9; 14:6). Such a person "becomes able to help others to salvation."[26] In what follows there are repeated references to how Moses gives this help to the children of Israel. The *Life of Moses* is as much an account of their journey as of his. After attaining the height of contemplation Moses returns from the mountain to lead the people toward the promised land. Gregory ends by saying that Moses became perfect by being the servant of God, and even though he makes no mention there of Moses' role in guiding the people, it seems unnecessary to omit this aspect of his journey.[27]

Does this mean that Moses' contemplation is imperfect? The answer must be a qualified yes, if for no other reason than that it must be completed by his role as guide and leader of the people. There may be, however, another reason for the imperfection of present contemplation. In *Homily 4 on Song of Songs* Gregory tries to interpret Song 2:7, "I adjure you, daughters of Jerusalem, by the powers and strengths of the field, not to rouse or awaken my love until he wills." The "field" is the world (cf. Matt 13:38), and the "powers and strengths" are the angels (cf. Ps 102:21 LXX). The bride's oath requires the daughters to look beyond this world to the angels. Thus, this life is a preparation for the next, so that those who live in the flesh and in the "field" of this world may not live according to the flesh or be conformed to this world (cf. Rom 8:12; 12:2). Instead, they should "meditate beforehand on the life for which they hope throughout their time of life in this world."[28] My suggestion is that contemplations given Christians in this world are imaginative "glimmers" of what can be supposed the characteristics of the

25. *Vit. Mos.* 1.21 (CWS 35; GNO 7.1:10).

26. *Vit. Mos.* 2.26 (CWS 60–61; GNO 7.1:41).

27. Cf. *In inscr. ps.* 1.7 (GNO 5:45). The title of Ps 89 is "A Prayer to Moses, the Man of God." Gregory tells the story of Moses and says that he offers prayers to God for others and carries God's mercies to them. He introduces the fourth ascent and "raises up with himself" those who have accomplished the first three ascents.

28. *In cant.* 4 (GNO 6:134). Cortesi, *Omelie*, 56, notes this passage, but employs it to speak of the angelic life of the resurrection.

age to come. Perhaps as well they are largely the product of meditation upon scripture. My suggestion may go too far, but it is clear enough that such meditation is a following of Christ that represents perpetual progress in the good, a progress that will continue in the age to come without the interruptions visionary leaders experience because of their followers. Even if there are some more perfect who may somehow already participate in the future beyond all futures, by the very fact that they still live in this world they still must anticipate it.

Indeed, it is not even clear whether there are very many Christians who have attained a sufficient purity of heart to qualify them for the incomplete perfection possible in this life. As I have noted Gregory makes no such claim for himself. I think we can assume he believes that for most if not all Christians the interaction of vision and virtue is dynamic and ongoing. What explains this, I think, is that the contest for virtue in its narrower sense never ceases and continues to involve the struggle to eradicate vice. Therefore, I want to turn attention to Gregory's homily *On the Dead*, even though it certainly appears to be an early work and includes ideas that Gregory elsewhere treats in different ways. Nevertheless, the homily does supply an understanding of the Christian contest with the devil and the passions that is fairly coherent throughout his writings.

THE CONTEST

In *On the Dead* Gregory's aim is to persuade his hearers not to mourn excessively for the departed. He makes no attempt to forbid grief altogether, but at the end of the homily cites 1 Thessalonians 4:13, "that you may not grieve, as others do who have no hope."[29] It is, however, the faithless who "confine the hopes of living to the present life." This is why "they make death the equivalent of a disaster" (*Mort.* 68). His argument begins with a definition of the good as what is good "both of itself according to its own nature, and likewise for everyone and at all times" (*Mort.* 30). Since the present life does not fit this definition, "removal from such a life is separation from nothing good" (*Mort.* 34). The reason for this assessment of the present life has to do with the contest that Gregory calls in *On Perfection* "the civil strife between virtue and vice" (*Perf.* 180). Only after death will the mind cease "being vexed and troubled"; it is only "when this war within us is destroyed by death that the mind maintains peace, having left the disputed frontier of the

---

29. See discussions of Gregory's treatment of grief in *Life of Macrina* and *On the Soul and the Resurrection*: Williams, "Macrina's Deathbed Revisited," 227–46; Smith, "Macrina, Tamer of Horses," 37–60; Smith, "Just and Reasonable Grief," 57–84.

battle." Here Gregory supposes that the contest is never totally won this side of the grave (*Mort.* 43–44).

This statement, of course, contrasts with other passages in Gregory's writings that appear to leave open the possibility of purity of heart and the triumph of moral virtue over vice. While he nowhere that I can find reconciles the apparent contradiction, it does seem possible that he does understand that the realities of this life almost always compromise the ideal and that even when victory seems assured the conflict remains hidden and apt to break open again. Perhaps the small victories along the way afforded the Christian in this life are all one should expect before the final victory over sin and death. Still more problematic is that Gregory in the passage just cited identifies "the disputed frontier" with "the body, and coming to be outside the battle lines drawn up by the elements against one another." By "elements" he apparently means the the body and the passions (cf. *Mort.* 34). Throughout the homily he disparages the body in a way that at first seems without qualification. At the same time he does speak of the purified body of the resurrection that "must be loved" (*Mort.* 62).

THE BODY, THE PASSIONS, AND THE SENSES

The problem of Gregory's assessment of the body is by no means confined to *On the Dead*. Throughout his writings there is an obvious tension between his account of the soul's ascent and his conviction that the body will be raised from the dead.[30] There may well be various ways of explaining this fundamental fault line in Gregory's thought. To some degree his possible philosophical sources help explain the problem, and one could speak of a Platonizing account of God's creation of humanity in his image and a Stoicizing account of the leavening process that leads to the resurrection. Perhaps more important, Gregory appears convinced both by aspects of Origen's contemplative notion of human (and angelic) destiny and of Irenaeus' anti-gnostic insistence upon the physical character of redemption. Moreover, the context in which he employs these two theological traditions can be considered his polemic against Eunomius and Apollinaris.[31] As will be obvious, my own approach involves shifting attention to how Gregory

30. See, e.g., Bouteneff, "Essential or Existential," 409–19. A solution depends upon seeing the body as "image by association" and by distinguishing this "coarse material body" from the "resurrection body," 417.

31. See Hübner, *Die Einheit*. Without altogether excluding the influences of Platonists and Stoics, he places the problem in the fourth-century controversies and gives importance to the influence of Marcellus of Ancyra together with Origenist themes.

uses these philosophical and theological themes and by damning a good many torpedoes to conclude that even though Gregory's themes cannot be systematized, there are ways of trying to see them as aspects of a coherent view.

To return to *On the Dead*, if the body is somehow at the root of the human predicament and helps explain the continuous contest experienced in this life, it is necessary to ask why this is so. The first part of Gregory's answer in *On the Dead* revolves around the fall of humanity. His discussion of this occurs in the context of his argument that "not even the nature of the body is useless with respect to the hope of good things we await." I shall return to this aspect of the matter later in my argument. For the moment, Gregory says that if humanity had not fallen, "we would certainly not have needed the coat of skin (Gen 3:21), since likeness to the divine would be shining upon us." But the devil's deceit resulted in "an inclination to what is bestial and irrational." That this could happen depended upon the fact that God created humanity "with free autonomy" (*Mort.* 53–54), and, as Milton's God says (*Paradise Lost*, 3.98–99), "I made him just and right, / Sufficient to have stood, though free to fall." What we notice first is not the coat of skin's positive use.

The coat of skin correlates with humanity's inclination to the bestial and irrational, and it "means becoming material." Gregory does not say so, but it is also the divine punishment that fits the crime. In this way "properties of the irrational nature belonging to animals were mingled with humanity," and these properties include or at least lead to the passions, "pleasure, anger, gluttony, greediness, and the like" (*Mort.* 55). The problem, then, is not merely the body but the bestial irrationalities associated with it. Later Gregory will identify the coat or coats of skin with mortality.[32] Here, however, he seems surprisingly close to Origen's account of the fall of the rational beings who take on "heavier" bodies and are divided into angels, humans, and demons. But Gregory does not explain here from what condition humanity fell; yet whether the body is the transformation of an originally pure one or there is a completely new one it is the consequence of the fall.

Gregory's homiletical purpose includes showing that the present phenomenal world is by no means a true good, and that death involves leaving it behind and being born to a new life that is truly good. Even the elements of this world are not good always and for all. Water nourishes, but it also produces floods; air is good for humans but lethal for fish. Fire, "though useful to us in some respects, is ruinous in many ways" (*Mort.* 30). Another point is that death delivers a person from "the inclement aspects of

---

32. See, e.g., *Or. cat.* 8 (LCC 3:283; GNO 3.4:130).

the atmosphere," from "all constraining evils" such as farming, seafaring, commerce, and the various arts. The dead need not fear war in any form, and the soul has no place "for slavery and lordship, poverty and wealth, noble and ignoble birth, private lowliness and dignified ruling power" and other things like them that constitute the divisions now found in human life (*Mort.* 35). The list continues and includes freedom from earthquakes, ship wrecks, captivities, the assaults of wild beasts and of the stings and bites of creeping and poisonous things, taxes, orphanhood and widowhood, and diseases (*Mort.* 35–37).

Part of these lists of evils has to do with a world plagued with vices or passions of one kind or another. The life to come will be one "in which no one is either heaped up with luxury or trampled down in humiliation, where no one is either made savage by rashness or frightened by cowardice; no one either swells in anger ... or is driven to confusion by fear" (*Mort.* 36). Opposite vices, characteristic of earthly life, appear to leave little room for any golden mean. The problem, though, is not merely the emotions or passions associated with the body, but also the world perceived by the senses. Even when the soul is infantile "the operation of the senses is born immediately perfect together with the body." As a result, "reasoning in judging of the good is prejudiced by sense perception," that is, "the soul accepts what has been prejudged by custom without testing it." Thus, we fail to realize that what is accounted good by the senses and custom is not really good at all (*Mort.* 48). Fallen human beings, then, are tied not merely to the body as such, but to the irrational emotions attached to it. And these emotions when provoked and activated by the senses, by the devil, or by the circumstances of life become the passions as the vices and diseases of the soul. This is because the passions, whether quiescent as emotions or active as vices, are the product of our present embodiment. It is unclear where Gregory locates the passions, but perhaps he thinks of them in the borderland between soul and body.[33]

In *On the Dead* Gregory speaks of the passions in several different ways, but all of them depend upon "some falsified illusion of the good." Early in the homily, without speaking of the passions, he specifies as false goods "externals such as strength and beauty, distinguished birth, property and ruling offices, distinctions," and the like. These are not truly good since "beauty and power are short lived ... ruling offices are easily overthrown ... reputation has no substance ... passionate attachment to property ... is vain" (*Mort.* 31). As Gregory says in the *Catechetical Oration*, seeking

---

33. Gregory suggests the idea that the passions exist on the "borderland" (*en methoriō*) between soul and body in *De anima et resurrectione* (PG 46:57b–c).

such false goods is like Aesop's story of the dog that dropped the real bone in his mouth in an attempt to grasp its reflection in water.[34] A second way of thinking of the passions is to note that "the life of our body is actualized in two ways, both by filling and emptying" (*Mort.* 32–34). The examples Gregory gives include eating and drinking, breathing, sleeping and waking. Neither filling nor emptying accords with Gregory's definition of the good. Filling is good sometimes, but "surfeit" makes filling destructive, while emptying can be not only of what is harmful but also of what is beneficial. The implication may be that "filling" in this life never satisfies, while emptying may be an emptying of the good. The idea resembles Gregory's interpretation of making bricks in Egypt in his *Life of Moses*.[35] The brick molds are constantly filled and emptied again. This means that "those who yearn after the pleasures of clay and keep on filling themselves with them never keep the space which receives them full; for though it is always being filled, it becomes empty again before the next pouring." Anyone can understand what this means "by looking at the appetitive part of the soul." In *On the Dead* Gregory says that this pattern never ceases "until after this life there is no longer "acquisition and deprivation," but a condition in which the soul "is always filled and never limits its fullness by satiety" (*Mort.* 36).

One further way in which Gregory describes how the passions are provoked has to do with the bodily needs of humans, including procreation, food and drink, clothing and shelter. "Appetite [ὄρεξις] is moved" for these needs, and its impulses are necessary in our present condition. Nevertheless, "whoever is the servant of pleasures has made necessary needs paths for the passions." The appetite for food can lead beyond what is sufficient to "sumptuous fare"; clothing can be sought not merely for covering the body but for "ornamentation"; procreation, designed for bearing children, can lead to "lawless and forbidden pleasures." In short, "greed with great gates has burst in upon human life, and effeminacy, luxury, frivolity, various kinds of profligacy, and such things like some withered offshoots of necessary needs have sprouted up because appetite has gone beyond the limits of need." Gregory's conclusion is that these vices are not the fault of the body, but "free choice produces them by turning aside the aim of need to the desire for wicked things" (*Mort.* 58–59).[36]

34. *Or. cat.* 21 (LCC 3:298; GNO 3.4:56).

35. *Vit. Mos.* 2.60–61 (CWS 68; GNO 7.1:50).

36. See Smith, *Passion and Paradise*, 89–94, where he discusses "Nyssen and Classical Views of the Passions." The whole of chapter 3 should be consulted, especially because it provides an excellent account of how the passions are treated in *On the Soul and Resurrection*.

FREE CHOICE

The fallen condition of humanity, associated with the body, the passions, and sense perception, is really to be located in the way they prejudice the mind in its judgments about the good. The mind is autonomous because it is self-moved and in principle ought to have access to the good because of its likeness to it as the image of God. As well, the motions of the mind result in its free choice (προαίρεσις), which is not to be regarded as a separate faculty but as the mind's activity. Free choice, then, should be the election of the truly good; and Gregory can even regard the freedom expressed in it as constituting the image of God.[37] But the impact of the fall and the coat of skin on the mind alters the picture. "Indeed," says Gregory, "since some natural relation to the good is inherent in all humans, and every free choice is moved toward this, proposing to itself aiming at the good of every pursuit in life, because of this it is a mistaken judgment concerning what is really good that customarily causes many mistakes to be made" (*Mort.* 29). This might imply that no one ever deliberately chooses evil, but in the *Catechetical Oration* Gregory leaves this possibility open: "If a man in broad daylight of his own free will closes his eyes, the sun is not responsible for his failure to see."[38] Evil is the privation of good and so has no ontological status. But there may be cases where humans, perhaps like the devil himself, deprive themselves of good by rebelling against it. In any case, mistaken judgment explains what must be regarded as the misuse of free choice, as well as the fact that our choices incline to both good and evil.[39] Later in the homily, speaking of the desire for power, greed, and anything else "because of which there are weapons and wars and mutual slaughters," Gregory says that all this is a "piling up of disasters introduced into life by free choice" (*Mort.* 39). This does not mean that human nature as such is changed, only that desire for good things is corrupted because "there comes into free choice the desire of alien things, the enjoyment of which gives pleasure not to the nature but to the passion of the nature" (*Mort.* 57).

At one point in the homily Gregory imagines a puzzled or hostile hearer asking whether we should "be displeased with our present life." The question is what "purpose and what function does the body serve for us, if indeed life has been demonstrated by your argument to be better apart from

37. See Leys, *L'image de Dieu*, 72: "La prérogative du libre arbitre n'apparaît seulement comme un des aspects de la royauté humaine: au plusieurs textes c'est elle qui constitue l'image divine." See also Wilken, "Free Choice and the Divine Will," 123–40; Gorday, "Paulus Origenianus," 141–63.

38. *Or. cat.* 7 (LCC 3:282; GNO 3.4:28).

39. See Smith, "Passion as Errant Judgment," in *Passion and Paradise*, 95–98.

it?" Gregory's fundamental answer is that "the present life becomes the path to what is hoped" (*Mort.* 48–49). Just as wheat matures in successive stages, so we pass through the stages of life; and death, "woven together with this life," is the way "nature trains us" (*Mort.* 52).[40] It is tempting to suppose that that here Gregory begins to shift attention from the body as tied to sense perception and the source of irrationality to the body as mortal because of the soul's weakness in governing it. However that may be, it is in trying, as it were, to make the best of a bad bargain that he turns to God's providential plan. As already noted, despite the fact that the coat of skin explains why humans misuse their freedom by making wrong choices, embodiment is the means by which God works out his merciful purpose. Gregory needs to explain how this can be so.

The argument begins by asserting that the greatest of goods given humanity by the Creator is free autonomy by which humanity was made "godlike and blessed." The allusion is to humanity as the image of God, because "ruling oneself and being without a master is the specific property of divine blessedness."[41] But "through the deceit of the enemy of our life" humanity "willingly had an inclination to what is bestial and irrational." Gregory treats the devil as the explanation for the fall, but not its cause, which is identified as the misuse of God's great gift by moving "willingly" away from good to becoming evil by its deprivation. It seems impossible to understand here—and perhaps elsewhere—how Gregory understands the condition of humanity before the fall. Does he mean that human freedom was unstable and for this reason humans chose to disobey God? If so, does this imply that God created humanity already fallen?

It is easier to understand what God's response to the fall is. Some may think that it would be "useful" for God "to remove those under constraint from the worse and to transfer them to the better by compulsion." But God sees through this superficial solution of the problem and is unwilling to

---

40. Cf. several passages in the *Homilies on Song of Songs* where mortification is associated with being buried with Christ (Rom 6) and with references to baptism. *In cant.* 6 (*GNO* 6:189) interprets "myrrh" in Song 3:6; *In cant.* 8 (*GNO* 6:249–50), summarizing the advance from "myrrh" to "frankincense" as "coming from Lebanon" (Song 4:8), identifies this with dying and rising with Christ in baptism; *In cant.* 12 (*GNO* 6:343–44) interprets "myrrh" (Song 5:5) as mortification of the passions, dying and rising with Christ, and "opening the door" to the Word.

41. Cf. *De hom. op.* 4.1 (PG 44:136b–c): God created human nature "for the exercise of royalty, preparing it at once by superior advantages of soul and by the very form of the body." The soul manifests its royal character "because it is without a master and freely autonomous, guided by its own wishes in a sovereign way." Cf. Gen 1:26: "have dominion."

violate his gift of freedom (*Mort.* 53–54).[42] Does this deny God's omnipotence? The answer is a qualified one. In the *Catechetical Oration* Gregory argues that the incarnation is God's decisive response to the fall and that it unites God's power with his goodness, wisdom, and justice. Granted God's omnipotence, the fact that his nature "was capable of descending to man's lowly position is a clearer evidence of power than great and supernatural miracles." The true marvel is the Word's "condescension to our weak nature."[43] Thus, God refuses to employ coercion and wisely resorts to the power of persuasion. What Gregory says both here and in the *Catechetical Oration* reflects his theodicy, which is elaborated by what can be called "the free will defense." One common way of posing the problem was first articulated by Epicurus.[44] Granted the existence of evil, if God is omnipotent, then he chooses not to remove evil and cannot be good; if he is good, but does not remove evil, he cannot be omnipotent. Gregory's solution is to argue that God, by renouncing coercive power, chooses to gain or regain power over all by the goodness of persuasion until at the final end all will be voluntarily subject to him. The apparent impotence of God at the present time is no more than that and is designed to bring all to a mature and free recognition of his sovereignty. Gregory does not say so, but God behaves like parents who allow their children freedom to grow in the hope that they will become friends when they mature.[45]

To return to *On the Dead*, God's response to the fall is one that refuses to deprive humanity of freedom and the capacity to make free choices. It is God's wise device "to permit humanity to become what it wished, so that by tasting the evils it desired and learning by experience what sort of things it had exchanged for the kinds it chose, it might return willingly by desire to its first blessedness, after shaking off from its nature like some burden passibility and irrationality." In other words, humans will learn by experience how to govern their passions, and by "moderating" them turn the passions into virtues. Gregory leaves open the possibility that some may fail to learn by their mistakes in this life, but they will undergo further education after death "by the purifying furnace of fire." Like a wise physician God has effective antidotes and knows how and when to use them (*Mort.* 54–55). Gregory appeals to the examples of the patriarchs and prophets, and after

42. See Gaïth, *La conception de la liberté*, 70–71, where he discusses this passage from *On the Dead*.

43. *Or. cat.* 20–24 (LCC 3:296–301; GNO 3.4:53–62).

44. His formulation is preserved in Lactantius, *De ira* 13, found most readily in *ANF* 7:271.

45. My own attempt to explain this may be found in "Augustine's Transformation of the Free Will Defense," 471–86.

them to "the disciples, apostles, and martyrs, and all those who have honored the virtuous life instead of the material life." These people, learning from their "voluntary acts" have "hastened upwards to perfection through virtue and philosophy" (*Mort.* 56). And by "philosophy" he probably means the ascetic life.

The question remains whether Gregory's insistence upon autonomy and free choice undermines any notion of divine grace.[46] It seems clear enough in *On the Dead* that he wants to hold together the importance both of God's providential dispensations and of human free choice. It is necessary to look elsewhere in his writings to discern the structure he employs to show how he treats grace and free will as complementary rather than contradictory. In broad terms the structure is one found in Book 3 of Origen's *On First Principles*, a discussion preserved in a Greek text by Basil and Nazianzen in their anthology of Origen's writings called the *Philocalia*. Origen's aim is to preserve free choice despite the scriptural texts that appear to deny it, for example, the hardening of Pharaoh's heart (e.g., Exod 4:21; 7:3). His solution is to argue that providence is a general and universal operation like the rain that falls alike on the just and the unjust (Matt 5:45; Heb 6:7–8), or like the sun that melts wax but hardens mud. Thus, we must distinguish providence as the context in which free choice is exercised from its effects which depend upon the use freely made of it. Providence assists and benefits those who use it wisely, while it "hardens" and punishes those who misuse it. Yet the punitive effect of providence has a remedial purpose, namely, to help us to learn by our mistakes. In principle, all divine punishments are healing and educative. It can be remembered that the same Greek word (παιδεύσις) means both punishment and education. Needless to say, this brief account of the structure of thought passes over complications, as well as Origen's apparent use of philosophical conventions.[47]

With Origen's structure in mind it is possible to discern its main lines in Gregory's argument in *On the Dead*. God's great gift of autonomy and

---

46. See Ludlow, *Gregory of Nyssa*, 119–22, where she discusses scholarly debates of the question.

47. Philosophical discussion of the problem appears to begin with attempts to reconcile the Stoics' insistence upon fate with their equal belief in "what is in our control." See Dillon, *Middle Platonists*, 44. He notes that "Chrysippus states the problem of determinism in its starkest form" at a time when "the question had not been one of great urgency." See also 168, where he notes that Philo, like all the middle Platonists he is studying, sought to preserve both "the autonomy of the will" and "to maintain the doctrine of God's providence." The treatise *On Fate*, falsely attributed to Plutarch, distinguishes fate from providence and argues that fate is both hypothetical and consequential. Dillon dates the treatise early in the second century CE and thinks it based on a source followed also by Apuleius, Calcidius, and Nemesius; see 295–98, 320–26.

free choice, together with his providential preservation of the gift, constitute the context in which humans make their free choices, a theme encountered in my earlier discussion of the gift of baptism. As Gregory says in the *Catechetical Oration*, "The Divine is present in everything, pervading, embracing, and penetrating it."[48] Nevertheless, the effect of God's grace depends upon how it is used, and it is important to note that Gregory understands God's grace to be persuasive rather than coercive. Love cannot compel. Free choice can be a path both to evil and wickedness and to the return to God. In the *Life of Moses* Gregory can speak of both effects. Interpreting Moses' meeting with Aaron (Exod 4:14), he says, "For truly the assistance which God gives to our nature is provided to those who correctly live the life of virtue."[49] On the other hand, while the Hebrews remain unaffected by the plagues, "The Egyptians' free will caused all these things . . . and the impartial justice of God followed their free choices and brought upon them what they deserved."[50] In *On the Dead* the contest between these two uses of grace by free will does not cease this side of the grave. But Gregory is convinced that "the desire for things alien to nature does not last forever . . . when the passion goes away, the desire of things contrary to nature goes away with it, and what is nature's own becomes again longed for and appropriate" (*Mort.* 57).

Gregory is thinking of what will be the case only after death when free choice will no longer incline to evil as well as to good. Instead, it will become an insatiable desire for God.[51] God created humans so that their free choice might coincide with his will, or, better, that his love might have the response of their undistracted love. But the instability of humans as mutable creatures means that God's creative purpose can be achieved only by his persuasive training of free choice so that it will become the voluntary and unitive choice of good. The idea is by no means peculiar to Gregory. In his long discussion of Gal 2:15–16, Theodore of Mopsuestia argues that "the Lord makes us rational and wishes to promote that very rationality in us and make it efficacious, because it could be manifested in no other way save by distinguishing contraries by which the choice of what is better can be acquired—for this is the highest knowledge for all rational beings."[52] It is

48. *Or. cat.* 25 (LCC 3:302; GNO 3.4:63).

49. *Vit. Mos.* 2.44 (CWS 64; GNO 7.1:45).

50. *Vit. Mos.* 2.86 (CWS 74; GNO 7.1:58).

51. See Smith, "Enjoyment and Holy Desire" and "Epectasy as the Transformation of the Erotic," in *Passion and Paradise*, 206–25. See also the discussion of *De mortuis* 53, 57, 61, in Hübner, *Die Einheit*, 217–18, where he notes that Gregory locates *Eros* in the final good. Also, Dal Toso, "La nozione di Προαίρεσις," 569–80.

52. See the edition by Swete, *Theodori Mopsuesteni in Epistolas B. Pauli Commentarii,*

even possible to think of Augustine's distinction between *liberum arbitrium* and *libertas* as the movement from conflicting choices to a unitary cleaving to God, whose service, as the Collect says, is perfect freedom. Gregory, suprisingly, can attribute free choice to the divine Word of God. In the *Catechetical Oration* he says that if "the Word has life because he *is* life, he certainly has the faculty of will [προαιρετικὴν δύναμιν]." Nevertheless, "the will [προαίρεσιν] of the Word, though capable of everything, has no inclination toward evil."[53] Perhaps the implication is that only when humans are finally united with the Word through his incarnation will they be able to make uninterrupted progress in the good.

VISION

In *On the Dead* Gregory so emphasizes the contest of this life that he has little to say about the contemplative aspect of the Christian life. Nevertheless, while he firmly locates what is to be contemplated on the other side of death, he does argue that a vision of what is to come then not only empowers the contestants but also establishes the necessary point that leaving this life is not merely leaving evil but is also transformation to a better life. Those who mourn the dead would better mourn those who fail to see beyond the confines of this world and the prison it represents. They are like prisoners whose "familiarity with darkness makes them suppose that the present life is gentle and free of pain." Like those in Plato's cave "they are ignorant of the brilliance awaiting those delivered from darkness"—the beauties of the sky, the earth, and the sea, the buildings that adorn the cities.[54] Similarly, those who treat this life as the final good "do not see what is above the world and its immaterial beauties, the thrones, rulers, powers, dominions (Col 1:16), the hosts of angels, the church of the holy ones, the city on high, and the festival gathering above heaven of those enrolled (Heb 12:22–24)" (*Mort.* 37–39). Presumably, imagining this while still in this life is a present vision that enables the contest for virtue.

Gregory then speaks on behalf of the departed "as though it were possible to be outside bodies by thought and to separate our soul from its passionate attachment to matter" (*Mort.* 39). The speech begins by appealing to the Delphic maxim, "know yourself," as though it were Moses' instruction to "pay attention to yourself" (cf. Deut 18:19). As Paul points out "we have an outer self and an inner one," and "when the former wastes away, the latter is

1:27. See also text and translation in Greer and Mitchell, *"Belly-Myther" of Endor*, 42–43.

53. *Or. cat.* 1 (LCC 3:271; GNO 3.4:9–10).

54. Cf. *In inscr. ps.* 1.6 (GNO 5:41–42).

renewed" (cf. 2 Cor 4:6). The inner self is not merely the soul, but includes the change of what is now mortal to immortality. Even so seeing oneself is not easy, since we see ourselves only when looking in a mirror. Similarly, the soul must look "to its own image." But the analogy breaks down, since when we look at ourselves we see only ourselves, but when we look at our soul by introspection we see "the divine beauty" of which it is an image, which Gregory goes on to say is "archetypal Beauty" beyond all conceptions based upon "the intervals of time and space." He concludes, however, that the soul 'is recognized by the same characteristic marks, so that it too is immaterial, invisible, intelligible, and incorporeal" (*Mort.* 40–42). This surely means that *On the Dead* is an early work somewhat lacking in a strong emphasis upon the incomprehensibility of God and the great gulf between Creator and creature. Gregory also says that "when by death we pass over to what is incorporeal, we draw near to that nature which has been separated from all bodily thickness . . . [and] ascend to our proper beauty by which we were shaped in the beginning when we were made according to the image of the archetype." Imagining our destiny may indeed help us in our contest in this life, but here Gregory has given an account of that destiny he will later be obliged to correct. It is true that at the end of the homily he speaks of the resurrection body as purified and spiritual, but it is hard to see that it has any clear connection with this body.

In conclusion, while Gregory's account of the contest on the whole coheres with what he will later say, his treatment of the body both before the fall and after this life seems very much to have the taint of views found in Origen's writings that came to be largely repudiated in Gregory's time. To be sure, Gregory is less than lucid in speaking of the condition of humans before the fall both in *On the Making of Man* and in the *Catechetical Oration*. There may still be the problem as to whether the soul or the body is responsible for the fall. The ancient rabbis may have had the right answer in one of their interpretations of "The horse and his rider has he thrown into the sea" (Exod 15:1). This can refer to the body and the soul that blame one another for sin before God's judgment seat. What will the Holy One Blessed be He do? It is like an earthly king who found his orchard robbed by his two guards, one lame and the other blind. They blame one another, and each uses his infirmity to claim innocence. How could a lame man climb the trees, or how could a blind man see in order to rob? Not fooled, the king puts the lame man on the back of the blind man and judges them both together. So God will judge body and soul together.[55] Gregory will end, I think, by supposing that the problem rests with the mutability of the soul

---

55. See *Mekhilta de-Rabbi Ishmael*, Tractate Shirata 2, 2:21–22.

because of which humans failed to govern their bodies and received the penalty of death.[56]

The other major problem in *On the Dead* that dissociates it from most of Gregory's other works is the virtual absence of any reference to Christ or to the body of Christ. Once in an account of the spiritual senses he refers to the sense of smell by which the Christian "grasps the fragrance of Christ" (cf. 2 Cor 2:14; *Mort.* 47). As well, in his discussion of the resurrection toward the end of the homily he says that "there will be one race for all when all of us become one body of Christ, having been shaped by one characteristic mark" (*Mort.* 63). In the next essay I wish to turn to the body of Christ and especially to how the different travelers on the one path are united with one another even in this life.

56. A similar problem is found in Plotinus. Is the descent of the soul its own fault or that of the body to which it is attracted? See Rist, *Plotinus*. In ch. 9, "The Descent of the Soul," he draws two contrary conclusions. According to Plotinus, "The fault lies not in the creation of the world, but in the attitude of the individual soul," 127. But "Hence we have to conclude that matter is the cause of weakness and of vice for the soul," 128. His conclusion is that Plotinus does not think "the creation and existence of the material world is evil *per se*." Nevertheless, "where he has failed to draw the conclusions of his own premises is in his account of the potentialities for evil in the individual soul."

3

HELPERS AND ALLIES

Even before Stephen's martyrdom the Holy Spirit had overturned the con-
sequences of building the Tower of Babel (Gen 11:1–10) by dispensing a
new form of uniting language for "the spiritual building of the church." At
Pentecost his grace "distributed the benefit common to humans to every
differing human language, lest the preaching of true religion, by being restricted to only a single language, should remain unavailing and ineffective
for those of other tongues" (*St.* 1 81). Ideally the whole world was to become
united in the faith in a way that at least relativized if it did not abolish all the
divisions that characterize human life in this world. But by the end of the
fourth century it began to be clear that the whole world would not become
Christian. People say that "our faith does not extend to all mankind." And
they ask what explains the fact that "the grace of the gospel has not reached"
everyone.[1] Gregory's answer is that humans retain free choice and that the
gospel can persuade belief but not compel it. Unbelievers include not only
pagans but also heretical Christians. Moses, early in the story, encounters
an Egyptian beating a Hebrew; he kills the Egyptian only to discover two
Hebrews fighting. The one in the wrong reproaches Moses for having slain
the Egyptian, and Moses is obliged to flee to Midian, where he later finds the
burning bush (Exod 2:11–15). Among other meanings Gregory interprets
the Egyptian as pagan idolatry and the Hebrew in the wrong as heresy.[2] The
church encounters opposition both from without and from within.

The problem for the church even apart from its relation to the wider
society and its struggle against those who have left the right path is also to

1. *Or. cat.* 30 (LCC 3:308; *GNO* 3.4:74).
2. *Vit. Mos.* 2.14–16 (CWS 58; *GNO* 7.1:37–38).

deal with those who have made little progress on it. Gregory recognizes the problem in several ways. Arguing against Eunomius and his understanding of language he insists that God has not produced the names for things, but the things themselves.[3] The words are the product and discovery of rational power, and they are designed to describe God's works. God's gift of rationality expresses itself in different languages, and God adapts his "word" to these languages as the "voice" heard at Jesus' baptism demonstrates.[4] The argument continues by pointing out that because of the Tower of Babel God confused the language that already existed, that this original language was not Hebrew, and that at Pentecost the Holy Spirit through the apostles adapted God's word to the different languages of those who were there assembled. So Paul, who imitated Christ, knew how to adapt his speech to the conditions of those to whom he preached, giving milk to babes and solid food to the perfect (cf. Heb 5:12–14).[5] In the *Life of Moses* the manna as the bread from heaven is the Word, and he adapts himself to become whatever "might be appropriate to and desired by the one who receives him" (cf. Wis 16:21). In the same way Paul makes "his message strong meat for the more mature but greens for the weaker and milk for little children."[6]

Respect for those who differ from one another because of the progress they have made is one way of binding Christians together on the same path. Another way does not involve teaching but rather care for the poor and the outcast. Gregory's homily on Matt 25:40 ("just as you did it to one of the least of these my brothers, you did it to me") paints a gruesome picture of the lepers that are apparently encountered by his hearers with some frequency. He recognizes even in himself the natural revulsion felt on seeing these outcasts, but he argues that to secure a blessing we must follow the Lord, "who reckons to himself zealous care for those in need." This is because "the commandment has great scope in the present life, and many are in need of life's necessities, while many are in a needy condition in their body itself."[7] Neither the angels nor the Lord loathe flesh and blood, and so "should you not have pity on one who belongs to the same race as yourself?"

---

3. See Mortley, *From Word to Silence*; Vaggione, *Eunomius of Cyzicus*, 251–57; Barnes, *Power of God*, 202–6; Laird, *Grasp of Faith*, 65–78; Van Dam, "'The Evil in our Bosom': Eunomius as a Cappadocian Father," in *Becoming Christian*, 15–45. For a detailed discussion of Gregory's critique of Eunomius' theory of language, see Kobusch, "Die Epinoia," and Studer, "Der Theologiegeschichtliche Hintergrund der Epinoiai-Lehre."

4. *C. Eun.* 2 (*GNO* 1:298–99).

5. *C. Eun.* 2 (*GNO* 1:302).

6. *Vit. Mos.* 2.140 (CWS 88; *GNO* 7.1:77–78).

7. *De paup. amand.* 2 (*GNO* 9:113).

Know who you are and "that you are a human being conceived by humans, and that you have acquired nothing special in yourself apart from the common nature."[8] The lepers may seem more like beasts than those created in the image of God, but "they sustain one another because of their distress. For each one, weak by himself, becomes a support to another, using the limbs of one another in the place of those that are missing."[9] To be sure, caring for these people is difficult; but no accomplishment of virtue is easy because "the way to life is hard to tread, since it is narrowed on all sides with the more laborious and harsher ways of life" (cf. Matt 7:14).[10] All humans are on the same voyage by sea, and though there may be fair sailing for some at some times, "hidden depths, rocks, headlands, and the rest of the evils of sailing through life supply equal fear." Therefore, "do not pass by without pity someone who has been shipwrecked."[11]

The homily, of course, envisages the Christ of Matt 25:31, who comes as judge of all the nations after the end of the world; and the eschatological perspective informs Gregory's exhortation. The same point can be made of ways in which Christians should treat those marginalized by society; and one can think, albeit in different ways, of slaves and women.[12] The idea implicit in how Christians should treat the simple, the poor, the outcasts, and the marginalized is, of course, that of the church as the body of Christ. Gregory often makes use of Paul's descriptions of its diversity in unity as found in Rom 12 and 1 Cor 12. For example, commenting on Song 3:11 (Solomon's crown) he identifies Christ's crown with the church, which surrounds his head with living stones. The universal church is one body with many members which have different functions (1 Cor 12:12–27).[13] In this way the unity of the body is preserved by functions that do not confer status, and that honor the fundamental conviction that all members of the church must care for one another. Nevertheless, the anticipation of what is really an eschatological reality does not entirely avoid turning the distinction of functions into a hierarchy that runs the risk of changing function into status. There are special people in the church, especially teachers and leaders such as bishops and the superiors of ascetic households and monasteries.

8. *De paup. amand.* 2 (*GNO* 9:115).

9. *De paup. amand.* 2 (*GNO* 9:119). See also Holman, "Healing the Social Leper," 283–309.

10. *De paup. amand.* 2 (*GNO* 9:125).

11. *De paup. amand.* 2 (*GNO* 9:126).

12. For slavery, see Hart, "'Whole Humanity,'" 51–69. For women, see the extended discussion of the secondary literature in Ludlow, *Gregory of Nyssa*, Part III, 161–227. See especially her own conclusion to ch. 11, 181.

13. *In cant.* 7 (*GNO* 6:214–16.)

These can only avoid claiming status by identifying themselves as fully as possible with those they teach and lead. Both tasks involve the paradox of assuming responsibility over others and yet finding identity with them and their interests.

TEACHERS AND LEADERS

Midway through his *Life of Macrina* Gregory describes his arrival at Annisa and his meeting with his dying sister. They remember their brother Basil, who had recently died; and this leads Macrina to speak of "the higher philosophy." Her subjects are the creation of humanity, God's dispensations hidden beneath life's sorrowful experiences, and the life to come. Her discourse is so inspired by the Holy Spirit that Gregory feels his soul lifted beyond human nature and guided by Macrina's words within the heavenly sanctuaries.[14] In *On the Soul and the Resurrection* in dialogue with Macrina Gregory calls his sister "the teacher."[15] Despite the difficulty of penetrating Gregory's rhetorical praise of Macrina, there can be little doubt that he regards her as his mentor.[16] This need not mean that Gregory thought of her primarily as a monastic even though by the time of her death the family household at Annisa had become what surely must be called a double monastery. The ascetical movement that in the fourth century swept through the church, first in the East and then in the West, was not necessarily confined to the emergence of monasteries; there were households like Macrina's that fostered the ascetical and spiritual life not only in the countryside but also in the cities. Gregory was in touch with other leaders of the ascetical movement as is indicated by his dedication of the *Homilies on Song of Songs* to Olympias of Constantinople, who by 391 had been ordained as a deaconess and was distributing her great wealth to the poor of the city.[17]

14. *Vit. s. Macr.* 17 (SC 178:198–99).

15. See Roth, "Platonic and Pauline Elements," 20–30. She points out, as others have, that the dialogue appears to be a Christian version of Plato's *Phaedo*, but also makes use of the *Symposium* and *Phaedrus*. Macrina is, as it were, a Christian Socrates or a Christian Diotima.

16. See Maraval's introduction (SC 178:102–3), where he underlines Macrina's role "de guide, d'éducatrice" and assesses Gregory's approach to asceticism as one contrasting with the harshness of the desert fathers—"peut-être la VSM répond-elle assez bien par une synthèse: culture et sainteté." See also Meredith, "Comparison," 191, where he argues that Gregory treats "the philosophical life" as "primarily, if not exclusively, the life of moral virtue."

17. See Brown, *Body and Society*, 203: "Female asceticism grew out of the Christian household." For Olympias, see his discussion on 282–84, and also, especially for her friendship with John Chrysostom, see Kelly, *Golden Mouth*, 111–14, 265–68. See also

The ascetical movement provoked strong opposition throughout the Roman Empire, as attested by the controversies over the opinions of Origen and his followers, and in the West over the teachings of Jovinian and Pelagius. The synod of Gangra in the middle of the fourth century reflects how the disputes affected Cappadocia. Gregory and his older brother Basil sought for a mean between the harsher forms of asceticism and mere acquiescence in the common norms of the surrounding culture. Basil, of course, was one of Gregory's teachers and mentors, even though there surely appear to have been difficulties in their relationship. Gregory does, however, portray Basil as a bishop formed by ascetical ideals.[18] The same ideal explains Gregory's interference in the episcopal election at Nicomedia, as noted in the introduction. Sanctity ought to be of more significance than rank, wealth, and a candidate's relationship with the power structures in society. It is better to have a patron connected with heaven than one well connected in earthly ways. Not all would agree, and the dilemma played itself out in various places.

There is an interesting episode in Gregory's *Life of Gregory Thaumaturgus* that illustrates Gregory's concern for an ascetical understanding of episcopal leadership—perhaps in an exaggerated form. The Wonderworker's fame has spread through the region from Neocaesarea. and he is invited by a commission from Comana "to support the church by his priesthood."[19] The commission is already deliberating about whom to present to the church for election as its bishop; and, failing to agree with one another, they ask for the Wonderworker's opinion. Like Samuel he decides "to search out a royal soul even if it happened to be in a contemptible body" (cf. 1 Kgdms 16:7). And so he asks the commission to continue its search and "to look at even the meaner ones according to their form of life." Offended by this advice, one of the commissioners with great irony said to the Wonderworker that

---

Cahill, "Date and Setting," 447–60. He gives a fuller account of Gregory's association with Olympias and suggests that the commentary is in part directed against the kind of exegesis found in Diodore's writings.

18. See Harl, "Moïse Figure de l'évêque," 71–119.

19. Gregory Thaumaturgus ("The Wonderworker") did not bring Christianity to Neocaesarea but was responsible for its spread in Cappadocia during the third century and for the conversion of Gregory of Nyssa's maternal grandmother, Macrina the Elder. A student of Origen's, Gregory pursued the life of a hermit in the desert before being ordained (*in absentia*) by Phaedimus of Amasia and designated bishop of Neocaesarea. Gregory of Nyssa's *De vita Gregorii Thaumaturgi* was written for the celebration of his feast (November 17) in Neocaesarea. See Abramowski, "Das Bekenntnis des Gregory Thaumaturgus," 145–66; Kochlamazashvili, "*De vita Gregorii Thaumaturgi*," 718–20; Van Dam, "Remembering the Future: Christian Narratives of Conversion," in *Becoming Christian*, 72–81.

he supposed this would mean choosing "someone from the vulgar mob." And he suggested that Alexander the charcoal-maker should be summoned. Presumably no one could be more vulgar.

The commissioner's retort inspires the Wonderworker to summon Alexander, clearly a providential decision. Alexander appears "in rags and covered with soot," and was immediately "a laughingstock to untrained eyes." It emerges that Alexander is not what he seems to be, but is a "philosopher," who has pursued "the higher and true life" in order to "achieve the goal of virtue." One version of the text specifies that Alexander was so beautiful a youth that he sought to disguise himself by "the ugly mask" of being a charcoal-maker so as not "to experience any involuntary passion" and "be placed as a basis for passion to the eyes of others." Needless to say, Alexander is elected bishop, and his first speech confirms the wisdom of the Wonderworker's advice. The speech is "filled with thought, since it had been less embellished with flowery diction." An "arrogant youth who was visiting from Attica" found the speech ridiculous, but changed his mind "when he saw a flock of doves conspicuous with unadorned beauty" and learned that they belonged to Alexander.[20]

MONASTICISM

In his *Life of Macrina* Gregory tells of meeting a high ranking soldier soon after the completion of Macrina's funeral rites. The soldier tells Gregory the story of how he and his wife brought their small daughter to Macrina. The little girl had an eye disease, which Macrina healed not by the medicine her parents thought Macrina had promised, but by the medicine of prayer—which was what Macrina had meant. The soldier's story gives us some hints concerning what he and his family found at Macrina's house in Annisa. They came to "the thinking shop of virtue," but the soldier and his wife were separated. He went to the "men's quarters," while his wife and daughter entered the "virgin's quarters." The Greek words apparently refer to a double monastery, one for men and the other for female virgins.[21] Presumably, then, by the late 370s Gregory is acquainted with a double monastery at Annisa. His brother Peter presided over the male monastery, while Macrina led the convent. Macrina's earlier experiment in domestic asceticism had blossomed into what we can probably regard as two somewhat larger monasteries situated near one another on the family estate in Pontus.

20. *Vit. Greg. Thaum.* (GNO 10.1:36–40).
21. See Maraval's introduction, *Vie de Macrine* (SC 178), 41–43.

Basil's retreat was apparently at some distance on the other side of the Iris river. He first found it after his return to Caesarea from Athens and following his tour of the monasteries in Egypt, Palestine, and Syria, probably in 357 or 358.[22] It is possible to assume that it was at this time that Basil wrote letters 14 and 2 to his friend and fellow student at Athens, Gregory Nazianzen. In letter 14 Basil tells Nazianzen that his brother Gregory had written to say that he longed to visit Basil in his retreat and that Nazianzen had the same wish. While it is certain that Nazianzen did finally accept Basil's invitation, there is no clear evidence that his brother Gregory did so.[23] Nevertheless, such a visit seems a real possibility; and, more importantly, it is reasonably sure that, though Gregory may never have become a monk in any formal sense, he was well aware of Basil's attempts to foster what became a monastic movement in Pontus, Cappadocia, and Armenia.

Basil was almost certainly not the original prime mover in establishing ascetic communities in Asia Minor. That honor probably goes to Eustathius of Sebaste, with whom Basil was obliged to part company by 375. It would take me far from my purpose and my competence to give any full account of Basil's work, but a brief sketch will supply a background for assessing Gregory's involvement. In general terms it seems likely that what Basil found after he became bishop of Caesarea in 370 was a complex network of ascetical communities, as well as a number of people willing to dedicate themselves to the ascetical life without becoming members of such communities. Clearly, the ascetical movement of the fourth century had spread in a fairly disorganized fashion to Asia Minor. Even Basil's work may well have been less institutional than hindsight made it.[24] To be sure, the Rules include many issues that do affect the institutional life of monasteries. Under what conditions should slaves and married men be admitted to a monastery? How should what a monastery produces be sold? What are the hours of prayer? What are the qualifications and responsibilities of the superiors?[25] One of the most interesting of the Longer Rules is number 35: "Whether several brotherhoods should be formed in the same parish." The issue re-

22. See Rousseau, *Basil of Caesarea*, 62–66.

23. *Ep.* 223, written in 375 to Eustathius of Sebaste, includes the following: "Ask yourself: How often did you visit us in the monastery [μονῆς] on the river Iris, when, moreover, our most divinely-favored brother Gregory was present with me, achieving the same purpose in life as myself." The Gregory Basil mentions is more likely to be Nazianzen than Gregory of Nyssa.

24. See Rousseau, *Basil of Caesarea*, 192. Cf., however, 196; and see 200: "So the distinction was not between classes of person within the Church but between Christians at differing stages of spiritual development."

25. See *Longer Rules* 12–13, 25–27, 30–31, 37–40, 43; translation in Clarke, *Ascetic Works of Saint Basil*, 145–228.

volves around what should be done when several "superiors" happen to be in one place, presumably forming a number of very small communities. In such a case the superiors, in humility, will be subject to one of their number in order to form a strong center in place of the dispersed communities in the place. Basil is not recommending the establishment of the sort of large communities characteristic of the Pachomian monasteries, but he is concerned to avoid what he seems to have regarded as a divided and less effective effort. Basil's institutional concern is to organize and so strengthen the existing as well as the newly founded communities, and to do so by holding them together by a unity of purpose and by drawing them into the patronage of the bishop. Like Athanasius and John Chrysostom, Basil is seeking to co-opt and to bind to the church what might otherwise have been a protest movement against the post-Constantinian church. The institutional arrangements appear to be embryonic, destined later to be regulated by canonical and imperial law.[26] And they take second place to the ascetical and spiritual ideals Basil wishes to inculcate.

That Gregory of Nyssa co-operated with Basil's larger purpose finds expression in his earliest work, *On Virginity*, written in 371.[27] This treatise is largely an extended praise of virginity as a spiritual ideal,[28] but at several points Gregory is obviously thinking of what we should call monastic communities. Chapter 23 has the title: "That whoever wishes to learn the exact disciplines of this life must be taught by one who has succeeded in it." Such a person may find detailed written instructions, even though "guidance by deeds is more effective than teaching based on words."[29] Basil is such a guide; and though Gregory does not name him, he is the model for the portrait of the ideal guide and master given in 23.5–6.[30] The written instructions to which Gregory refers are probably Basil's earliest ascetical writings. His insistence upon the necessity of an exemplary guide is related to two opposed dangers. Some who have chosen the way of life he recommends have done so with excessive rigor, going so far as to condemn marriage altogether.

26. Jones, *Later Roman Empire*, 2:933.

27. Following Aubineau, *Traité de la Virginité*, 31. *Pace* Staats, "Basilius als Lebende Mönchsregel," 228–30.

28. Not all would agree, and there are various ways of construing "spiritual ideal." See Ludlow, *Gregory of Nyssa*, 195–201; also Harrison, "Male and Female," 441–71.

29. *De virg.* 23 (SC 119:520–60). See esp. Aubineau's note 1 on p. 522 and his introduction, 58–61, 79.

30. See Staats, "Basilius," 228–55. For Gregory's complicated personal, ecclesial, and theological relationship with Basil, see Ditmars, "Gregory the Theologian's Panegyric on Saint Basil," 199–210; Radde-Gallwitz, "Epinoia and Initial Concepts," 21–26; Howard, "Familial Askesis in the *Vita Macrinae*," 33–38.

Others embrace the opposite error of laxity, living openly with women (*virgines subintroductae*) and calling their community a "brotherhood."[31] Those who are lax include ascetics who fail to work for their own bread, "making their indolence an art of living" (23.3). The golden mean that Gregory seeks between the excesses of rigorism and laxity (cf. 7.2) can be correlated with Basil's ascetical writings and could be understood as excluding both the rigorist followers of Eustathius of Sebaste and those who are often labeled Messalians.[32] Gregory's chief concern in *On Virginity*, however, is to articulate a spiritual ideal for ascetics and for those who have chosen a higher form of life. Virginity is by no means tied to sexual abstinence; indeed, marriage should not be condemned (ch. 7), while virginity in the strict sense is a means toward a larger end.[33]

There is another possible piece of evidence for Gregory's attitude toward monasticism. A treatise titled *On the Goal in Accord with God and the Training in Accord with Truth*, commonly called *De instituto christiano*, is attributed to Gregory in part of the manuscript tradition. Werner Jaeger's argument for the authenticity of this attribution has been disputed by many, who see in its emphasis upon constant prayer, which seems suspiciously like Messalianism, reason to doubt Gregory's authorship.[34] Despite its doubtful authenticity *On the Goal* in many ways reflects Gregory's thought as found elsewhere; and for this reason let me venture a few remarks and for the sake of convenience call the author Gregory.

He begins the work by speaking in general terms of "knowledge of the truth," given by "the Savior's grace" so as to destroy error. It is "while the dishonorable mind of the flesh is quenched" that "the soul that has received

31. *De virg.* 23.4. The lax may be pre-Messalians; see Aubineau's notes in SC 119 on 534, 536, and 540. As for the rigorists, the synod of Gangra condemned those who rejected marriage, as well as those who rejected eating meat, who taught slaves to despise their masters, and who held assemblies apart from the church. See Rousseau, *Basil of Caesarea*, 75. A translation of the canons of Gangra may be found in Morison, *Saint Basil and His Rule*, 146–48.

32. For Gregory's efforts to distinguish the understanding of monastic practices in Basil's and Macrina's communities from the view of the Messalians, see Meyendorff, "Messalianism or Anti-Messalianism," 585–90; Staats, "Messalianism and Antimessalianism," 27–44; Hunt, *Clothed in the Body*.

33. See Aubineau's introduction to SC 119, on page 148: ". . . la polyvalence envahissante du mot παρθενεία, signifiant tour à tour l'intégrité d'un corps voué à Dieu, la continence absolue, l'exclusion de toute faute morale, la vie vertueuse considérée dans sa totalité, la plénitude de la vie divine communiquée à l'homme, enfin un état de vie tranchant sur la vie du commun . . ."

34. See Jaeger, *Two Rediscovered Works*. See also May, "Die Chronologie," 60 nn. 2 and 3. He notes some of the literature and Daniélou's change of opinion to a judgment of inauthenticity.

knowledge is led by the light of truth to the divine and to its own salvation." It is with this common aim in mind that those who have "eagerly assembled" have written Gregory, asking for a discourse from him as "a kind of guide and teacher for life's journey." The request clearly comes from a brotherhood or monastery, and it includes particular inquiries that reflect the special conditions attaching to a common life under superiors. The request also presupposes that the brothers wish to employ ascetical disciplines in order "to ascend to the summit of virtue and to prepare their own souls to be worthy for a receptacle of the Spirit."[35] The first part of Gregory's treatise concerns "the goal of true religion," one that is presumably common to all Christians.[36] Gregory implies that this goal is also that of "philosophy," that is the life of the brotherhood. The goal may be pursued in a special way, but it is not a goal that differs from the one all are meant to set before themselves.

Early in his advice Gregory refers to "the washing," which furnishes "the worthy with the pledge of immortality, so that the talent entrusted to each one might gain unseen wealth." Holy baptism is "great for the acquisition of spiritual goods," but this is true only of "those who receive it with fear." The gift is given "according to the partaker's measure of faith" (cf. Rom 12:3).[37] The argument continues by describing the intended use of the gift of baptism. The new born soul must grow to maturity, and this means that "one must always advance to 'the perfect man,' according to the apostle, until all of us come to the unity of faith . . . to the measure of the full stature of Christ, so that we may no longer be infants . . . but, speaking the truth, let us grow up in every way with him, who is the head, Christ" (Eph 4:13–15). Following this long citation Gregory appeals to Rom 12:2, where Paul exhorts his readers not to be conformed to this world, but to be transformed by a renewed mind that can discern the will of God.[38]

It is hard not to be reminded of the baptismal renunciation of Satan and the promise of alliance with Christ. At one point Gregory cites Rom 1:28–32 with its list of vices, and he argues that these include "passions that lie hidden in the soul." Christians should arm themselves with "pious thought, fortified by the fear of God, the grace of the Spirit, and the works of virtue," thereby putting to flight "the assaults of the tyrant," that is, the

---

35. *De inst.* (*GNO* 8:41).

36. *De inst.* (*GNO* 8:63).

37. *De inst.* (*GNO* 8.1:44). I find only one place in Gregory's undisputed writings where he refers to the parable of the talents (Matt 25:14–30; Luke 19:11–27), namely *In cant.* 15 (*GNO* 6:462–63). Here he discusses Song 6:8 (sixty queens, eighty concubines, numberless virgins). There are six commandments which are accomplished by good works, and these when multiplied by the ten talents yield the sixty queens.

38. *De inst.* (*GNO* 8.1:45–46).

devil.[39] As well, Christians must remember that familiarity with someone
expresses itself in imitation. "Therefore, it is also necessary for the soul longing to be Christ's bride to be made as far as possible like Christ's beauty
by virtue." Gregory cites Paul's injunction, "Be imitators of me, as I am of
Christ" (1 Cor 11:1).[40] The double promise, then, requires a contest, and
one that should not allow vice to be mixed together with virtue.[41] The aim
of the contest is purity of heart, and Gregory cites Matthew's beatitude (5:8)
among other texts. A little later, citing Ps 23:34 ("who will go up to the
mountain of the Lord? The one guiltless in hands and pure in heart."), he
says that the Lord "leads up to the mountain of God whoever is altogether
pure."[42] Purity of heart appears to be the "summit" of the Christian life,[43]
and nothing explicit is said of "seeing God," as in the beatitude. It could be
that prayer takes the place of contemplation. "Whoever perseveres in prayer
has fellowship with him [God] and is joined to him by mystical sanctity and
spiritual working and an ineffable disposition." With the Spirit "as his guide
and ally he is inflamed with love for the Lord, and he boils with longing because he finds no satiety in prayer."[44] Gregory asks, "Do you see how many
ways of salvation he [Paul] has pointed out to you, ways that aim at a single
path and the single grace of being a perfect Christian?"[45]

After describing what applies to all Christians, Gregory then turns to
ways in which those whom he is addressing should strive to put the ideal
into practice. The special disciplines of the monastic life do suggest that
monks are further along the path of the Christian life than others who may
lag behind. Despite the special character of the monastic life two themes
block any radical distinction between the monks and other Christians. The
first of these, as noted, is Gregory's repeated admonition of the grave danger
attached to accomplishments in discipline and virtue. There is a risk that
those "who suppose the entire crown depends upon their own disciplines"
may "take pride in human efforts."[46] Such pride may result from pursuing
"good repute from humans"—choosing poverty "for outward show," giving
alms "to be praised." Gregory is thinking of Matt 5–6, and he alludes to
Christ's implied command (Matt 5:16) to "glorify your Father in heaven"

39. *De inst.* (*GNO* 8.1:53–56).
40. *De inst.* (*GNO* 8.1:50).
41. *De inst.* (*GNO* 8.1:46, 56–57).
42. *De inst.* (*GNO* 8.1:48–49).
43. *De inst.* (*GNO* 8.1:61).
44. *De inst.* (*GNO* 8.1:78).
45. *De inst.* (*GNO* 8.1:63).
46. *De inst.* (*GNO* 8.1:47).

rather than to chase after glory from humans.[47] The greater the progress someone has made, the greater the danger of pride and vainglory. "For it is the greatest achievement of philosophy that someone who is great in works should abase himself in his heart and find fault with his way of life . . . so that he may reap the fruit of his profession because by believing he has loved it, rather than by embracing discipline he has worked for it."[48] The Christian profession, attended and lived out by faith and love, is what matters. Those who have made greater progress along the Christian path must beware lest, thinking they stand, they should fall; and this attitude allies them with those who have made less progress.

The other theme in *On the Goal* that drives against any division between people who have made greater progress and those who have failed to do so applies particularly to the superiors of the monastery. Those who are "the superiors of this spiritual chorus" must take account of a right understanding of their office and of the devices used by the devil "to ambush the faith." The danger lies in "lifting up proud thoughts with respect to their authority," and "there are already some who think they stand ahead of others and have forgotten to guide them to heavenly life, destroying themselves by pride."[49] The functional hierarchy that distinguishes superiors from the other monks must not undermine an equality of status attaching to all, no matter where they find themselves on the one path:[50]

> If those of you set in charge and those of you employing them as teachers have this disposition toward one another, some gladly obedient to what has been ordered and others with pleasure leading the brothers to perfection, and if you consider one another the first in honors, you will be living the life of angels on earth.

Gregory establishes his point by citing Christ's words about humility (Luke 14:11; 18:14; Matt 9:35; 23:12; Mark 9:35; 10:45).

Gregory in *On the Goal* is also concerned for "those still young and in need of teaching."[51] He recognizes that there may be some monks "who lack the intensity of the highest form of prayer or the zeal and ability owed to the matter." These monks should be allowed to "fulfill their obedience in other ways as far as they can." What Gregory has in mind are good works, and he

47. *De inst.* (GNO 8.1:51–52).

48. *De inst.* (GNO 8.1:66).

49. *De inst.* (GNO 8.1:69).

50. *De inst.* (GNO 8.1:70).

51. *De inst.* (GNO 8.1:82).

is convinced that God "has supplied each person with the ability to do some good and has granted that no one eager to be saved should entirely fail of the possibility." Christ has promised to give a reward to anyone who "gives only a cup of cold water in the name of a disciple" (Matt 10:42).[52] Some people may be special because they have journeyed further along the one path, but Gregory's emphasis is upon the single path and the equality of status possessed by all who travel on it. Two final points occur to me. The monastic life involves Gregory's more general notion of perpetual progress in the good, the "stretching forward" or epectasy Paul speaks of in Phil 3:13.[53] Next, there is certainly the recognition that the ideal portrayed is difficult, if not impossible, to accomplish.

THE MARTYRS AND SAINTS

Occasionally Gregory in his writings gives us hints about what it was like to preside over the actual body of Christ entrusted to his care as bishop. In one of his letters he describes his return to Nyssa, possibly after he was recalled from exile by the emperor Valens probably in 379, perhaps a little earlier.[54] Delayed by thunder storms from which they were obliged to take shelter, Gregory and his companions draw near to Nyssa along a road following the course of a river. The road is crowded with villagers who greet their bishop with joyful tears. When Gregory's entourage reaches the town itself, they find themselves thronged with a great welcoming crowd. About to enter the church Gregory sees "a torrent of fire" flowing into the church. It turns out to be "the chorus of virgins," carrying their torches.[55] Liturgical occasions must have been like this. At the beginning of his homily *On the Day of Lights* Gregory rejoices to see his "flock." The crowd is so great that not everyone can "enter the sacred precincts." Like bees some "work inside, while others buzz outside the hive."[56] Similarly, in his *Praise of Theodore* Gregory's flock has streamed into Euchaita from the cities and the countryside. They are from many "different fatherlands," and have traveled during the harsh winter conditions to make their pilgrimage to the martyr's shrine (*Th.* 61). The road to the shrine has been so filled with people that Gregory thinks of a swarm of ants (*Th.* 70).

---

52. *De inst.* (GNO 8.1:87–88).

53. The text is cited, *De inst.* (GNO 8.1:65).

54. See Rousseau, *Basil of Caesarea*, 360–63.

55. *Ep. 6* (GNO 8.2:34–36).

56. *In diem lum.* (GNO 9:221). Cf. *In sanct. Pasch.* (GNO 9:249–50).

The crowds were not always easy to manage. In his first homily on the Forty Martyrs Gregory claims that his "shepherd's eye is gladdened" when he sees "the flock crushed by its multitude and overflowing its fold" (*FM. 1a* 137). But Gregory can scarcely be heard over the tumult caused by the crowd, "because your sound drowns out my speech" (*FM. 1a* 141). He is finally obliged to stop, hoping for "a second leisure time for speaking with quiet hearing" (*FM. 1a* 142). The next day he has better luck and reminds the crowd where he was in his homily "when the prayerful and sweet uproar from the multitude of those assembled prevented hearing what was said, when that living sea of the church, in flood tide with the multitude of those pouring in, seethed with the motion of people constantly hard pressed" (*FM. 1b* 145).

Perhaps Gregory had somewhat mixed feelings about the pilgrimages to the shrines of the martyrs. That certainly seems to be the case with his attitude toward the increasingly popular pilgrimage to Jerusalem and the Holy Land.[57] Two of Gregory's letters[58] at first seem to give contradictory assessments of such pilgrimages.[59] Both letters reflect Gregory's trouble shooting mission to Jerusalem and Arabia, which took place either immediately before or shortly after the Council of Constantinople in 381. The first letter, commonly called "On Pilgrimages," is addressed to someone otherwise unknown who may have been a monastic superior. In it Gregory begins by pointing out that nowhere in the (monastic?) rules, nor even in Christ's beatitudes is there any commandment or blessing concerning such pilgrimages.[60] Moreover, no one can escape the pollution of vice found not only on the journey but even in Jerusalem itself; women are especially vulnerable. Gregory excuses his own pilgrimage by the necessity of his mission, and he argues that he escaped the worst of the hazards he describes because he and his companions traveled in a carriage furnished by the emperor, which became, as it were, a moveable church or monastery. He did not find that the sight of the holy places either helped or hindered his faith in Christ. We do not draw nearer to God by changing places, and Cappadocia has many sanctuaries where one can find God's presence in visible things.[61]

---

57. For one account of this with a focus upon Egeria, see Wilkinson, *Egeria's Travels*.

58. *Ep.* 2 and 3 (*GNO* 8.2:13–27). See Maraval (SC 363) for text, French translation, introduction, and notes. In his introduction, 36, he refers to *Ep.* 3 as addressed "dès son retour de Palestine à des correspondents de Jérusalem."

59. See Ludlow, *Gregory of Nyssa*, 138–41.

60. See Ulrich, "Wallfahrt und Wallfahrtkritik," 87–96; Pullan, "'Intermingled until the End of Time,'" 387–409.

61. See Maraval, *Lieux saints et pèlerinages d'Orient*. For shrines in Cappadocia and the surrounding area, see 371–79. Also see Wilken, *Land Called Holy*, 117–18. Here the

The second letter (*Ep.* 3) is written to three pious "sisters," and the implication is that they are residing in Jerusalem. Gregory rejoices because he has seen both the tokens of Christ in the holy places and, more to the point, their sign in these women. The basilicas in Bethlehem, on the Mount of Olives, and the Anastasis and Golgotha on the site of Christ's death and resurrection are spiritually in their hearts. "Therefore, when I saw with my senses the holy places and saw also in you clear signs of such places, I was filled with such joy that words cannot describe that good."[62] But he immediately continues by saying that bitter is always mixed with sweet and that on his journey home he saw the truth in the Lord's words, "the whole world lies under the power of the evil one" (1 John 5:19). He is saddened by the fact that even the places where Christ walked prove no exception to this judgment. The rest of the letter is concerned with defending right doctrine and probably refers to controversies over Gregory's view of Christ that took place in Jerusalem while he was there. While Gregory does change his tune somewhat in this letter, giving his own experience of the holy places more positive expression than in the first letter, nonetheless in both letters he insists upon the importance of a spiritual understanding of Christ and of the holy places, and in both letters he laments the sorry moral condition of Jerusalem. Perhaps the real difference between the two letters has to do with their recipients. It would have been offensive to denigrate the holy places in any explicit way to women who presumably lived saintly lives in the holy city.

It may be that Gregory has mixed feelings about the crowds that thronged the churches, the holy places, and the martyrs' shrines, but he has no hesitation in holding up the ascetics and martyrs as helpers and models. Indeed, he can treat the ascetics as martyrs and the martyrs as ascetics.[63] The martyrs, however, are special people in a more obvious way than the ascetics and monks. They have passed beyond the immediate goal of the Christian path in this world, and like Theodore the martyr have left this world and embarked on their "fine and blessed journey to God" (*Th.* 69).[64] Their souls have been separated from their bodies by death, and Gregory

---

apparent contradiction of the two letters is unresolved, but Wilken points out that the first, *Ep.* 2, was a favorite of the Protestant Reformers.

62. *Ep.* 3 (*GNO* 8.2:20).

63. See Alexandre, "Les nouveaux martyrs," 33–70.

64. See Esper, "Enkomiastik und Christianismos," 145–59. His concern is with how Gregory transforms the conventions of Hellenistic rhetoric, but he points out that the homily must have been delivered at Euchaita, where Theodore's shrine was, not far from Amasea, where he was martyred. The date of the homily must be after 369 and the first insurrection of the Goths and before 379 when they crossed the Danube.

displays a degree of uncertainty about how to describe "the present condition of the saints." To be sure, it must be "very beautiful and magnificent." The soul, having ascended, "delights in its own inheritance and lives without a body together with those like it, while the body, its revered and spotless instrument, which never harmed the incorruptibility of its indwelling soul by its own passions," is preserved on earth in holy places. "It is kept for the time of the new creation like some highly valued treasure, quite incomparable to other bodies" (*Th.* 62).[65] The souls of the saints can be thought to have entered paradise. Adam and Eve, the first to contend against the devil, "through sin brought down human nature when it was standing." The martyrs "raised it up again by their endurance." Adam and Eve were driven out of paradise, while the martyrs "have found again their dwelling in paradise," where they await reunion with their bodies at the general resurrection (*FM. 1b* 151). The "turning sword" (Gen 3:24) guarding the entrance to paradise was made by God so that it "might be turned back for the worthy, opening for them an unhindered entrance into life." The martyrs will surely have had no less than the penitent thief to whom Christ said, "Today you will be with me in paradise" (Luke 23:43; *FM. 1b* 155–56).

Gregory is not thinking of paradise as a specific location, but understands it as one of many scriptural terms by which the condition of righteous souls after death is described. Another term for this condition is "Christ's hands" (*St.* 2 100):

> The longing for martyrdom not only bestows angelic worth, but also opens the gates of the heavens, no longer escorting souls to death, but commending the spirit into Christ's hands. For the Savior's dominical man called upon his own Father on the cross, when he said, "Father, into your hands I commend my spirit" (Luke 23:46). And Christ's servant, Stephen, reaching up to the Master, said, "Lord Jesus, receive my spirit" (Acts 7:59). With these words he put off his soul.

The pattern Gregory describes correlates with his solution to the problem how Christ after his death could be in paradise with the thief, in hell with the souls of the departed, and in the hands of the Father. The solution is to identify paradise with the Father's hands and to say that Christ's spirit or soul "went" there, while his body went to the tomb and to Hades. The divine Word, present to both soul and body, reunited them at the time of Christ's

65. See Brown, *Cult of the Saints*, 70, where he argues that despite the special bodies of the martyrs that removed any cause for grief, "yet the sadness of the tomb survived." He refers to Gregory's reaction to placing Macrina's body in the family tomb in which "an ancient horror of the dead gripped him."

resurrection.[66] For humans the reunion of soul and body will take place only at the general resurrection, and that is why the souls of the martyrs are in a condition preliminary to that time.

The bodies of the martyrs, as noted, are kept on earth until the day of resurrection, treasured there as an assurance of their presence. The binding together of relics with the continuing presence of the martyr was a joining of paradise to earth and a breaking of the barriers separating the dead from the living.[67] It is a great gift to be allowed to touch a martyr's remains (*Th.* 63):

> For those who look at the body as though it were living and flourishing kiss the eyes, the mouth, and the ears, approaching all the senses; and then, shedding tears of reverence and emotion, they offer supplication to the martyr as though he were in complete health and appearing.

Here Gregory is thinking of the martyr Theodore, whose relics were apparently undivided. In contrast, the relics of the Forty Martyrs of Sebaste[68] have been "distributed everywhere." Nevertheless, "no one who has taken up a partial gift of their remains has failed to receive in its entirety the manifestation of the martyrs" (*FM. 1a* 142; *FM. 2* 166). Indeed, "almost the whole earth is blessed by these holy relics."[69] Gregory himself has "a portion of

66. See my discussion in Greer and Mitchell, *"Belly-Myther" of Endor*, lxxvi–lxxxii.

67. See Brown, *Cult of the Saints*, ch. 1, 1–22. He notes that graves were excluded from ancient cities, a taboo that Christians overturned by placing graves in the cities or by establishing new cities surrounding burial places. See also Kötzsche-Breitenbruch, "Zum Ring des Gregor von Nyssa," 291–98.

68. The Forty Martyrs of Sebaste in Armenia were forty soldiers serving under the Emperor Licinius and were put to death by the emperor circa 320 (Sozomen, *Ecclesiastical History* 9.2). See Van Dam, "Small Details: The Cult of the Forty Martyrs," in *Becoming Christian*, 132–50; Leemans, "On the Date of Gregory of Nyssa's First Homilies," 93–97.

69. Gregory's point is confirmed by a story told by Sozomen (*Ecclesiastical History* 9.2). A deaconess belonging to the Macedonian sect, named Eusebia, possessed a house and garden outside the walls of Constantinople, and also a casket of relics of the Forty martyred under Licinius in Sebaste. She left the property to monks with the proviso that she be buried there with the relics and that this be kept secret. The monks built an underground shrine for Eusebia and the relics, but disguised the entrance and built a structure above it. The property was later bought by an imperial official as a place for his wife's burial and his own; and he built a shrine to the martyr Thyrsus, thereby obliterating any memory of Eusebia and her relics. But Thyrsus appeared to the empress Pulcheria, Theodosius II's elder sister, as did the Forty Martyrs themselves. This precipitated a search for the relics, which proved successful and resulted in a public celebration sometime in the 430s. For the distribution and translation of relics, see Brown, *Cult of the Saints*, 78–79, 88–90.

the gift" and has "deposited the bodies of my forebears" next to relics of the Forty Martyrs (*FM. 2* 166). Gregory's view is in agreement with that of Theodoret of Cyrus:[70]

> The noble souls of the victors traverse heaven, united with the chorus of incorporeals [angels]. A single grave for each does not guard their bodies hidden. Instead, the cities and villages to which they have been distributed call them the saviours and healers of bodies and souls and honor them as guardians and protectors. . . . Though the body is divided, the grace has remained undivided; and that small and very tiny relic has a power equal to the martyr even if he had never in any way been divided.

The relics, then, function to guarantee the martyr's presence with those who have not yet begun their journey from the end of this life to the final goal of the single path, and they are spread throughout the Roman Empire as, so to speak, an irrigation system of holiness.

The martyrs, then, occupy a special place in the larger understanding of the Christian path, since their condition marks the boundary area that includes both its destination in this life and the beginning of its continuation in the age to come. The martyrs, without losing their connection with those journeying behind them, are allied with the angels. I have already noted Stephen's "angelic grace" (*St. 1* 87; Acts 6:15), but similarly, when the Forty Martyrs displayed their contempt of death, they showed they were "people far above human limits" (*FM. 1b* 149). As we have seen Paul say in 1 Cor 4:9 the martyrs are a "spectacle to the world, to angels and to mortals." The angels had seen with dismay "the first wrestling match, when the serpent overthrew Adam." But when they saw the victory of the Forty "there was applause and praise from above—acclamation from the citizens of the heavenly city who applauded the achievement, and joy from the entire festal throng in heaven" (*FM. 1b* 150). The angels were also "waiting for the separation of their souls so that they might receive them and take them up to their own allotted place" (*FM. 2* 163).

Gregory's emphasis, of course, is upon the great victory won by the martyrs. They are the "athletes" who have won the race or bested their demonic opponents in a wrestling match.[71] They have won the victory in their warfare against the devil. Theodore was in actual fact a soldier, who came from the East "to our land with his own legion." But this new recruit was one "whom Paul armed, whom angels anointed for his combat and Christ

---

70. Theodoret of Cyrus, *Graec. aff. cur.* 8.10 (SC 75:317).

71. See, e.g., *Th.* 62, 63, 70; *St. 1*, 76, 80, 85, 89; *FM. 1b* 150.

crowned when he won the victory" (*Th.* 64). The Forty Martyrs, who were in the Roman army, were really "Christ's soldiers, the Holy Spirit's armed men, faith's champions, the divine city's towers." In doing battle against the devil they did not arm themselves with sword and shield, but instead "put on the whole armor of God" (Eph 6:11–17; *FM. 1b* 149). They were "Paul's soldiers, Christ's bodyguards" (*FM. 2* 163). And their confession of Christ was "the noble soldier's sling" by which they slew the devil in order to decapitate him, fulfilling, Gregory implies, the type of David slaying Goliath (*FM. 1b* 150).

In praising the Forty Martyrs Gregory restricts the metaphor of the crown to the triumph of their martyrdom. The day of their feast is one on which they are commemorated just as "some loud-voiced herald . . . proclaims the crown of the martyrs." Their wonders "outweigh the world," since "they are adorned with the beauty of crowns" (*FM. 1a* 141). Before the Forty were placed on the ice to freeze to death they were bound together with iron chains. "Such a numerous distinguished band of youths, conspicuous for its nobility, in stature above the others—all of them at the same time were joined together with one another by the chain, like some crown or necklace having pearls of equal size distributed in a circle." The saints were "both united in faith and bound together with one another by the chains" (*FM. 1b* 148). After all but one of the Forty had frozen to death, Gregory describes their fate with another metaphor of victory. Their bodies were carried off to be burned. "What speech will describe that divine procession, when their bodies were led in triumph to the fire on wagons?" By this time the converted jailer has filled up the number of the Forty, replacing the one soldier who had apostasized. There follows the story of the mother of the one soldier who still lives. She tells her dying son that he was "begotten according to God" and urges him to hasten to his Father, "lest you be left behind your comrades, lest you come in second place to your crown." The mother then puts her son "into the covered chariot with the rest, marching before the bright countenance of the athlete" (*FM. 1b* 154–55). Gregory alludes to the conventions of the Roman triumph, and it seems possible to me that the shift in terminology from "wagons" to "covered chariot" is meant to imply that while the Forty are victims or captives carried in the triumphal procession, they are also the victors who ride in the triumphal chariot.

When Gregory tells the stories of Theodore, Stephen, and the Forty, he must emphasize their victory and the claim that their noble deaths have given them true life in their association with the angels. At the same time this aspect of his rhetoric serves the larger purpose of describing how the martyrs continue to serve those still in this life. His aim is to paint in words "an accurate portrait of the combat, so that the list of marvels through the sequence of events could be displayed in its relation to our path" (*St. 1* 77).

The mediatorial character of the martyrs enables them to bind together the living and the dead. The martyrs, who have passed beyond the summit of virtue in this life and have begun their journey to God in the life to come, remain tied to those still striving for the summit of virtue here below. Throughout his homilies on the martyrs Gregory underlines their close relation to Christians in this life. Theodore's fatherland was in the East, but "now he is a martyr in the whole world, a fellow citizen for all who dwell beneath the sun" (*Th.* 65). From another perspective Theodore's fatherland is "the place of his suffering," the town of Amaseia. But "his fellow citizens, brothers, and kindred are those who have cherished it [his place of suffering] and who hold and honor it" (*Th.* 70). There seems to be a paradox. What is local has at least the potential of becoming universal, and we can think of the scattering of the relics of the Forty Martyrs. Perhaps it is possible to think of this paradox as a shadow of the paradox of the incarnation, of the particular human life of Christ that has universal significance because that life is also God's with us. Gregory is able to underline the theme of the universality of the gospel in his homilies on the martyrs because he can set their stories in the larger context of the church's mission. As already mentioned, when the apostles at Pentecost speak in different tongues, this marked the beginning of "the Holy Spirit's dispensation," which was designed to undo the fragmentation of human languages that took place at the time of the tower of Babel. The Holy Spirit distributed "the benefit common to humans to every differing human language, lest the preaching of true religion, by being restricted to only a single language, should remain unavailing and ineffective for those of other tongues" (*St. 1* 78).

The saints that can be most clearly associated with the universal scope of the gospel are the apostles, and Gregory thinks chiefly of Peter, James, and John. They were "not lamps or beacons or stars," but "lights shining not in one region or in one corner, but illuminating the whole world beneath heaven." Peter, when nailed to a cross, "modeled the Master's image of a king (and I mean by kingly image the cross), unashamed of his passion, but exalted on the great trophy of victory." Peter honored Christ by being crucified head down so as not to claim equality with the Savior, "who was crucified for all mankind and with hands stretched out, and who encompasses the world with his hands, just as he did with his hands stretched out on the cross" (*St. 2* 102). When we honor the saints, it is not for their profit, "but so that we may have fellowship with them when we are benefited." Commemorating Peter, James, and John involves the larger fellowship with "the entire concord of the apostles" (*St. 2* 104). By extension Gregory's idea is that Christians in this life have fellowship with all the saints and martyrs. Though they are unseen, they are our friends. Gregory addresses Theodore, saying: "You have come here for a short time at the appeal of those who honor you as their unseen friend" (*Th.* 70).[72] Gregory ends his first homily on Stephen by claiming "that we have not only become spectators of Stephen's struggle, but also partakers of his grace by being filled with the Holy Spirit for putting down those at war against us and for the glory of our Lord Jesus Christ" (*St. 1* 94). In his last homily on the Forty Martyrs, Gregory cites the reference in Heb 12:1 to the great "cloud of martyrs surrounding us," concluding from it, "let us bless ourselves, rejoicing in hope, persevering in prayer, sharing in the memorial of the saints" (*FM. 2* 169). To have fellowship with our unseen friends[73] is to share in their grace, to find blessing, hope, and perseverance in prayer.

What this means is that the martyrs and saints, as friends, benefit Christians in this life in various ways. They carry our prayers to God, since "whoever has so many ambassadors would never leave prayer and supplication without success, even if he were quite heavily weighed down with sin" (*FM. 2* 169). In his homily in praise of Theodore, Gregory implores the martyr: "We need many services. Be an ambassador on behalf of our fatherland to our common King" (*Th.* 70). Those who approach Theodore's body "offer supplication to the martyr as though he were in complete health and appearing, asking him to be their ambassador and beseeching him as God's attendant, as the one receiving gifts and, once summoned, bestowing them when he is willing" (*Th.* 63–64). Thus, as ambassadors the martyrs are mediators between those on earth and God. They not only carry the Christians' prayers to God, but also bring God's gifts to them. It is this second aspect of their work, "their embassy," that strengthens us "for the good confession of our Lord Jesus Christ" (*FM. 1b* 156). The first passage I have cited in this paragraph is closely followed by a description of how the Forty Martyrs exercise their role as ambassadors, bringing God's help to us (*FM. 2* 169):

> For the Forty Martyrs are strong defenders against our enemies
> and faithful advocates of our prayer to the Master. With hope
> in them let the Christian take courage against the devil when
> he contrives temptation, against evil people who rise up against
> us, against tyrants seething with anger, against the sea when
> it becomes wild, against the earth when it does not bear what
> it is ordained to produce for humans, against heaven when it
> threatens disasters. For the power of these martyrs is sufficient
> for every need and circumstance, since it has received rich grace
> from Christ.

72. See also *Th.* 62, 64.

73. See Brown, *Cult of the Saints,* ch. 3, "The Invisible Companion," 50–68.

Gregory has himself deposited the bodies of his forebears beside the relics of the Forty Martyrs, "so that at the time of the resurrection they may be raised with helpers speaking with the boldest freedom" (*FM*. 2 166).

One particular form that the help of these unseen friends and ambassadors takes is that of miracles that benefit Christians. Gregory's last homily in praise of the Forty Martyrs describes two such miracles. A lame soldier entered the martyrs' shrine, and "after praying to God he also implored the saints to be his ambassadors." A man appeared to the soldier that night in a dream, touched his foot and put the soldier's leg back in joint. The soldier awoke healed of his infirmity. The second story is of Gregory's own dream of the forty soldiers barring his entrance to the vigil that was honoring their relics, an experience that seems to have been one of conversion (*FM*. 2 166–68).[74] Theodore, interceding in heaven, has already "stilled the storm of the barbarians and put a stop to the savage Scythians' war by threatening them . . . with the cross of Christ which wards off evil and is all powerful, and for which he also suffered and gained this glory" (*Th*. 61–62). The danger is not passed, and Gregory asks Theodore to continue his help against the barbarians. "Fight for us as a soldier; as a martyr use your boldness on behalf of your fellow servants" (*Th*. 70). Stephen's role as an unseen friend is rather different from Theodore's. He is like an athlete who has "retired from contests," but continues to "train the young by athletic exercises" (*St*. 1 89). It is no surprise that the martyrs can now work miracles, since even before their death this power was theirs. Gregory identifies the story of the "Thundering Legion" with the miracle performed by the Forty, who as Christians formed their own company and by prayer called down rain, which both assuaged the thirst of the trapped soldiers and overcame their enemies (*FM*. 1b 146–47).[75] Gregory also notes that Stephen performed miracles before his martyrdom (Acts 6:8; *St*. 2 98). As well, during his trial Theodore miraculously set on fire the temple of the Mother of the gods in Amaseia (*Th*. 67), and his prison was marvelously filled with singing and shining lamps

---

74. In his *Life of Macrina* (15) Gregory tells of a visionary dream, repeated three times, in which he finds himself holding the relics of the Forty Martyrs, from which a dazzling and blinding light emanates. This is immediately before his arrival at Annisa.

75. Eusebius (*Hist. eccl.* 5.5) places the miracle during Marcus Aurelius' campaign against the Germans circa 174 CE, attributing it to a Christian legion from Melitene in eastern Cappadocia. He notes the wide currency of the story, both in writers "foreign to our faith" and in Christian writings. He notes Apolinarius of Hierapolis and Tertullian (*Apol*. 5). The story also appears in a spurious letter of Marcus Aurelius to the Senate, appended to Justin's first *Apology*. The fullest version is to be found in Dio Cassius 72.8, where Xiphilinus, Dio's epitomizer, corrects the pagan version by giving the Christian one. See also the life of Marcus Aurelius, section 24, in the *Historia Augusta*; Marcus performs the miracle himself.

(*Th.* 69). The miraculous power displayed during their lives continues after the martyrs' victory; and this is the more important claim.

One way in which Gregory describes the role of the martyrs is found in his account of the function of Theodore's martyr shrine (*Th.* 69–70):

> He [Theodore] has made this place a hospital for many kinds of diseases, a harbor for those tempest-tossed by afflictions, a thriving storehouse for the poor, a free lodging place for travelers, an unceasing place of assembly for those celebrating festivals.

The miracle of victory against the barbarians is now the miracle of what we should think of as the social gospel. The role of the martyr's shrine, while it does include miraculous healing, is also a place where the poor can be fed and travelers given lodging. It may be difficult for us to understand the connection between the social work of the church and the cult of the saints, perhaps because we think of that work as our own rather than that of Christ and the saints. But the example of the shrine at Lourdes is at least one way of trying to imagine what Gregory and others in the ancient church describe.

While Gregory's emphasis in his accounts of the martyrs is upon their role as unseen friends and helpers capable of benefiting Christians both in a miraculous way and by their service to those in need, he does not entirely ignore what appears to have been much earlier the chief motive for telling their stories. The *Martyrdom of Polycarp*, perhaps the oldest martyrology, is a letter meant to circulate widely, composed by the church in Smyrna in the middle of the second century. It is designed to portray Polycarp's conduct and martyrdom as an example to be imitated, since he demonstrated "a martyrdom in accordance with the Gospel."[76] This was because, in accordance with Gregory Nazianzen's much later rule of martyrdom,[77] he neither sought it nor refused it when it came to him. The letter of the church in Smyrna expresses the conviction that Christ will permit "us" to assemble and "celebrate the birthday of his [Polycarp's] martyrdom, both in memory of those who have already contested, and for the practice and training of those whose fate it shall be."[78] Polycarp's is a "martyrdom all desire to imitate."[79] Of course, by Gregory's time martyrdom was no longer something anyone could expect. But that by no means meant that Christians were no longer able to emulate the virtue and steadfastness of the martyrs by living their lives with loyalty to Christ as their chief aim. Like the martyrs they, too,

---

76. *Martyrdom of Polycarp* 1 (LCL 2:313).

77. Gregory of Nazianzus, *Or.* 43.6.

78. *Martyrdom of Polycarp* 18 (LCL 2:337).

79. *Martyrdom of Polycarp* 19 (LCL 2.339).

could define their journey by following in Christ's steps. There is much to be said for treating the spread of the ascetic ideal in the fourth century as a way of preserving the old martyr spirit.

In his homily in praise of the Forty Martyrs delivered at the shrine near Annisa Gregory says that it is "in every way best and quite profitable for youths to be brought up and men to flourish by stories of virtue." Hearing is "no less instructive than sight," since it teaches souls and "leads a person to desire to do what is thought." The example of the martyrs is more than merely the story of their fate. It has the power to motivate Christians, and Gregory asks for calm attention to his homily "so that the blessed martyrs may be honored with what is fitting and so that you may be taught devotion and the love of God by their memory" (*FM. 2* 159). Gregory continues by making the same point about Basil, who had preceded him some years ago in praising the Forty Martyrs. Basil "was adorned with all the beauty of virtue. Exalted, then, he praised those who were exalted; a saint he was the servant of saints because in accordance with his own power he completed the prize for those who gained it by their valor" (*FM. 2* 160). Perhaps we can remember Paul's words: "Be imitators of me, as I am of Christ" (1 Cor 11:1). The imitation of Christ that should dominate the Christian life can include imitating those who are Christ's; and this idea applies in a special way to the saints.

Gregory also strikes the theme of imitating the martyrs toward the end of his second homily in praise of Stephen. After speaking of the apostles and, specifically, of Peter, James, and John, he concludes that "in this one thing we are deemed worthy to share in the commemoration of the saints, that is, by imitating and being zealous for their virtues, not publishing their life in words, but preserving their manner of living in our purpose." Only that will make us their true disciples. "Do you honor the memory of the martyrs? Honor also their purpose, for agreement with their purpose is sharing in their memory." Christ's gospel and his grace are for all Christians. "The commandments are in common; the manner of life is in common; there is one judge of the contests; there is one prize of truth" (*St. 2* 105). The relation of Christians to the saints and martyrs is a reciprocal one. They give to Christians their powerful help and their example, but Christians must respond not only by honoring them, but also by imitating them.

What takes pride of place in the martyrs' example is their confession of Christ despite all the various ways in which they are urged or compelled to deny him (e.g., *Th.* 65). All the stories Gregory tells in his homilies focus upon this. Moreover, his account of that one of the Forty who was seduced by the devil and who betrayed Christ like Judas and who nonetheless died, represents a cautionary tale that underlines the kind of endurance necessary for martyrdom (*FM. 2* 164). The sight of the Forty Martyrs was "beautiful to angels . . . but bitter to the demons." They were human beings, but endured "far above human limits." "They mocked every punishment meted out by tortures, every swelling up of fear, every threatening assault, as though they were some childish folly" (*FM. 1b* 149). Gregory treats Stephen's endurance rather differently. As already noted, Stephen displayed forbearance, disdain of threats, contempt for life, love, beneficence, and disclosure of the truth. He "prevailed by the true wisdom, struggling against fear by boldness, against threats by disdain, against bitter enmity by beneficence, against falsehood by truth." He addressed his enemies as brothers. At the moment of his death, "repaying their bloodthirstiness with kindness," he said "in the hearing of his murderers, 'Lord, do not hold their sin against them'" (Acts 7:60; *St. 1* 84–86). This was because his vision of Christ was of "the lawgiver of forbearance," and he remembered Christ's law "commanding us to love our enemies" (Matt 5:44; *St. 1* 88).

CONCLUSION

Gregory's account of the ascetics and martyrs does treat them as special Christians. The ascetics are different not only if they live in a community to some degree separated from the world around them, but even if they do not live this way they aspire to traveling further along the Christian path than others. Still more obviously, the martyrs and saints are special because they have attained the summit of virtue in this life and have passed beyond it in a journey toward the final goal and destination of the Christian path. At the same time, Gregory wants to insist that what is special about both groups in no sense divides them from the main body of Christians in this life. Just as ascetical directors and monastic superiors have no status higher than the people they serve, so the ascetics and monks serve the whole church by holding up a high ideal for the Christian life and by helping along those who have not traveled so far. The martyrs and saints, though dead, are still very much a part of the Christian communities that remember and honor them. They function as ambassadors and mediators, binding the dead to the living and the realm of the angels to those still on earth. Gregory appears to recognize that in this world the distinctions involved have a way of becoming divisions rather than differences. But surely he wants to argue that the whole church, the living and the dead, is moving toward its final destiny, when there will no longer be a distinction between the church and the world and when all divisions will cease, enabling the differences that remain to be ones that will build up the body of Christ. That body will be the completion and perfection of the corporate humanity of Christ, and it will fulfill God's intention for humanity by binding together the visible and the invisible creation. Finally, since the incarnate Word has united God with humanity, the whole of creation will become not merely a harmony, but also a divinized one. It is, I think, this large vision that explains Gregory's treatment of special Christians. They are special, but the role they play is one in service to the body of Christ and to Gregory's mystical understanding of that body's destiny. It is to his understanding of what will take place after death and after the consummation of this world that I wish to turn in the last essay.

4

THE LAST THINGS

> But, as it is written [cf. Isa 64:4], What no eye has seen, nor ear
> heard, nor the human heart conceived, what God has prepared
> for those who love him.

Gregory cites this verse, 1 Cor 2:9, at a number of places in his writings. In *On the Christian's Profession* he speaks of placing "our merchandise," that is, our accomplishments in the virtuous life, in the treasury of heaven (Matt 6:19), where what we have managed to do will accrue interest, since we shall receive more than we deserve, and "great things will be given back for small ones, heavenly things for earthly, and eternal things exchanged for those that quickly die." It is these things that Paul describes in the verse from 1 Corinthians (*Prof.* 141–42). In his treatise *Against Eunomius* Gregory insists upon God's incomprehensibility; we must not think more highly than we ought to think (cf. Rom 12:3). Paul with his speech untrained by rhetoric must be our teacher for "mysteries beyond knowledge." He says that God's judgments are unsearchable and his ways inscrutable (Rom 11:33), and that his promises in return for their achievements in this life for those who love him are beyond comprehension since they cannot be grasped by the eye, received by the ear, or contained in the heart.[1] The Psalms, according to Gregory, teach us the way to blessedness; and they always "urge on to what is greater and loftier in the journey to virtue those they guide toward what is on high, until someone attains that measure of blessedness beyond which neither understanding can give an account by any guesses and conjectures,

1. *C. Eun.* 3.1 (*GNO* 2:39). Gregory twice refers the verse from 1 Corinthians to the incomprehensibility of the Word or of God: *In cant.* 8 (*GNO* 6:247) and *Vit. Mos.* 157 (*CWS* 93; *GNO* 7.1:84).

nor reason find what is next by logical consequence." Hope outstrips our desire, and when it reaches "incomprehensible things," it remains idle. At the time in the age to come when humans will be reunited with the angels, the guesses of understanding as well as "the working of our hope" will lie idle. What follows will be "the ineffable and incomprehensible establishment of what is better than all understanding, which neither eye has seen, nor ear heard, nor the human heart grasped."[2] As Gregory says in the *Catechetical Oration*, "the promised blessings, held out to those who have lived a good life, defy description. For how can we describe what the eye has not seen, or the ear heard, or what the heart of man has not entertained?"[3] In his funeral oration for Pulcheria Gregory says that Sarah would have mourned the sacrifice of Isaac had she not seen with her eyes what is unseen and known that the end of fleshly life is the beginning of a more divine one, where there are those good things that are above eye, ear, and heart.[4]

In *Homily 11 on Song of Songs* Gregory contrasts our present wonder at creation, one that leads us to worship God, with what will be after heaven and earth pass away (Matt 24:35) and we shall no longer know in part (1 Cor 13:12). Then we shall pass over to "that life which is above eye, hearing, and thought." Then "in another way the form of ineffable blessedness will certainly be grasped, as well as another way of enjoyment that does not have a nature able to go up to the human heart," Meanwhile we must be content with the bridegroom's "hand" (Song 5:4).[5] At the same time Gregory can leave room for at least a partial apprehension in this life of the good things to come. In his homily on the Easter Vigil he speaks of the rites and says, "We have welcomed joy by what we have seen, by what we have heard, by what has entered our heart." We have seen the light of the lamps lit at the Vigil and heard the psalms and hymns. "And the heart, illuminated by what was said and seen, was marked with ineffable blessedness, led by what appeared to what is unseen, so that there was an image of those good things which neither eye has seen, nor ear heard, nor the human heart conceived."[6]

I have begun the essay in this way because Gregory's use of the verse from 1 Corinthians supplies a perspective from which to assess what he has to say about the last things after death and the consummation of this world. It seems to me necessary to make this preliminary assessment in relation to what follows in my discussion for at least two reasons. First, everything

2. *In inscr. ps.* 1.7 (*GNO* 5:67–69).

3. *Or. cat.* 40 (*LCC* 3:325; *GNO* 3.4:105).

4. *In Pulch.* (*GNO* 9:469).

5. *In cant.* 11 (*GNO* 6:336). Cf. Smith, *Passion and Paradise*, 211.

6. *In sanct. Pasch.* (*GNO* 9:309).

Gregory says about what transcends this life is speculative, glimmers of the truth and partial apprehensions, not at all doctrines that he would insist must be believed. To be sure, he is committed to the credal affirmation of the resurrection of the dead and eternal life; but that does not mean that these doctrines require no explanation. The rule of faith may place limits on what can be said, but it is also a basis for speculation. Second, Gregory's "glimmers" are not all of a piece. That is, it is not easy to see how he wants his various insights to be assembled. It is not so much that these insights are incoherent as that his guesses tempt the reader to put them together in a way that would defy his repeated insistence that only the Truth knows how to solve the puzzles and problems that provoke his ruminations.[7]

ON THE MAKING OF MAN:
THE BEGINNING IS LIKE THE END

It may be foolish of me to rush in by trying to interpret Gregory's treatise *On the Making of Man*, but it seems worthwhile to speculate on the speculations he offers in this complex work.[8] Let me begin with some comments on Gregory's covering letter to his brother Peter, in which he explains what he will attempt. The treatise is an Easter gift to Peter and is meant to complete Basil's homilies *On the Six Days of Creation*. Basil "made the orderly arrangement of the universe easy to grasp for the many through his own spiritual interpretation [θεωρία]," but his work was incomplete and did not include the creation of humanity.[9] Gregory, however, does not intend his treatise for the many, but wishes only to contribute what was lacking in Basil's spiritual exegesis.[10] His aim is no small one since it is only humanity that has been made in the image of God, and so he must leave nothing about humanity unexamined—what is "believed" to have happened beforehand, and what is "expected" to come about later on, and what is "now" contemplated. Here he

---

7. Cf. Mosshammer, "Disclosing but Not Disclosed," 99–123. He treats Gregory's understanding of language and focuses upon his interpretation of scripture.

8. For two important discussions of *On the Making of Man*, see Corsini, "Plérôme humain et plérôme cosmique," 111–26, and Zachhuber, *Human Nature*, especially ch. 4, 145–86. Corsini rejects the idea that Gregory had a view of a double creation, whereas Zachhuber thinks he did and attributes the difficulties in Gregory's argument to his "rudimentary Origenism" (172).

9. The very nature of Gregory's project as θεωρία follows the speculative tradition of Origen. The task of *theoria* is to move beyond the letter of the text to the spiritual meaning, even though these interpretations are no more than contingent judgments. See Daniélou, "La theoria," 130–45, and Böhm, *Theoria-Unendlichkeit-Aufstieg*.

10. *De hom. op.* (PG 44:125a–b).

does not seem to me to be setting out an outline of the treatise, but rather to be alerting the reader to a fundamental contrast between what humans are now and, on the other hand, what they were in the beginning and will be at the final end beyond this life, a contrast by no means limited to chapter 16.[11] This contradiction must be resolved on the basis of scripture and reasoning "so that the entire subject may cohere in an orderly sequence when what seems contradictory is brought together to one and the same goal, and when in this way the divine power discovers hope for those beyond hope and a pathway for those without resources."[12] T. S. Eliot may have it right: "The end is where we start from. . . . And the end of all our exploring / Will be to arrive where we started / And know the place for the first time."[13]

Gregory appears to depend upon the idea that the end is like the beginning and that humanity after the resurrection will be like humanity before the fall of Adam and Eve. "Like" may be the operative word, and it is surely clear enough that Gregory supposes the end to be an increment on the beginning if for no other reason than that it will be stable, or better, a "stable motion" without the possibility of a fall.[14] At any rate, as already observed, Gregory often speaks of human destiny as a return to its beginning. But is it the "believed" beginning that explains the end, or the "expected" end that defines the beginning? Obviously, Gregory begins with creation, but there is at least the possibility of arguing that his vision of the life to come informs his account of creation. At any rate the first chapter takes as its text Gen 2:4, which Gregory treats as a summary of Gen 1, which he briefly interprets. Two points emerge in his discussion. The marvelous order of the visible universe binds together the four elements, earth, air, fire, and water. As well, the luminaries in heaven and the creatures on earth are mutable, though in different ways, since the heavenly bodies move but are not corrupted, while

11. Cf. the translation in *NPNF²* 5:387: "of what we believe to have taken place previously, of what we now see, and of the results which are expected afterwards to appear." Notice the reversal of "now" and "expected." The translation gives the impression that the treatise moves from creation to our present condition and then to the age to come. Gregory's contrast between human nature now as opposed to how it was in the beginning and will be at the end allows him to address the troubling question that is at the heart of the treatise: how can creatures made in the image of God be so miserable? See *De hom. op.* (PG 44:181a).

12. *De hom. op.* (PG 44:128a–b).

13. Eliot, *Four Quartets*, ll. 216, 240–42.

14. Cf. Gregory's comment regarding Moses, who stands in the cleft of the rock and sees God's back: ". . . the progress is a standing still, for it says, 'You must stand on the rock.' This is the most marvelous thing of all: how the same thing is both a standing still and a moving. For he who ascends certainly does not stand still, and he who stands still does not move upwards. But here the ascent takes place by means of the standing" (*Vit. Mos.* 2.243 [CWS 117; GNO 7.1:118]).

things on earth are stable but subject to decay. Thus, all creation is mutable, while only the Creator is immutable. Gregory ends the chapter with a lyrical account of the beauties of heaven and earth, and he concludes there was as yet no one to share in them.

This leads to the question posed in chapter 2: why was humanity created last? Gregory's answer is complex. In the first place it would not have been right for God to introduce the ruler before his subjects, and so he prepared a lodging for the ruler that was to come; then God displays humanity in the world with all its marvels. Of some of them humanity is the contemplator (θεατήν); of others, the lord (κύριον).[15] As the provider of the feast God welcomes humanity not to acquire what was absent, but to enjoy the banquet he had prepared. "And because of this God founds the origins of a double fashioning [διπλῆς τῆς κατασκευῆς] for humanity, mixing the divine with the earthly so that by both it might have enjoyment with each by kinship and appropriation, enjoying God through a more divine nature, and the goods on earth through sense perception of the same kind as theirs."[16]

Chapter 3 underlines the special character of humanity by pointing out that only in its case does God deliberate about its fashioning (κατασκευῆς βουλὴ προηγεῖται) and consider "to what sort of archetype it would bear the likeness and for what purposes it would come into being, what its operation would be when it came to exist and what it would govern." Gregory cites Gen 1:26: "God said, let us make humanity according to our image and likeness, and let them rule over the fish of the sea and the beasts of the earth and the birds of heaven and the cattle and all the earth." The verse reflects Gregory's understanding of the double constitution of humanity; the soul as the image of God allies humanity with God, while the dominion humanity is destined to exercise depends upon the body as the soul's instrument allying humanity to the lesser creation.[17] This becomes clearer in chapter 4 where we learn that just as craftsmen form a tool or instrument for their use, so God, the Chief Craftsman created our nature "as a kind of implement for the exercise of kingship, having fashioned it with superior advantages in the soul and by the very form of the body to be such as would be prepared for kingship."[18] In the rest of chapter 4 and chapter 5 Gregory calls attention to the soul and its royal character. The soul is "without a ruler, freely autonomous, governed autocratically by its own wishes." In this way humanity is, as it were, God's vicegerent in creation. Its vocation is to be the mediator of

---

15. *De hom. op.* 2 (PG 44:133a).

16. *De hom. op.* 2 (PG 44:133b).

17. *De hom. op.* 3 (PG 44:133c–d).

18. *De hom. op.* 4 (PG 44:136b).

the created order, binding the intelligible creation to the perceptible one. This is implicitly one reason Gregory might have given for his denial that humanity is a microcosm.[19]

It seems reasonable to conclude that in his first five chapters Gregory establishes the claim that God's deliberative purpose in the beginning was to make humanity in his image but with the body as the instrument through which the soul or mind is enabled to exercise its function to "have dominion" over the rest of creation (Gen 1:26a and 26b). As we should expect he continues in chapters 6 through 15 to explore the way in which the mind is related to the body. Here, I think, the basic problem implicit in his discussion is the way the present condition of humanity fails to accord with how and why it was to be created and with what will be its destiny. In chapter 6 Gregory raises the problem whether the mind really is an image of God, since God's operation (ἐνεργεία) in relation to creation is unitary, reflecting his "simplicity" (ἁπλότης), whereas the human mind approaches the phenomenal world with separate faculties, the senses.[20] Gregory's solution is to argue that the mind itself remains single because it controls and unifies the data given it by the senses. He returns to this idea in chapter 10, where he treats the mind as productive of speech but also as a receptacle for sense impressions. In this function the mind sorts out all the sense perceptions it receives, like a city with many gates that welcomes to their appropriate places those who enter. Sometimes there is "one knowledge from differing senses," while it is also possible from one sense "to learn many various things."[21]

So far so good. But with chapter 7 we begin to see something of a contrast with what we have learned up to this point. The title of the chapter, one that Gregory gives it in his letter to Peter, raises the question why humanity is bereft of natural weapons and coverings. Humans lack the defenses common to animals, since they do not have horns, claws, sharp teeth, or venom. Humans do not even have a covering of hair, and surely we should expect that if humanity was introduced to have rule over the rest of creation, it would have been provided with the natural gifts for defense and protection we see in other creatures. "How, someone might say, has such a one been allotted rule over all?" Gregory's answer is that what seems a deficiency is really the basis for "exercising power" (κρατεῖν) over humanity's subjects.[22]

19. Cf. Corsini, "Plérôme humain et plérôme cosmique," 112–13, where he points out that this idea supplants that of a purely spiritual mediator between God and the world, an idea found not only in Platonism but also in Origen's notion of the mediatorial Logos.

20. *De hom. op.* 6 (PG 44:137d).

21. *De hom. op.* 10 (PG 44:152a–53c).

22. *De hom. op.* 7 (PG 44:141a–b).

Earlier he spoke of humanity's task as one of "governing" (ἡγεμονεύσει).[23] Now he speaks of the use of force rather than of leading or guidance. He goes on to describe the way humans make up for their deficiencies by compelling animals to serve them in various ways, horses to enable swift movement, sheep to provide wool for clothing, beasts to carry burdens, oxen to tend the fields, and dogs to protect them like "a living sword." Even the crocodile yields its hide for protective armor.[24] All this sounds more like the Stoic arguments Cicero has Balbus present in Book 2 of *On the Nature of the Gods*.[25] However that may be, here Gregory gives us a picture of "nature red of tooth and claw," and humanity compels obedience. The beginning of chapter 8 reinforces this conclusion because he interprets the upright stature of humans as a sign of humanity's "royal worth." The lower creatures bow down before humanity's mighty power (δυναστεία). This does not seem to be a description of the peaceable kingdom.

One other—and clearer—example of the way Gregory mixes together what appears in humanity now with what characterizes its condition before and after this present world will suffice. In chapter 12 he begins a long discussion of where we should locate the mind, the rational soul that acts as a governing principle. In the previous chapter he has cleverly argued that since we do not know our own mind, its incomprehensibility is indeed an image of God's incomprehensibility. Therefore, the argument that begins with chapter 12 must be regarded as speculative. Nevertheless, Gregory makes his conclusion clear midway through this chapter. The mind is not to be located in the heart, the brain, or any particular part of the body. Instead, it is like a musician that requires an instrument for his use. "So the mind, by pervading the whole of its instrument [the body] and by touching each one of its parts in succession with the intelligible activities that are its by nature, activates what belongs to all of them when they are naturally disposed."[26] Instead of stopping with this conclusion Gregory continues his discussion of the topic of the mind's relation to the body to the end of chapter 15, digressing somewhat from the main point along the way.

23. *De hom. op.* 3 (PG 44:133c).

24. *De hom. op.* 7 (PG 44:140d–41d).

25. Cf. Alexandre, "La théorie de l'exégèse," 101. See also Balás, Μετουσία Θεοῦ, 36–37. He is speaking here of Gregory's divisions of corporeal nature "as reflecting a dynamic process." But he says, "Both doctrine and terminology point to Posidonius as the ultimate source, but other sources (e.g. Panaetius) cannot be excluded, and it is possible that Gregory's immediate sources in this case were manuals or doxographical collections." Cicero, of course, knew Posidonius; and Balbus' account probably reflects Posidonius' teaching.

26. *De hom. op.* 12 (PG 44:161b).

The passage just cited leads Gregory to what he calls "one of the nobler teachings." "Since the good that is most beautiful of all and most exceptional is divinity itself, to which all things that have a longing for the good incline, for this reason we say that the mind also, since it came to be according to the image of the most beautiful, as long as it participates in its likeness to the archetype as much as it can, abides itself in the good." Contrariwise, if the mind turns away from its archetype, it is stripped of its beauty. The mind, then, ought to be a mirror reflecting God and his true beauty, while, as well, the body ought to be, as it were, the mirror of this mirror. When the mind governs the body, it too reflects the divine beauty.[27] The idea is an important one, and had Gregory only pursued it more thoroughly throughout his writings it would prove a solution to the problem of how to relate his account of the mind's ascent to God with his insistence upon the resurrection of the body. In principle the mind's participation in God empowers it for its task of governing the body. But, of course, as Gregory recognizes in this chapter, if the mind loses its participation in God by turning away from him, it loses its power over the body and "it impresses upon itself the formlessness of matter." This explains the origin of evil, as well as the way the passions often disturb the mind.[28] More could be said about the first part of the treatise, but two conclusions may be drawn. First, Gregory clearly includes the body in what he wants to say about the creation of humanity; the body is the mind's necessary tool for its function to govern the lower part of creation. Second, he has already set up the problem he attacks more directly in chapter 16 by contrasting the way the human compound should function with the way it fails to do this now after the fall.

Gregory begins chapter 16 by citing the first part of Gen 1:26 in order to deny that humanity is a microcosm. He does not in fact appeal to humanity's function as mediator, but focuses upon humanity as the image of God. Thus, its primary relationship is not to the world, but to God. He then draws a contrast between what is obviously our present embodied state and what should characterize the image. "Perhaps you will say that there is no likeness of the body to what is bodiless, the temporal to the eternal, the changeable to what is unchanging, what is subject to passion and corruption to the impassible and incorruptible, what is constantly associated with evil to what is pure of all evil." The contrast, then, is oriented to the embodied mind which has failed in its task to govern the body. Only Truth itself can solve

27. *De hom. op.* 12 (PG 44:161c–d). It is likely that Gregory is drawing on Plotinus' hylomorphic view of the soul's communication of form (i.e., beauty) to the body through its contemplation of the beauty of the One manifest in the multiplicity of the forms in Nous. See *Enneads* 1.6.2; 2.4.4–5; 4.8.2.

28. *De hom. op.* 12 (PG 44:164a; cf. 157b).

the puzzle, but Gregory will offer his guesses, based upon two presuppositions; scripture does not lie when it says that humanity was made according
to the image of God, nor can we deny that the present miserable condition
of humanity is not at all like "the blessedness of impassible life." And so he
begins with scripture, citing Gen 1:26a ("Let us make humanity in our image and likeness") and alluding to 1:26b by speaking of "for what purposes
let us make him," and then citing the whole of Gen 1:27.[29]

After a brief digression, apparently arguing that the heretics fail to
observe that Gen 1:26 by using the first person plural ("our") alludes to the
three persons of the Trinity, while "image" in the singular refers to the single
divine essence, Gregory turns to Gen 1:27. The first half of the verse "completes" (τέλος ἔχει) the "creation" (κτίσις) of what is to be made according
to the image, while the rest of the verse is a "resumption of the account
according to the fashioning [κατασκευήν]." Since verse 26 refers to God's deliberation and his purpose, it would seem that Gregory identifies this with
the "creation," that is, with God's plan. Verse 27, then, refers to the actual
"fashioning" of this purpose; and the first part of the verse accords with
the "creation" God planned. But the second part of the verse does not quite
accord with the "creation" of the preceding verse, since even though God's
intended creation, as we have seen, included the body, there was no mention
of "male and female." So, I should argue, the problem is not the body as such
but rather the distinction of gender.[30] Gregory goes on to say that this does
not accord with Christ in whom there is neither male nor female (Gal 3:28).
Surely Gregory is thinking of the risen Lord and supposing that his glorified
body transcends the male-female distinction. And this, somehow accords
not with what we find in verse 27, but with God's deliberation or intent in
verse 26.[31]

Gregory tries to solve the puzzle he has introduced by a long and complicated argument. He begins by saying that Gen 1:27 implies "a certain
great and lofty teaching," and he starts his exposition by saying that there are
two extremities divided from one another and that humanity is the mean or
mediator (μέσον) between them, namely, between "the divine and incorporeal nature" and "the irrational and bestial life." This means that humanity
binds together the angelic creation on the one hand, and the lower corporeal
creation on the other. The human soul or mind is incorporeal, while the
human body is not. So far Gregory has repeated what can be learned from

29. *De hom. op.* 16 (PG 44:180).

30. See Coakley, "Eschatological Body," 61–73; see also Harrison, "Gender Reversal," 34–38; Harrison, "Male and Female," 441–71.

31. *De hom. op.* 16 (PG 44:180d–81b).

the first art of the treatise, but he has not yet addressed the problem of "male and female." And so he takes a deep breath and begins an "argument from afar."[32] He starts with human freedom. God's ungrudging goodness explains his creation of humanity, and he gave it a whole list of goods for which "image" is the shorthand. Of these gifts one is "freedom from necessity"; humans are freely autonomous and cannot be compelled because their nature is without a master and acts voluntarily. The next point is that the image is a likeness, but that does not mean that humanity is identical with God. Unlike God humans are mutable, as their very passage from non-being to being demonstrates.[33] Of course, this means that human freedom and the free choices it makes are mutable, capable of moving toward God or away from him. God foresees that humanity will fall by misusing its capacity to make free choices; and we need to remember that speaking of God's foreknowledge is misleading because God, since he is outside time and space, knows all without any reference to past or future.[34]

There is one more piece to be added to this long argument. Again Gregory underlines the speculative character of what he is going to say, but he notes that in the two verses from Gen 1 the word used for humanity (ἄνθρωπος) is an indefinite term and refers to all of humanity (ἅπαν τὸ ἀνθρώπινον). Here there is no mention of Adam as in the narrative that follows in Gen 2, since the name given the man to be created (τῷ κτίσθεντι ἀνθρώπῳ) is not individual but general. Notice that Gregory speaks of "the man to be created," and so if he is observing the distinction he has made between "creation" and "fashioning," we are obliged to think of this general humanity in the context of God's deliberation in Gen 1:26, not in the context of his actual fashioning of humanity in the next verse. That is, the fact that God's eternal purpose or intent has as its object the "plenitude" of humanity does not exclude the idea that Adam represents the first beginning of that plenitude.[35] As well, the image of God applies to the plenitude of humanity rather than to individuals. "In a similar way both the man displayed with the first fashioning of the world [Adam?] and the one that will come to be at the consummation of the universe [Christ] equally bear in themselves the divine image.[36] I see no reason not to understand Gregory to mean that Adam before the fall bears the image of God, while what is potential in him

32. *De hom. op.* 16 (PG 44:181b–d).

33. *De hom. op.* 16 (PG 44:184a–c).

34. *De hom. op.* 16 (PG 44:185a, d).

35. For a discussion of the plenitude, see Balás, "Plenitudo Humanitatis," 115–31.

36. *De hom. op.* 16 (PG 44:185c–d).

is actualized in the plenitude of humanity in the age to come, thereby fulfilling God's purpose.[37]

Gregory appears to realize that he needs to specify the means by which
the plenitude is to be completed, and so he says, "Therefore, the entire nature
extending from the first ones [Adam and Eve?] to the last ones [the body
of Christ?] is a certain single image of he who is, while the distinction of
kind with respect to male and female was last of all fashioned as an addition
to the formation [προσκατασκευάσθη τῷ πλάσματι]."[38] "Formation" is the
operative word and looks very much like an allusion to Gen 2:7, "And God
formed the man as dust from the earth" (cf. Gen 2:15, 19). Gregory apparently understands the addition of the sexual difference as somehow a change
or an adaptation of God's purpose. To be sure, a body without this difference
would have been the instrument necessary for humanity's governance of the
lower creation; but, granted the fall of Adam and Eve, it would not have suf-
ficed for the procreation of the humans destined to fill up the plenitude of
humanity. Gregory has in fact already explained his solution, but in chapter
17 he repeats and elaborates it. Gregory realizes that the true answer to the
problem he is exploring can be known only by those who like Paul have
been initiated into the mysteries of paradise (2 Cor 12:4).[39] His tentative
answer begins by citing Christ's answer to the Sadducees that in the resurrection there will be neither marriage nor the giving in marriage, for they
will not die and will be equal to the angels (Matt 22:30; Mark 12:28; Luke
20:34–36).[40] Thus, Gregory clearly attempts to define the life in paradise
before the fall on the basis of what he believes about the resurrection from
scripture. He entertains the rather strange idea that had Adam and Eve not
fallen, the human race might have multiplied without gender in an angelic
fashion, whatever that might be. But God, whose all-embracing knowledge
included the realization that humans would fall by misusing their freedom,
thereby depriving themselves of their angelic condition, "fashions in our
nature a device for increase appropriate for those who would fall into sin."[41]

37. See *De an. et res.* (PG 46:156c–57b), where Macrina argues that the resurrection
is our nature's restoration to its original state. But just as in the scriptural account of
creation and in Paul's analogy of the seed (1 Cor 15:36–38) the grain produces a seed, so
"the first grain was Adam." Zachhuber, *Human Nature*, 156–57, distinguishes "man" in
Gen 1 from Adam in Gen 2. But in his later article, "Once Again," he revises his opinion.
See 96 n. 63 and his conclusion, 96–97: "I should, then, suggest that the 'potential'
creation of humanity described in Gen. 1:27 is . . . nothing other than the creation of
Adam." See the whole of his persuasive discussion.

38. *De hom. op.* 16 (PG 44:185d).

39. *De hom. op* 17 (PG 44:188b).

40. *De hom. op.* 17 (PG 44:188c).

41. *De hom. op.* 17 (PG 44:189d).

This solution raises more problems than it solves. How are we to relate this explanation of how the plenitude of humanity will be completed to the idea that humanity's role is to govern the lesser creation? More important, granted that sexual procreation is meant as a remedy for the fall, how can it be prevented from being regarded as the occasion of the fall? Did God create humanity already fallen?[42]

There is one passage in the chapters that follow (18–30) that must be examined. In this last part of the treatise Gregory discusses the passions as vices that when moderated can be transformed to virtues (18), the life in paradise (19–20), the resurrection (21–22, 25–27), the beginning and the end (23), matter as not co-eternal with God (24), the denial of pre-existent souls and a traducianist understanding of the soul (28–29), and the construction of the human body (30). But in chapter 22 he gives what looks like a summary of his earlier arguments. The problem he addresses is why the resurrection appears to be delayed. After making his usual disclaimer that only the Truth knows the answer, his own understanding begins by "taking up again" his "first argument." He then cites the first half of the two verses in Gen 1 (vv. 26 and 27). Both refer to God's creation of humanity in his image, and the image is contemplated "in the entire human nature." There the half verses stop (τὸ τέλος ἔσχεν). Not yet is there any mention of Adam, the earthly formation (ὁ δὲ Ἀδαμ οὔπω ἐγένετο). "Humanity in the image, then, came into being, the whole nature, the godlike thing. And it came into being by the all powerful Wisdom not as part of the whole, but as the entire plenitude of the nature all at once."[43] We might suppose that Gregory here speaks of an actual fashioning, but he immediately continues by appealing to God's timeless knowledge, which includes how great a number would comprise the plenitude of the nature.[44] Here the plenitude is restricted to the image in some contrast to what he has said earlier. At any rate, his conclusion seems to be that the first part of Gen 1:26 ("creation" as God's purpose) is actualized in the first part of verse 27 (the "fashioning").

Gregory continues by saying that since God knew "in forming us" (ἐν τῷ πλάσματι ἡμῶν) that there would be an inclination to the worse and a voluntary falling away from angelic honor, he mingled something irrational with his own image, that is, the sexual distinction enabling humans to

---

42. Here I agree with Zachhuber, *Human Nature*, 186, where he says, "Gregory all but says that God himself created the 'fallen' state in anticipation of the Fall." Hans Urs von Balthasar does see the creation of humanity with passions as tantamount to creating humanity in a fallen state; see *Presence and Thought*.

43. *De hom. op.* 22 (PG 44:204c–d).

44. *De hom. op.* 22 (PG 44:204d–5a).

multiply.[45] "For it was not when [the verse says] 'he made according to the image' that he then added to humanity the power of increasing and multiplying, but when he made the distinction by the difference according to male and female." Thus, I want to argue that the second half of Gen 1:26 refers to God's intention to create the image embodied, while the second part of verse 27 adapts God's actual fashioning of humanity to accommodate God's knowledge of the fall that is still to come and can be equated with the "forming" of Adam in Gen 2. Only after his provision of the sexual capacity for procreation does God then say, "Increase and multiply and fill the earth" (Gen 1:28). God also knows "the time measured out for the fashioning of humans"; and once the fashioning has been completed and the plenitude of humanity actualized, time will cease, as Paul says, "in the twinkling of an eye, at the last trumpet" (1 Cor 15:52).[46] Let me admit that my account has been highly interpretive, and I cannot claim to have solved all problems. But the basic structure I discern in Gregory's long and complicated argument rests upon distinguishing God's "creation" as his eternal purpose from his actual "fashioning" as the way he works that purpose out in time and space by the formation of Adam and the procreation of Adam's descendants. God's purpose certainly includes the body as well as the soul or mind as specifically his image. But he adds to the fashioning of the body the male-female distinction that will somehow disappear in the resurrection after it has served its purpose with respect to the plenitude. The formation of Adam is God's fashioning in embryo of the human race destined to grow from Adam into its plenitude.

THE RESURRECTION AND PARADISE

Gregory can identify the resurrection with the restoration of paradise. Chapter 21 of *On the Making of Man* argues "that the resurrection is hoped for in logical sequence not as much from the preaching of scripture as from

45. Mark Hart's positive assessment of Gregory's view of sex and marriage in "Reconciliation of Body and Soul" triggered debate around the relationship between the views of sex and marriage in *De virginitate* and *De hominis opificio*. See Barnes, "Burden of Marriage," 12–19; Behr, "Rational Animal," 111–21; Behr, "Sex/Gender in Gregory of Nyssa's Eschatology," 363–68; Smith, "Body of Paradise," 207–28.

46. *De hom. op.* 22 (PG 44:205c–d). The reference must be to time as we know it in this life and not a passage into God's eternity. See Balás, "Eternity and Time," 128–55, especially 152–53: "It is true, however, that he sometimes restricts the meaning of χρόνος to the time of empirical history, whereas the αἰών or αἰῶνες (in the sense explained above) include both the material and the spiritual creation, the present time and the future blessedness."

the necessity of things."[47] The chapter is really a discussion of evil, which is the deprivation of good and is therefore bounded and limited by good. Since humanity is always moving and becoming, if it enters evil it will inevitably come to evil's limit and go beyond it back to good. The metaphor Gregory employs identifies evil with the shadow cast by an eclipse, which is surrounded on all sides by light. Moving into darkness, then, is temporary, since sooner or later one will move beyond the darkness to light. "Paradise, then, will be once more, once more that tree which is indeed the tree of life, once more the grace of the image and the dignities of dominion."[48] As well, in his homily *On the Day of Lights* Gregory describes the destiny God has prepared for us as the restoration of paradise. Addressing God he says, "You righteously turned away from us and generously had pity. You cast us out of paradise and summoned us back again; you stripped off the fig leaves that covered our shame, and you put around us a costly robe." God has made "both paradise and heaven . . . accessible to humanity."[49] Another example may possibly be found in his homily *On the Three Day Period of the Resurrection*. One problem Gregory addresses is how the Lord after his death can be at the same time in Hades, in paradise welcoming the penitent thief (Luke 23:43), and in the hands of the Father (Luke 23:46). Since the Word remained present with both Christ's soul and his body when they were separated by death, the body is the means through which he harrows Hades, while the soul is that through which he ushers the thief into paradise, which is to be identified with the Father's hands.[50]

At the same time another explanation of the Easter homily is possible. After all Christ's entrance into paradise and into the hands of the Father presumably takes place before Easter morning, and what Gregory may have in mind is the common notion of paradise as a condition of the soul before the general resurrection.[51] Perhaps the thief will have to wait for that day, while Christ himself anticipates it by his own resurrection. In any case, in his funeral oration for Meletius, Gregory speaks of the "chasm" between the departed bishop and the church. He now rests in "the bosom of Abraham" (Luke 16:23–26). And yet Meletius still intercedes "for us," even though he has put off the coat of skin of which there is no need in paradise.[52] Similarly,

47. *De hom. op.* 21 (PG 44:201a).
48. *De hom. op.* 21 (PG 44:204a).
49. *In diem lum.* (*GNO* 9:241).
50. *In diem lum.* (*GNO* 9:293–94). See Daniélou, *L'être et le temps*, 182–83.
51. See Daley, *Hope of the Early Church*, 88: "He does, however, occasionally speak in more concrete and traditional terms of the reward of individuals immediately after death." See the whole of his discusion, 85–89.
52. *In Mel.* (*GNO* 9:451–52, 454).

the deceased empress Flacilla is "in the bosom of Abraham, the father of faith, beside the spring of paradise."[53] The same idea is to be found in Macrina's prayer as Gregory records it in chapter 24 of his *Life*.[54] The prayer includes the following assertions: "You have opened for us the way to the resurrection. Place beside me the luminous angel to conduct me to the place of refreshment where the water of repose is found (Ps 22:2), beside the bosoms of the holy patriarchs (Luke 16:22). You who have broken the flame of the fiery sword (Gen 3:24) and restored the man crucified with you to paradise . . . remember me in your kingdom (Luke 23:42–43). . . . Let not the terrifying chasm separate me from your elect." There can be little doubt that here paradise is a condition of the soul prior to the general resurrection, and it is significant that paradise is associated with the parable of the rich man and Lazarus in Luke 16 with its references to "the bosom of Abraham" and to the "chasm" separating Lazarus from the rich man, who is in fiery torment.[55]

More ambiguity attaches to the references to paradise in Gregory's homilies on the Forty Martyrs. In his homily *In Praise of Theodore* we do learn of the "present condition of the saints, how very beautiful and magnificent it is. For the soul that has gone up delights in its own inheritance and lives without a body with those like it, while the body . . . lies with reverence in this holy place . . . kept for the time of the new creation" (*Th.* 62). Here Gregory does not give a name to the soul's waiting place, and the question becomes whether we should use what he says here to explain the references to paradise in the homilies on the Forty Martyrs. In the second part of his first homily he points out that after the first humans were expelled from paradise "a sword, flaming and turning, was assigned to guard the entrance" and prevent access to the tree of life (Gen 3:24). Why then does Christ promise the penitent thief that he will be with him in paradise? The solution is that the sword "turns" to allow the entrance of the martyrs, and Gregory prays that we also "may come to be within paradise" (*FM. 1b* 156). If he has remembered that the relics are on earth and the souls in paradise, this would be how we could understand what he says. Similarly in the second homily he speaks of the Forty as "a noble planting, the ornament of

---

53. *In Flac.* (GNO 9:489).

54. *Vit. s. Macr.* (SC 178:218–25). See Maraval's notes *ad loc.* and his introduction at SC 178:74–77. He gives an excellent account of the liturgical background of the prayer.

55. See also the spiritual interpretations Macrina gives to the parable in *On the Soul and the Resurrection* (PG 46:80b–81a, 84c–85b); see Virginia Woods Callahan's translation, FC 58:231–32, 234–35. Macrina assumes that Lazarus and the rich man are souls after their death and before the resurrection; the problem triggering the spiritual interpretations is why they are described in bodily terms.

paradise" (*FM. 2* 163). Perhaps the ambiguity is understandable, since it is possible to speak of someone's destiny without reference to the resurrection.

Whether paradise is a preliminary condition or the final destiny of Christians (and others), Gregory often treats it as the object of contemplation and the goal of "epectasy." One reason for this is that Paul speaks of being "caught up to the third heaven, caught up into paradise" (2 Cor 12:2–4).[56] In homily four *On the Beatitudes* ("those who hunger and thirst after righteousness will be satisfied," Matt 5:6) Gregory claims that whoever "has received God into himself, becomes full of that for which he has thirsted and hungered." This fulfills Christ's promise that he and his Father will make their abode with such a person (John 14:23), a promise that presupposes the indwelling of the Holy Spirit. "So I believe great Paul too, who has enjoyed a taste of those secret fruits of Paradise, and is full of what he had tasted, is also for ever hungry." That he has been filled is proved by Galatians 2:20, "Christ lives in me," while "as hungering he is for ever reaching out to what lies ahead." And Gregory cites Phil 3:12–13. So what we have come to call epectasy, the stretching or straining forward of Phil 3:13, is a hunger that is always satisfied, but when satisfied becomes greater because there can be no satiety in the soul's movement toward God, who is infinite good.[57] It is needless to ask how this understanding of paradise accords with the others. Presumably it represents a glimpse of what will come to be in the age to come, a glimpse partial and intermittent in this life, but complete and continuous in the new age.[58]

EXPLAINING THE RESURRECTION

Gregory's discussion in *On the Dead* is almost certainly his earliest attempt to understand the resurrection. The chief passage begins with an exhortation that "the body not be reproached by thoughtless people." This may come as something of a surprise because of his earlier denigration of the body. But what he means is that the soul "will be adorned with it in its more

---

56. See Canévet, *Herméneutique*, 200, where she speaks of the "profonde empreinte" of this passage and of 2 Cor 3:18 on Gregory's spirituality. For Phil 3:13, see Daniélou, *Platonisme*, 291–307.

57. *De beat.* 4 (*GNO* 7.2:122–3). Translation by S. G. Hall in Drobner and Viciano, *Homilies on the Beatitudes*, 56.

58. Many other examples can be given of paradise as the object of epectasy, e.g., *Vit. Mos.* 247 (CWS 118; *GNO* 7.1:119), where the cleft in the rock (Exod 33:22) is identified with "the crown of righteousness" (2 Tim 4:8), which has numerous other names, including "pleasure of paradise." See also *Vit. Mos.* 178 (CWS 99; *GNO* 7.1:92–93); *In cant.* 1 (*GNO* 6:24 and 40); *In inscr. ps.* 1.7 (*GNO* 5:43).

divine condition, when afterwards the body's elements will be changed by regeneration, when death has cleansed it of what is superfluous and useless for the enjoyment of the life to come." The condition and structure of the body will be changed (*Mort.* 59–60). An analogy Gregory employs earlier in the homily helps to explain what he means. His argument is that this life is not useless with respect to that to come, but "becomes the path to what is hoped." The analogy meant to support this claim is the growth of a seed to ripe wheat, and it is impossible not to be reminded of Paul's argument in 1 Cor 15:35–44, where the analogy contrasts the physical body that is sown with the spiritual body that is raised.[59] Gregory's use of the analogy specifies the various stages of growth involved in producing the grain, and he notes that certain of the stages perish once their contribution has been made. One might object that since "the blossom drops off and the grass dries up," they are unnecessary. But this is obviously not so even though they are left behind when the grain has matured (*Mort.* 49–51). The same contrast, then, obtains between the condition and structure of this body and the "more divine condition of the resurrection body." Gregory appears to be reading Paul's use of the analogy not so much to deny the continuity between the seed and the grain it produces as simply to emphasize the contrast between the present physical body and the future spiritual body of the resurrection.

To return to the passage with which I began, Gregory continues by using the analogy of a blacksmith fashioning a lump of iron ore into some finished product. The lump of iron is nothing but a rock at first, but once it has been purified (smelted) by fire and its slag has been removed, it is fit for the blacksmith's art. Similarly, the body "has many slag-like qualities that in the present life contribute what is useful for some purpose, but are altogether useless and alien in the blessedness expected hereafter." It is death that smelts the body and removes everything useless. Gregory then expounds his fuller interpretation of the analogy. The lump of iron ore is the appetite (ὄρεξις) which now directs its impulses (ὁρμὰς) to the "slag," that is, to "pleasures, wealth, love of reputation, offices, angers, luxuries, and such things." Death purifies the appetite of all this and enables it to have "immaterial participation in good things. For there love for true beauty is unceasing" (*Mort.* 60–61). Putting these two analogies together implies that the transition to the resurrection, while it involves an organic development, represents a fairly radical shedding of the attributes of this body and one that involves the purification that death effects. What is striking about this account is its resemblance to what we can know of Origen's teaching about

---

59. For patristic treatments of 1 Cor 15, see Bynum, *Resurrection of the Body*, 59–114; Ludlow, *Universal Salvation*, 64–76; Ramelli, "'In illud: tunc et ipse Filius,'" 259–74.

the resurrection and the absence of Gregory's later insistence upon the resurrection body as continuous with its present elements and structure, an emphasis surely the product of Methodius' repudiation of Origen's teaching and his insistence that somehow it must be this body that is raised. If I am correct, Gregory's view shifts from an understanding of the resurrection as a sort of organic growth to the idea that it represents the reassembling of the scattered elements of this body.[60]

To be sure, Gregory continues by discussing the great change made by the resurrection and does say that "there, the elements of whose bodies have been changed to a more divine condition, will travel through the air with the incorporeal nature [the angels]" (*Mort.* 62; 1 Thess 4:17). But the change is a radical one. If it does not involve the abolition of the male-female distinction, it will certainly transform procreation into giving birth to "the spirit of salvation," as Isaiah says (26:18). Certainly left behind will be the different stages of life from infancy to old age, and still more, the various diseases and handicaps that now afflict humans (*Mort.* 63–64). Gregory then suggests a way of understanding what the resurrection body will be like, a fascinating speculation and one he seems to realize will prove provocative. What will "characterize the form [μορφήν] of each" will be "the special properties of vice and virtue." Gregory points out that in this life we are accustomed to discern the inner emotional disposition of a person by outward signs. So he thinks "that when the nature has been changed to what is more divine, the person is endowed with a form [εἰδοποιεῖσθαι] through his moral character with no difference between what this is and what he appears to be." Since what supplies the "form" can be vice as well as virtue, and since the various virtues differ in various people both in kind and degree, the resurrection is preliminary to the time "when the last enemy has been destroyed" (*Mort.* 65–66; 1 Cor 15:26), a point to which I shall want to return.

Gregory discusses the resurrection in greater length later on in *On the Making of Man* and *On the Soul and the Resurrection*, and his homily *On the Sacred Pasch* could be included.[61] He treats the usual problems: what about the dead who have been cremated or eaten by wild beasts, vultures, or fish? Since humans grow from infancy to old age, at which stage of life will a person be raised? What about those who die as infants, those who die incapacitated by old age, disease, or some disability? But the big difference

60. On Methodius' view of the resurrection, see Bynum, *Resurrection of the Body*, 63–71; Dechow, "Origen and Corporeality," 508–18; Henri Crouzel, "Les Critiques adressées par Méthode," 679–716; van Eijk, "'Only That Can Rise,'" 517–29.

61. See *De hom. op.* 22, 25–27 (PG 44:204b–9a and 213c–29a), *De an. et res.* (PG 46:44b–48b, 72c–88c, 105a–9a, 129a–60c; FC 58:212–15, 227–36, 244–46, 256–72), *In sanct. Pasch.* (GNO 9:245–70).

in these later works is that he shifts attention to the preservation in the next life of the elements (στοιχεῖα) and form (εἶδος) characterizing this body. The assembling of the body's scattered parts replaces the idea of growth. In *On the Soul and the Resurrection*, Macrina cites 1 Cor 15:35–38, but her interpretation focuses upon God's power to give the "bare seed" a body "as he has chosen." The person who has made the objection to which Paul is responding is measuring God's power by his own and supposes that it is impossible once the body's elements have been dissolved they could be reassembled.[62] Let me refer the reader to the article by T. J. Dennis titled "Gregory on the Resurrection of the Body."[63] He carefully explains Gregory's later view, contrasting it with what he said earlier in *On the Dead*, and convincingly demonstrates the impact of Methodius' critique of Origen on Gregory's thought.

AFTER THE RESURRECTION

In *On Perfection* Gregory argues that if we are going to call ourselves brothers of Christ, we must "present clear tokens of our noble birth," since scripture tells us that "those who have done good will go the resurrection of life, and those who have done ill, to the resurrection of condemnation" (John 5:29; *Perf.* 204).[64] Here Gregory is unconcerned with the resurrection of condemnation and leaves open the possibility that those who experience it will simply be condemned. But in *On the Dead, On the Soul and the Resurrection,* and the *Catechetical Oration* he deals with the idea of the text from John by redefining what "condemnation" means. As already noted, in *On the Dead* he argues that God chooses to preserve his great gift of freedom. This was so that humanity "might return willingly by desire to its first blessedness . . . either having been purified during the present life . . . or after removal from here by the purifying furnace of fire" (*Mort.* 54). Condemnation, then, is a divine punishment that will have a remedial effect, not before, but after the general resurrection. This idea accords with Gregory's conviction that "there will be one kind for all when all of us become one body of Christ" (*Mort.* 63). Presumably the "fire" will be the harsh medicine for the soul that will persuade it to ally itself with Christ's body. In this way "the last enemy" will be destroyed (1 Cor 15:26), and evil will be "completely banished from all existing things," and "there will lighten upon all the single godlike beauty in which we were found in the beginning" (*Mort.* 65–66).

62. *De an. et res.* (PG 46:152d; FC 58:268).

63. Found in Spira and Klock, *Easter Sermons of Gregory of Nyssa*, 55–80.

64. The only other place Gregory cites the text from John is *In sanct. Pasch.* (GNO 9:269). But here too he says nothing about the resurrection of condemnation.

Several passages in *On the Soul and the Resurrection* repeat and elaborate this idea. There will be some who are raised from the dead who will experience great harshness from their judge. This can be explained by the parable of the wheat and the tares (Matt 13:36–43); some will be raised to immediate blessedness, while others will require fire for their purification.[65] Earlier in the dialogue in one of her spiritual interpretations of the parable of Lazarus and the rich man Macrina argues that in this life people should detach themselves from it by virtuous conduct that will enable them to escape the necessity of a "second death" (cf. Rev 2:11; 20:6, 14; 21:8) for their later purification. The rich man in the parable requires such a purification because even after death he remains attached to this world.[66] God's punishment is to be imagined as like refining gold with fire; its aim is "to purge the soul of evil." The process will be shorter or longer depending upon the degree of evil that must be removed.[67] When all have been purified, God will be "all in all" (1 Cor 15:28), that is, he will be all things to each and in everyone.[68] This will mean not only the annihilation of evil but also the perfection of the entire human race from the first human to the last, the plenitude of humanity.[69] In the *Catechetical Oration* Gregory's brief comments add another idea. Those baptized, at least if they have rightly used their baptism, will not need the purifying "fire." Having been saved by water, they do not need to be saved by fire.[70]

In *On Christ's Subjection* Gregory makes no reference to a resurrection of condemnation and to its purifying function. His polemical purpose is to refute the use of 1 Cor 15:28 by the Eunomians to prove that Christ's subjection proves that he is inferior to the Father. But Gregory's exposition supplies a positive interpretation of the passage and one that he sets in the larger context of Paul's argument for the resurrection in the entire chapter.[71] Gregory focuses upon verse 22: "For as in Adam all die, so also in Christ will all be made alive." The aim of Paul's argument is to assert "that at some

---

65. *De an. et res.* (PG 46:157c–d; FC 58:271).

66. *De an. et res.* (PG 46:85d–88a; FC 58:235–36).

67. *De an. et res.* (PG 46:100a–c; FC 58:241–42).

68. *De an. et res.* (PG 46:104a–b; FC 58:243–44).

69. *De an. et res.* (PG 46:149d–52a; FC 58:267).

70. *Or. cat.* 36 and 40 (LCC 3:317, 325; GNO 3.4:91–92, 105–6.)

71. See Canévet, *Herméneutique*, 272–73, where she treats Gregory's method here as parallel with that found in the prologue to *Contra Eunomium* 3. Both passages argue from "l'enchaînement logique d'un texte" by examining it in context. She argues that this is "une méthode inventée à l'époque de la querelle eunomienne et maintenue par la suite." The passage from *C. Eun.* 3, "c'est la première fois que Grégoire la pratique," 268–69.

time the nature of evil will pass over to what does not exist, completely annihilated of being; and divine and pure goodness will embrace in itself the
entire rational nature." This will happen when the evil "mixed with existing
things has been destroyed like some kind of base matter consumed by a
furnace of purifying fire" (*Subj.* 13–14).[72] How does this come about? Gregory's answer depends upon his account of Christ and his work. With respect
to the "subjection" of 1 Cor 15:28 none of the various possible meanings
of subjection found in scripture can possibly apply to the Only Begotten
God. Even if we can understand subjection to God as salvation, we must
remember that the divine Christ wrought salvation through "the one in the
likeness of humans," that is, the man of Christ.Even Christ's subjection to
his parents (Luke 2:51) refers to "the one who in every respect was tested,
yet without sin" (Heb 4:15; *Subj.* 7). Gregory also argues that the subjection
Paul mentions is confined to the last things and is by no means a changeless
good appropriate to God and to the divine Son. No adventitious good can
be associated with God. The Son will be subject "then," and so the subjection
must refer to the incarnate Lord and the man of Christ (*Subj.* 9–10).

The subjection, then, has to do with the man of Christ, who became
the first fruits of our nature by receiving divinity in himself, who is also "the
first fruits of those who have fallen asleep" (1 Cor 15:20), "the firstborn from
the dead" (Col 1:18), and "the one who loosed the pains of death" (Acts
2:24). This implies that Christ's death and resurrection is the destruction
of the last enemy, death; and death can be construed as the limit of evil.
The logic is that of one drawing to himself the many, and Gregory thinks of
imitating Christ in the way Paul and Timothy did. Thus, the body of Christ
is formed both by the incarnate Lord's work and by the free choices of those
who become his. Gregory is not thinking of some kind of physical process.
"When, therefore, we all come to be outside evil by imitating our first fruits,
then the whole batch of our nature, mixed with the first fruits and made
one in accord with the conjoined body, will receive in itself the governance
of the good alone." And so "the subjection successfully accomplished in his
body refers to him who worked in us the grace of subjection." That is, the
divine Word accomplished this through the man he assumed (*Subj.* 15–16).
Since Christ "exists with the Father and came to be among humans, by this

---

72. See Mosshammer, "Non-Being and Evil," 136–67. His excellent discussion
draws widely on Gregory's writings, shows how evil is related to the misuse of free
choice, how it is associated with death as its limit, and how the conquest of evil is in
principle accomplished by Christ. Thus, evil exists, despite its ontological "non-being,"
from the first misuse of free choice until all rational beings exercise free choice rightly
by choosing the good at the "restoration of all things."

he fulfills his role as mediator (1 Tim 2:5) by uniting all people to himself and through himself to the Father" (*Subj.* 21).

My discussion has probably created the impression that Gregory's account of the last things that will take place from the general resurrection to the *apokatastasis* or restoration of all things is somehow systematic. Granted that there is a certain coherence in what he says, he does not in fact make that explicit in his writings. There is no single passage in which he unites all the themes I have mentioned. An illustration of the point stems from three further ideas that at least ought to be related to his understanding of the final end. The first of these has to do with the way he describes the hierarchical structure of reality.[73] He makes the common Platonizing distinction between the intelligible and the perceptible and, influenced by Aristotle, orders perceptible things from lifeless to sentient to rational. As we have seen, humanity belongs to both orders, and "the great and lofty teaching" of Moses' account is that "humanity is the mediator of two realities divided from one another as highly as possible, that is the divine and incorporeal nature [the angels] and the irrational and bestial life."[74] The other distinction Gregory makes transcends this one and represnts not a difference of degree but one of kind. This is the biblical distinction between God as Creator and all else as created. Here, of course, it is the incarnate Lord, the Word of God who appropriates humanity in its first fruits, the man of Christ, who represents the mediator between the uncreated and the created. The obvious implication is that the incarnate Christ not only enables humanity, his body, to fulfill its task as mediator, but by his mediation of God to humanity enables the divinization as well as the harmonization of the created order.[75] The closest Gregory comes to putting these pieces together is in the *Catechetical Oration*. In chapter 6 he says, "the divine nature produces in man a blending of the intelligible and the sensible, just as the account of creation teaches." And in chapter 32, discussing the meaning of the cross, he says. "Through himself he [Christ on the cross] brings the diverse natures of existing things into one accord and harmony."[76]

The second idea that seems to be a piece of the larger puzzle is the possible salvation of the devil. To be sure, in *On Christ's Subjection*, there seems to be a universalism that might include Satan and his host of demons.

73. See Balás, Μετουσία Θεοῦ.

74. *De hom. op.* (PG 44:181c).

75. Cf. Balás, Μετουσία Θεοῦ, 52: Gregory's emphasis upon the distinction of created and uncreated excludes any intermediary, but "is actually a presupposition of his well-developed theology of the 'Mediator' (μεσίτης): the incarnate Logos, truly God and truly man."

76. *Or. cat.* 6 (LCC 3:278–79; GNO 3.4:21–22); 32 (LCC 3:311; GNO 3.4:80).

Gregory does oppose two meanings of "subjection," that is voluntary sub-
mission and absolute annihilation. While death appears to be the only thing
totally destroyed, we could remember that the devil is the one who has the
power of death (*Subj.* 26–28). Nevertheless, two passages in the *Catechetical Oration* envisage the devil's salvation. At one point Gregory raises the
question whether Christ's defeat of the devil involved the use of deceit.
The answer is yes, but "he who first deceived man by the bait of pleasure is
himself deceived by the camouflage of human nature."[77] Gregory has earlier
explained what he means. The devil baited "the fishhook of evil" with "an
outward appearance of good." Though deceived, Adam and Eve fell of their
own free choice. Similarly, the divine Christ "was veiled in flesh, so that
the enemy, by seeing something familiar and natural to him, might not be
terrified at the approach of transcendent power." Seeing what he supposed
was an exceptional and unique human being, and thinking that this was a
"bargain which offered him more than he held," that is, all the rest of humanity, the devil took the human bait and was caught by the fishhook of
Christ's divinity.[78] The devil's defeat, of course, benefited humanity by free-
ing humans from the power of death, but it also benefited "the very one who
had brought us to ruin." The devil's defeat was his punishment, and he could
not complain provided he recognized that his punishment was remedial, a
dose of his own medicine designed to heal him. Gregory actually goes on by
omitting the proviso and saying that Christ "freed man from evil and healed
the very author of evil himself."[79]

    Gregory also speaks of the reunion of humanity with the angels, and
this is what I have thought of as a third loose piece of the puzzle. Here he
says nothing about the salvation of the devil and the demons, but is concerned with humanity's restoration to its angelic state. At one point in *On
the Soul and the Resurrection* Macrina alludes to Lev 23:39–43, which refers
to the feast of Tabernacles.[80] Spiritually understood the passage from scripture points to "a feast at which the dissolved tabernacles will be reformed
through the coming together again of the elements of our bodies" (cf. 2
Cor 5:1–5). Humans were once excluded from the heavenly tabernacle, but
when "our nature is reconstituted through the resurrection" and when "all
corruption caused by evil will be annihilated," then a feast common to all
will be established. That is, after the resurrection and after the purification

---

77. *Or. cat.* 26 (LCC 3:303; *GNO* 3.4:65).

78. *Or. cat.* 22–23 (LCC 3:299–300; *GNO* 3.4:57–60). See the discussion of scholarly
reaction to the analogy in Ludlow, *Gregory of Nyssa*, 108–19.

79. *Or. cat.* 26 (LCC 3:303–4; *GNO* 3.4:66–67).

80. *De an. et res.* (PG 46:132a–37b; FC 58:257–60).

of those raised to condemnation is completed, the feast will take place at the *apokatastasis.* This is what Paul means in Phil 2:10–11, where "he speaks of the angelic and celestial beings; and, with other words he refers to those created after them, that is, to us; and he says that one harmonious feast will prevail for all."

In *On the Titles of the Psalms* Gregory explains the title found in the Septuagint for Pss 52 and 87, "Of Maeleth." As his reference to 1 Kgdms 18:6–7 shows, the word is a transliteration of the Hebrew word *meholah,* which means "dancing." This word, says Gregory, is rightly associated in the titles with "To the End," which is a reference to victory. In 1 Kgdms 18:6 "women in a choral dance from all the cities of Israel came out to meet David." This was after David had killed Goliath. "Thus, the title concerning Maeleth means that every victory achieved by sweat and toil receives rejoicing and a choral dance when the entire rational creation joins itself together in the harmony of a chorus for the victors." Once there was a single chorus of the rational natures, but sin slipped in and tripped up the first humans, and so "fallen humanity needs much sweat and toil" to conquer the devil "who brought about its fall." Then they receive "the divine choral dance as the prize for victory against the wrestler. Since Gregory goes on to speak of Lazarus, who was carried away by the angels (Luke 16:22) to join them in the dance, he is not thinking here of the final reunion of humans and angels.[81] Earlier in the treatise, however, he interprets Psalm 150 as "the praise of God, accomplished among all the saints." These include the whole of human nature, and the phrase "praise the Lord with tuneful cymbals" (Ps 150:5) refers to the coming together of the angelic order and humanity "when human nature is brought back to its ancestral portion."[82]

Human destiny, then, involves many things—the resurrection, the purification of those raised to condemnation, the restoration of paradise and humanity's original condition, the completion of the plenitude of humanity and of the body of Christ, the fulfillment of humanity's vocation to harmonize creation and through Christ to divinize it, the reunion of humans with the angels. All these are various glimmers Gregory offers as ways of imagining what eye has not seen or ear heard. The different themes are coherent in the sense that they can be regarded as complementary rather than contradictory. But, it seems, their true coherence will become apparent only when human hopes are finally replaced by their fulfillment.

---

81. *In inscr. ps.* 2.6 (*GNO* 5:86–87).
82. *In inscr. ps.* 1.9 (*GNO* 5:65–67).

A Brief Postscript

What has provoked this short addendum to the preceding translations and to the essays, largely annotated by Warren Smith, is the recent publication of Richard Norris' translation of Gregory of Nyssa's *Homilies on the Song of Songs*.[1] With the privilege that may be granted to old age, let me begin with a personal explanation of why this has been so. Norris, as in his Oxonian way he preferred to be called, was in an informal sense one of my teachers more than fifty years ago. I first became intrigued by the church fathers at the General Seminary of the Episcopal Church under the tutelage of Dr. Norman Pittenger. He persuaded many of us to see our tradition in the light of the "Liberal Catholicism" of the *Lux Mundi* school and of William Temple. This "High Church" perspective owed much to a reading of the church fathers. Through Dr. Pittenger I was introduced to Norris and to Lloyd Patterson, and I vividly remember long and argumentative conversations between them that I could only partly understand. Over the years I did not see much of Norris, since I eschewed the noise and confusion of the City, while he found the countryside boring. At any rate, though I do not remember any conversation with him about Gregory of Nyssa—discussion focused on Irenaeus, Methodius, and Theodore of Mopsuestia—nevertheless, I was pleased to discover in Norris' introduction to the work I have mentioned an endorsement of the major suggestions I have tried to make. It is not that great minds think alike, but that a small mind rejoices when it discovers its conclusions better expressed by a great mind.

As I hope has been made clear in the essays, my chief contention has been that Gregory describes the Christian "path" or "way" as one common to all Christians, and is by no means concerned only with "advanced" Christians. As well, I argue that he understands baptism as paradigmatic of the Christian path as both promise and challenge. In his own way Norris has agreed with these conclusions that I had already reached. In his introduction

---

1. Norris, *Homilies on the Song of Songs*.

227

he persuasively argues (*pace* Daniélou) that the *Homilies on the Song of Songs* "were originally addressed to the regular congregation at Nyssa in the season of Lent, presumably on weekdays" (xxi). Immediately afterwards he says, "From Gregory's point of view, the 'way' that his homilies discern as the theme of the Song of Songs is not a way reserved for the 'advanced' but one that is meant to be trodden by all serious Christians" (xxi–xxii). Later, in his discussion of the *skopos* of the homilies, Norris points out that Gregory "announces" his aim in his dedicatory note "where he explains to Olympias that his homilies are not intended to be 'of assistance to [her] in the conduct of [her] life' but are on the contrary to give 'some direction to more fleshly folk for the sake of the spiritual and immaterial welfare of their souls.'" Despite passages in which Gregory appears to be describing "persons who are advanced in the spiritual life . . . the language he employs belongs to the sphere of customary accounts of the meaning of baptism and therefore conveys no more (or less) than that his hearers were indeed 'in Christ' if only as beginners in their exercise of this identity" (xxxv).

In one respect, however, there may be an emphasis upon the eschatological character of Gregory's thought that I have made that is at least partially obscured in Norris' introduction. One of his dominant concerns is to show how Gregory relates the distinction between the perceptible and the intelligible to the larger contrast he makes by appealing to the biblical distinction between the created and the uncreated. However much humans may ascend to the higher reaches of the intelligible and thereby gain access to the triune God and the "vision of God," they will never lose their creaturely status in finding what could be called a redeemed becoming. Norris can be read as supposing that this is sometimes possible in this life, and I should not disagree. Nevertheless, at one point in his discussion of *akolouthia* he speaks of "another dimension" that "governs (as Gregory sees it) the progressive restoration of the Bride to her paradisal state." The Bride symbolizes "not only the exemplary believer but also the collective 'church,' and indeed the human species as such, for as Gregory sees it these two are in the end—that is, in the age to come—to coincide (since as he repeatedly notes, 'God our Savior . . . desires all to be saved and to come to knowledge of the truth' [1 Tim 2:3–4])" (liii).

While Norris' work appeared too late for me to take account of it, this postscript is meant to be not only a tribute to him but also a recognition of ways in which he has had a decided influence upon my thinking and upon what in my less exacting way I have been able to do.

BIBLIOGRAPHY

EDITIONS OF ANCIENT WORKS

Apostolic Fathers. Translated by Kirsopp Lake. 2 vols. Loeb Classical Library. Cambridge: Harvard University Press, 1912–13.

Basil of Caesarea. *Letters.* Translated by Roy J. Deferrari. 4 vols. Loeb Classical Library. Cambridge: Harvard University Press, 1926–34.

Gregory of Nyssa. *Grégoire de Nysse: Lettres.* Edited by Pierre Maraval. Sources chrétiennes 363. Paris: Cerf, 1990.

———. *Grégoire de Nysse: Traité de la Virginité.* Edited by Michel Aubineau. Sources chrétiennes 119. Paris: Cerf, 1966.

———. *Grégoire de Nysse: Vie de Macrine.* Edited by Pierre Maraval. Sources chrétiennes 178. Paris: Cerf, 1971.

———. *Gregorii Nysseni Opera.* Edited by Werner Jaeger et al. 10 vols. Leiden: Brill, 1952–.

Mekhilta de-Rabbi Ishmael: A Critical Edition on the Basis of the Manuscripts and Early Editions with an English Translation, Introduction, and Notes. Edited by Jacob Z. Lauterbach. 2 vols. Philadelphia: Jewish Publication Society, 1933–61.

Patrologia graeca. Edited by J.-P. Migne. 162 vols. Paris, 1857–86.

Theodore of Mopsuestia. *Theodori Mopsuesteni in Epistolas B. Pauli Commentarii.* Edited by H. B. Swete. 2 vols. Cambridge: Cambridge University Press, 1880–82.

Theodoret of Cyrus. *Théodoret de Cyr, Thérapeutique des Maladies Helléniques.* Edited by P. Canivet. Sources chrétiennes 57. Paris: Cerf, 1958.

MODERN SCHOLARSHIP AND TRANSLATIONS

Abramowski, Luise. "Das Bekenntnis des Gregor Thaumaturgus bei Gregor von Nyssa und das Problem seiner Echtheit." *Zeitschrift für Kirchengeschichte* 87 (1971) 145–66.

Alexandre, Monique. "Les nouveaux martyrs: Motifs martyrologique dans la vie des saints et thèmes hagiographiques dans l'éloge des martyrs chez Grégoire de Nysse." In *The Biographical Works of Gregory of Nyssa*, edited by Andreas Spira, 33–70. Patristic Monograph Series 12. Cambridge: Philadelphia Patristic Foundation, 1984.

———. "Perspectives eschatologiques dans les *Homélies sur les Béatitudes* de Grégoire de Nysse." In *Gregory of Nyssa: Homilies on the Beatitudes*, edited by Hubertus

R. Drobner and Albert Viciano, 257–91. Supplements to Vigiliae Christianae 52. Leiden: Brill, 2000.

———. "La théorie de l'exégèse dans le *De hominis opificio* et l'*In Hexameron.*" In *Écriture et culture philosophique dans la pensée de Grégoire de Nysse*, edited by Marguérite Harl, 87–110. Leiden: Brill, 1971.

The Ante-Nicene Fathers. Edited by Alexander Roberts and James Donaldson. 1885–1887. 10 vols. Reprint, Peabody, MA: Hendrickson, 1994.

Aubineau, Michel, trans. *Traité de la virginité*. Sources chrétiennes 119. Paris: Cerf, 1966.

Babcock, William S., ed. *Paul and the Legacies of Paul*. Dallas: Southern Methodist University Press, 1990.

Balás, David L. "Eternity and Time in Gregory of Nyssa's *Contra Eunomium.*" In *Gregor von Nyssa und die Philosophie*, edited by Heinrich Dörrie et al., 128–55. Leiden: Brill, 1976.

———. Μετουσία Θεοῦ: *Man's Participation in God's Perfections according to Saint Gregory of Nyssa*. Rome: Libreria Herder, 1966.

———. "Plenitudo Humanitatis: The Unity of Human Nature in the Theology of Gregory of Nyssa." In *Disciplina Nostra: Essays in Memory of Robert F. Evans*, edited by Donald F. Winslow, 115–31. Patristic Monograph Series 6. Cambridge: Philadelphia Patristic Foundation, 1979.

Baldovin, John F. "The Empire Baptized." In *The Oxford History of Christian Worship*, edited by Geoffrey Wainwright and Karen B. Westerfield, 77–130. Oxford: Oxford University Press, 2006.

Balthasar, Hans Urs von. *Presence and Thought: An Essay on the Religious Thought of Gregory of Nyssa*. Translated by Mark Sebanc. San Francisco: Ignatius, 1995.

Barnes, Michael R. "'The Burden of Marriage' and Other Notes on Gregory of Nyssa's *On Virginity.*" *Studia Patristica* 37 (2001) 12–19.

———. *The Power of God: Dynamis in Gregory of Nyssa's Trinitarian Controversy*. Washington, DC: Catholic University of America Press, 2001.

Beeley, Christopher A. *Gregory of Nazianzus on the Trinity and the Knowledge of God*. Oxford: Oxford University Press, 2008.

Behr, John. "The Rational Animal: A Re-reading of Gregory of Nyssa's *De hominis opificio.*" *Journal of Early Christian Studies* 7 (1999) 219–47.

———. "Sex/Gender in Gregory of Nyssa's Eschatology: Irrelevant or Non-existent?" *Studia Patristica* 41 (2006) 363–68.

Böhm, Thomas. *Theoria-Unendlichkeit-Aufstieg: philosophische Implikationen zu "De vita Moysis" von Gregor von Nyssa*. Leiden: Brill, 1996.

Bouchet, Jean-René. "La vision de l'économie du salut chez S. Grégoire de Nysse." *Revue des Sciences Philosophiques et Théologiques* 52 (1968) 613–44.

Bouteneff, Peter C. "Essential or Existential: The Problem of the Body in the Anthropology of Gregory of Nyssa." In *Gregory of Nyssa: Homilies on the Beatitudes*, edited by Hubertus R. Drobner and Albert Viciano, 409–19. Supplements to Vigiliae Christianae 52. Leiden: Brill, 2000.

Bovon, Francois. "The Dossier on Stephen the First Martyr." *Harvard Theological Review* 96 (2003) 279–315.

Brown, Peter. *The Body and Society: Men, Women, and Sexual Renunciation in Early Christianity*. New York: Columbia University Press, 1988.

———. *The Cult of the Saints*. London: SCM, 1981.

Bynum, Caroline Walker. *The Resurrection of the Body in Western Christianity, 200–1336*. New York: Columbia University Press, 1995.

Cahill, J. B. "The Date and Setting of Gregory of Nyssa's *Commentary on the Song of Songs*." *Journal of Theological Studies* 32 (1981) 447–60.

Callahan, Virginia Woods, trans. *St. Gregory: Ascetical Works*. Fathers of the Church 58. 1967. Reprint, Washington, DC: Catholic University of America Press, 1999.

Canévet, Mariette. *Grégoire de Nysse et l'Herméneutique Biblique: Études des rapports entre le langage et la connaissance de Dieu*. Paris: Études Augustiniennes, 1983.

Cassin, Matthieu. "*De deitate filii et spiritus sancto et In Abraham*." In *Gregory of Nyssa: The Minor Treatises on Trinitarian Theology and Apollinarism*, edited by Volker Henning Drecoll and Margitta Berghaus, 277–311. Supplements to Vigiliae Christianae 106. Leiden: Brill, 2011.

Cavarnos, John P. "The Relation of Body and Soul in the Thought of Gregory of Nyssa." In *Gregor von Nyssa und die Philosophie*, edited by Heinrich Dörrie et al., 61–78. Leiden: Brill, 1976.

Chapa, Juan, ed. *Signum et Testimonium: Estudios ofrecidos al Profesor Antonio García-Moreno en su 70 cumpleaños*. Pamplona: Ediciones Universidad de Navarra, 2000.

Clarke, W. K. L., trans. *The Ascetic Works of Saint Basil*. London: SPCK, 1925.

Coakley, Sarah. "The Eschatological Body: Gender, Transformation, and God." *Modern Theology* 16 (2000) 61–73.

———. *Re-thinking Gregory of Nyssa*. Oxford: Blackwell, 2003.

Constas, Nicholas. "The Last Temptation of Satan: Divine Deception in Greek Patristic Interpretations of the Passion Narrative." *Harvard Theological Review* 97 (2004) 139–63.

Corsini, Eugenio. "Plérôme humain et plérôme cosmique chez Grégoire de Nysse." In *Écriture et culture philosophique dans la pensée de Grégoire de Nysse*, edited by Marguérite Harl, 111–26. Leiden: Brill, 1971.

Cortesi, Alessandro. *Le Omelie sul Cantico dei Cantici di Gregorio di Nissa: Proposta di un intinerario battesimale*. Rome: Institutum Patristicum Augustinianum, 2000.

Crouzel, Henri. "Les Critiques adressées par Méthode et ses contemporains à la doctrine origénienne du corps ressuscité." *Gregorianum* 52 (1972) 679–716.

Daley, Brian E. "'Heavenly Man' and 'Eternal Christ': Apollinarius and Gregory of Nyssa on the Personal Identity of the Savior." *Journal of Early Christian Studies* 10 (2002) 469–88.

———. *The Hope of the Early Church: A Handbook of Patristic Eschatology*. Cambridge: Cambridge University Press, 1991.

Dal Toso, Giampietro. "La nozione di Προαίρεσις in Gregorio di Nyssa." In *Gregory of Nyssa: Homilies on the Beatitudes*, edited by Hubertus R. Drobner and Albert Viciano, 569–80. Supplements to Vigiliae Christianae 52. Leiden: Brill, 2000.

Daly, Robert J., ed. *Origeniana quinta: historica, text and method, biblica, philosophica, theologica, Origenism and later developments*. Leuven: Leuven University Press, 1992.

Daniélou, Jean. "La theoria chez Grégoire de Nysse." *Studia Patristica* 11 (1972) 130–45.

———. *L'être et le temps chez Grégoire de Nysse*. Leiden: Brill, 1970. 1953.

———. *Platonisme et théologie mystique: doctrine spirituelle de saint Grégoire de Nysse*. Paris: Aubier, 1944.

Dassmann, Ernst, ed. *Tesserae: Festschrift für Josef Engemann*. Münster: Aschendorff, 1991.

Dechow, Jon F. "Origen and Corporeality: The Case of Methodius' *On the Resurrection*." In *Origeniana quinta: historica, text and method, biblica, philosophica, theologica, Origenism and later developments*, edited by Robert J. Daly, 508–18. Leuven: Leuven University Press, 1992.

Dennis, T. J. "Gregory on the Resurrection of the Body." In *The Easter Sermons of Gregory of Nyssa: Translation and Commentary*, edited by Andreas Spira and Christoph Klock, 55–80. Patristic Monograph Series 9. Cambridge: Philadelphia Patristic Foundation, 1981.

Dillon, John. *The Middle Platonists*. London: Duckworth, 1977.

Ditmars, Ron. "Gregory the Theologian's Panegyric on Saint Basil: A Literary Analysis of Chapters 72–81." *The Greek Orthodox Theological Review* 39 (1994) 199–210.

Dörrie, Heinrich, et al., eds. *Gregor von Nyssa und die Philosophie*. Leiden: Brill, 1976.

Drecoll, Volker Henning, and Margitta Berghaus, eds. *Gregory of Nyssa: The Minor Treatises on Trinitarian Theology and Apollinarism*. Supplements to Vigiliae Christianae 106. Leiden: Brill, 2011.

Drobner, Hubertus R., and Christoph Klock, eds. *Studien zu Gregor von Nyssa und der Christlichen Spätantike*. Leiden: Brill, 1990.

Drobner, Hubertus R. and Albert Viciano, eds. *Gregory of Nyssa: Homilies on the Beatitudes; An English Version with Commentary and Supporting Studies*. Supplements to Vigiliae Christianae 52. Leiden: Brill, 2000.

Dunstone, A. "The Meaning of Grace in the Writings of Gregory of Nyssa." *Scottish Journal of Theology* 15 (1962) 235–44.

Eliot, T. S. *Four Quartets*. New York: Harcourt, Brace, 1943.

Elsner, Jaś, and Ian Rutherford, eds. *Pilgrimage in Graeco-Roman and Early Christian Antiquity: Seeing the Gods*. Oxford: Oxford University Press, 2005.

Esper, Martin. "Enkomiastik und Christianismos in Gregors Epideiktischer Rede auf den Heiligen Theodor." In *The Biographical Works of Gregory of Nyssa*, edited by Andreas Spira, 145–59. Patristic Monograph Series 12. Cambridge: Philadelphia Patristic Foundation, 1984.

Ferguson, Everett. *Baptism in the Early Church: History, Theology, and Liturgy in the First Five Centuries*. Grand Rapids: Eerdmans, 2009.

———. "The Doctrine of Baptism in Gregory of Nyssa's *Oratio Catechetica*." In *Dimensions of Baptism: Biblical and Theological Studies*, edited by Stanley E. Porter and Anthony R. Cross, 224–34. London: Sheffield Academic, 2002.

———. "Preaching at Epiphany: Gregory of Nyssa and John Chrysostom on Baptism and the Church." *Church History* 66 (1997) 1–17.

Field, Lester L., Jr. *On the Communion of Damasus and Meletius: Fourth-Century Formulae in the Codex Veronensis LX*. Studies and Texts 145. Toronto: Pontifical Institute of Medieval Studies, 2004.

Frank, Georgia. "Macrina's Scar: Homeric Allusion and Heroic Identity in Gregory of Nyssa's *Life of Macrina*." *Journal of Early Christian Studies* 8 (2000) 511–30.

Gaïth, Jérome. *La conception de la liberté chez Grégoire de Nysse*. Paris: J. Vrin, 1953.

Gorday, Peter J. "Paulus Origenianus: The Economic Interpretation of Paul in Origen and Gregory of Nyssa." In *Paul and the Legacies of Paul*, edited by William S. Babcock, 141–63. Dallas: Southern Methodist University Press, 1990.

Grantfeld, Patrick, and Josef Andreas Jungmann, eds. *Kyriakon: Festschrift Johannes Quasten*. Münster: Aschendorff, 1970.

Greer, Rowan A. "Augustine's Transformation of the Free Will Defence." *Faith and Philosophy* 13 (1996) 471–86.

———. "The Man from Heaven: Paul's Last Adam and Apollinaris' Christ." In *Paul and the Legacies of Paul*, edited by William S. Babcock, 165–82. Dallas: Southern Methodist University Press, 1990.

———. *Theodore of Mopsuestia: Commentary on the Minor Pauline Epistles*. Writings from the Greco-Roman World. Atlanta: Society of Biblical Literature, 2010.

Greer, Rowan A., and Margaret M. Mitchell, trans. *The "Belly-Myther" of Endor: Interpretations of 1 Kingdoms 28 in the Early Church*. Writings from the Greco-Roman World. Atlanta: Society of Biblical Literature, 2007.

Hammerich, Holger. "Taufe und Askese: Der Taufaufschub in Vorkonstantinischer Zeit." PhD diss., University of Hamburg, 1994.

Hardy, E. R., ed. *Christology of the Later Fathers*. Library of Christian Classics 3. Philadelphia: Westminster, 1964. [The *Catechetical Oration* is translated under the title "An Address on Religious Instruction"] 268–325.

Harl, Marguérite, ed. *Écriture et culture philosophique dans la pensée de Grégoire de Nysse*. Leiden: Brill, 1971.

———. "Moïse, figure de l'évêque dans l'Éloge de Basile de Grégoire de Nysse (381)." In *The Biographical Works of Gregory of Nyssa*, edited by Andreas Spira, 71–119. Patristic Monograph Series 12. Cambridge: Philadelphia Patristic Foundation, 1984.

Harrison, Verna E. F. "A Gender Reversal in Gregory of Nyssa's First Homily on the Song of Songs." *Studia Patristica* 27 (1993) 34–38.

———. *Grace and Human Freedom according to St. Gregory of Nyssa*. Studies in the Bible and Early Christianity 30. Lewiston, NY: Mellen, 1992.

———. "Male and Female in Cappadocian Theology." *Journal of Theological Studies* 41 (1990) 441–71.

Hart, David Bentley. "The 'Whole Humanity': Gregory of Nyssa's Critique of Slavery in Light of His Eschatology." *Scottish Journal of Theology* 54 (2001) 51–69.

Hart, Mark. "Reconciliation of Body and Soul: Gregory of Nyssa's Deeper Theology of Marriage." *Theological Studies* 51 (1990) 450–78.

Heine, Ronald E. "Gregory of Nyssa's Apology for Allegory." *Vigiliae Christianae* 38 (1984) 360–70.

———. *Gregory of Nyssa's Treatise on the Inscriptions of the Psalms*. Oxford: Clarendon, 1995.

———. *Perfection in the Virtuous Life: A Study of the Relationship between Edification and Polemical Theology in Gregory of Nyssa's* Vita Moysis. Patristic Monograph Series 2. Cambridge: Philadelphia Patristic Foundation, 1975.

Holman, Susan R. "Healing the Social Leper in Gregory of Nyssa's and Gregory of Nazanzus's *peri philoptōchias*." *Harvard Theological Review* 92 (1999) 283–309.

Howard, Nathan D. "Familial Askesis in the *Vita Macrinae*." *Studia Patristica* 47 (2010) 33–38.

Hübner, Reinhard M. *Die Einheit des Leibes Christi bei Gregor von Nyssa: Untersuchungen zum Ursprung des "Physichen" Erlösungslehre*. Leiden: Brill, 1974.

Hunt, Hannah. *Clothed in the Body: Asceticism, the Body, and the Spiritual in the Late Antique Era*. Burlington, VT: Ashgate, 2012.

Jaeger, Werner. *Two Rediscovered Works of Ancient Christian Literature: Gregory of Nyssa and Macarius*. 1954. Reprint, Leiden: Brill, 1965.

Jones, A. H. M. *The Later Roman Empire, 284–602: A Social, Economic and Administrative Survey.* 2 vols. Norman: University of Oklahoma Press, 1964.

Karfíková, Lenka, et al., eds. *Gregory of Nyssa: Contra Eunomium II; An English Version with Supporting Studies.* Leiden: Brill, 2007.

Karras, Valerie A. "A Re-evaluation of Marriage, Celibacy, and Irony in Gregory of Nyssa's *On Virginity.*" *Journal of Early Christian Studies* 13 (2005) 111–21.

———. "Sex/Gender in Gregory of Nyssa's Eschatology: Irrelevant or Non-existent?" *Studia Patristica* 41 (2006) 363–68.

Kees, Reinhard Jacob. *Die Lehre von der Oikonomia Gottes in der Oratio catechetica Gregors von Nyssa.* Supplements to Vigiliae Christianae 30. Leiden: Brill, 1995.

Kelly, J. N. D. *Early Christian Creeds.* London: Longmans, Green, 1950.

———. *Golden Mouth: The Story of John Chrysostom, Ascetic, Preacher, Bishop.* London: Duckworth, 1995.

Kobusch, Theo. "Die Epinoia: Das Menschliche Bewusstsein in der Antiken Philosophie." In *Gregory of Nyssa: Contra Eunomium II; An English Version with Supporting Studies,* edited by Lenka Karfíková et al., 3–20. Leiden: Brill, 2007.

Kochlamazashvili, Tamaz. "*De Vita Gregorii Thamaturgi.*" In *The Brill Dictionary of Gregory of Nyssa,* edited by Lucas Francisco Mateo-Seco and Giulio Maspero, translated by Seth Cherney, 718–20. Supplements to Vigiliae Christianae 99. Leiden: Brill, 2010.

Kötzsche-Breitenbruch, Lieselotte. "Zum Ring des Gregor von Nyssa." In *Tesserae: Festschrift für Josef Engemann,* edited by Ernst Dassmann, 291–98. Münster: Aschendorff, 1991.

Krueger, Derek. "Writing and the Liturgy of Memory in Gregory of Nyssa's *Life of Macrina.*" *Journal of Early Christian Studies* 8 (2000) 483–510.

Laird, Martin. *Gregory of Nyssa and the Grasp of Faith: Union, Knowledge, and Divine Presence.* Oxford: Oxford University Press, 2004.

Leemans, Johan. "'At That Time the Group around Maximian Was Enjoying Imperial Power': An Interpolation in Gregory of Nyssa's Homily in Praise of Theodore." *Journal of Theological Studies* 57 (2006) 158–63.

———. "On the Date of Gregory of Nyssa's First Homilies on the Forty Martyrs of Sebaste (Ia and Ib)." *Journal of Theological Studies* 52 (2001) 93–97.

———. "Reading Acts 6–7 in the Early Church: Gregory of Nyssa's First and Second Homilies on Stephen the Protomartyr." *Studia Patristica* 47 (2010) 9–19.

Leys, Roger. *L'Image de Dieu chez saint Grégoire de Nysse.* Paris: Desclée de Brouwer, 1951.

Ludlow, Morwenna. "Demons, Evil, and Liminality in Cappadocian Theology." *Journal of Early Christian Studies* 20 (2012) 179–211.

———. *Gregory of Nyssa, Ancient and Post(modern).* Oxford: Oxford University Press, 2007.

———. *Universal Salvation: Eschatology in the Thought of Gregory of Nyssa and Karl Rahner.* Oxford: Oxford University Press, 2000.

Macleod, Colin W. "Allegory and Mysticism in Origen and Gregory of Nyssa." *Journal of Theological Studies* 22 (1971) 362–79.

———. "The Preface to Gregory of Nyssa's *Life of Moses.*" *Journal of Theological Studies* 33 (1982) 183–91.

Maddox, Randy. *Responsible Grace: John Wesley's Practical Theology.* Nashville: Kingswood, 1994.

Malherbe, Abraham J., and Everett Ferguson, trans. *Gregory of Nyssa: The Life of Moses.* Classics of Western Spirituality. New York: Paulist, 1978.

Maraval, Pierre. *Lieux saints et pèlerinages d'Orient: Histoire et géographie des origines à la conquête arabe.* Paris: Cerf, 1985.

Maspero, Giulio. "The Fire, the Kingdom, and the Glory: The Creator Spirit and the Inter-Trinitarian Processions in the *Adversus Macedonianos* of Gregory of Nyssa." In *Gregory of Nyssa: The Minor Treatises on Trinitarian Theology and Apollinarism,* edited by Volker Henning Drecoll and Margitta Berghaus, 226–76. Supplements to Vigiliae Christianae 106. Leiden: Brill, 2011.

———. *Trinity and Man: Gregory of Nyssa's Ad Ablabium.* Leiden: Brill, 2007.

Mateo-Seco, Lucas Francisco. "Imágenes de la imagen: Génesis 1, 26 y Colosenses 1,15 en Gregorio de Nisa." *Scripta Theologica* 40 (2008) 677–93.

———. "La unidad y la gloria: Jn 17:21–23 en la pensiamento de Gregorio de Nisa." In *Signum et Testimonium: Estudios ofrecidos al Profesor Antonio García-Moreno en su 70 cumpleaños,* edited by Juan Chapa, 179–200. Pamplona: Ediciones Universidad de Navarra, 2000.

Mateo-Seco, Lucas Francisco, and Giulio Maspero, eds. *The Brill Dictionary of Gregory of Nyssa.* Supplements to Vigiliae Christianae 99. Leiden: Brill, 2010.

Mathews, Thomas. *The Clash of Gods: A Reinterpretation of Early Christian Art.* Princeton: Princeton University Press, 1993.

May, Gerhard. "Die Chronologie des Lebens und der Werke des Gregor von Nyssa." In *Écriture et culture philosophique dans la pensée de Grégoire de Nysse,* edited by Marguérite Harl, 51–67. Leiden: Brill, 1971.

McCambley, Casimir. "On the Profession of a Christian: Τι τὸ Χριστιανοῦ Ἐπάγγελμα." *The Greek Orthodox Theological Review* 30 (1985) 434–45.

———. *Saint Gregory of Nyssa: Commentary on the Song of Songs.* Brookline, MA: Hellenic College Press, 1987.

Meredith, Anthony. *The Cappadocians.* London: Chapman, 1995.

———. "A Comparison between the *Vita Sanctae Macrinae* of Gregory of Nyssa, the *Vita Plotini* of Porphyry, and the *De Vita Pythagorica* of Iamblichus." In *The Biographical Works of Gregory of Nyssa,* edited by Andreas Spira, 181–95. Patristic Monograph Series 12. Cambridge: Philadelphia Patristic Foundation, 1984.

———. *Gregory of Nyssa.* London: Routledge, 1999.

Meyendorff, John. "Messalianism or Anti-messalianism: A Fresh Look at the 'Macarian' Problem." In *Kyriakon: Festschrift Johannes Quasten,* edited by Patrick Grantfeld and Josef Andreas Jungmann, 585–90. Münster: Aschendorff, 1970.

Morison, E. F. *Saint Basil and His Rule.* London: Froude, 1912.

Mortley, Raoul. *From Word to Silence.* Bonn: Hanstien, 1986.

Mosshammer, Alden A. "Disclosing but Not Disclosed: Gregory of Nyssa as Deconstructionist." In *Studien zu Gregor von Nyssa und der Christlichen Spätantike,* edited by Hubertus R. Drobner and Christoph Klock, 99–123. Leiden: Brill, 1990.

———. "Gregory's Intellectual Development: A Comparison of the *Homilies on the Beatitudes* with the *Homilies on the Song of Songs.*" In *Gregory of Nyssa: Homilies on the Beatitudes,* edited by Hubertus R. Drobner and Albert Viciano, 359–87. Supplements to Vigiliae Christianae 52. Leiden: Brill, 2000.

———. "Non-Being and Evil in Gregory of Nyssa." *Vigiliae Christianae* 44 (1990) 136–67.

The Nicene and Post-Nicene Fathers. Edited by Philip Schaff. 1886–1889. 28 vols. Reprint, Peabody, MA: Hendrickson, 1994.

Norris, Richard A., Jr., trans. *Gregory of Nyssa: Homilies on the Song of Songs.* Writings from the Greco-Roman World 13. Atlanta: Society of Biblical Literature, 2012.

———. "The Soul Takes Flight: Gregory of Nyssa and the Song of Songs." *Anglican Theological Review* 80 (1998) 517–32.

O'Connell, Patrick F. "The Double Journey in Saint Gregory of Nyssa: The Life of Moses." *The Greek Orthodox Theological Review* 28 (1983) 301–24.

Plant, Stephen, and Marcus Plested. "Macarius, St. Gregory of Nyssa, and the Wesleys." *Epworth Review* 33 (2006) 22–30.

Porter, Stanley E., and Anthony R. Cross, eds. *Dimensions of Baptism: Biblical and Theological Studies.* London: Sheffield Academic, 2002.

Pullan, Wendy. "'Intermingled until the End of Time': Ambiguity as a Central Condition of Early Christian Pilgrimage." In *Pilgrimage in Graeco-Roman and Early Christian Antiquity: Seeing the Gods,* edited by Jaś Elsner and Ian Rutherford, 387–409. Oxford: Oxford University Press, 2005.

Radde-Gallwitz, Andrew. "*Ad Eustathium de sancta trinitate.*" In *Gregory of Nyssa: The Minor Treatises on Trinitarian Theology and Apollinarism,* edited by Volker Henning Drecoll and Margitta Berghaus, 89–109. Supplements to Vigiliae Christianae 106. Leiden: Brill, 2011.

———. "Epinoia and Initial Concepts: Re-assessing Gregory of Nyssa's Defense of Basil." *Studia Patristica* 47 (2010) 21–26.

———. "Gregory of Nyssa on the Reciprocity of the Virtues." *Journal of Theological Studies* 58 (2007) 537–52.

———. "Gregory of Nyssa's Pneumatology in Context: The Spirit as Anointing and the History of the Trinitarian Controversies." *Journal of Early Christian Studies* 19 (2011) 259–85.

Ramelli, Ilaria. "'In illud: tunc et ipse Filius': Gregory of Nyssa's Exegesis, Its Derivation from Origen, and Early Patristic Interpretations Related to Origen." *Studia Patristica* 44 (2010) 259–74.

Rapp, Claudia. *Holy Bishops in Late Antiquity: The Nature of Christian Leadership in an Age of Transition.* Berkeley: University of California Press, 2005.

Rist, J. M. *Plotinus: The Road to Reality.* Cambridge: Cambridge University Press, 1977.

Roth, Catharine P. "Platonic and Pauline Elements in the Ascent of the Soul in Gregory of Nyssa's *Dialogue on the Soul and Resurrection.*" *Vigiliae Christianae* 46 (1992) 20–30.

———, trans. *St. Gregory of Nyssa: On the Soul and the Resurrection.* Crestwood, NY: St. Vladimir's Seminary Press, 1993.

Rousseau, Philip. *Basil of Caesarea.* Berkeley: University of California Press, 1994.

Smith, J. Warren. "The Body of Paradise and the Body of the Resurrection: Gender and the Angelic Life in Gregory of Nyssa's *De hominis opificio.*" *Harvard Theological Review* 99 (2006) 207–28.

———. "A Just and Reasonable Grief: The Death and Function of a Holy Woman in Gregory of Nyssa's *Life of Macrina.*" *Journal of Early Christian Studies* 12 (2004) 57–84.

———. "Macrina, Tamer of Horses and Healer of Souls: Grief and the Therapy of Hope in Gregory of Nyssa's *De anima et resurrectione.*" *Journal of Theological Studies* 52 (2001) 37–60.

————. *Passion and Paradise: Human and Divine Emotion in the Thought of Gregory of Nyssa.* New York: Crossroad, 2004.

Spira, Andreas, ed. *The Biographical Works of Gregory of Nyssa.* Patristic Monograph Series 12. Cambridge: Philadelphia Patristic Foundation, 1984.

Spira, Andreas, and Christoph Klock, eds. *The Easter Sermons of Gregory of Nyssa: Translation and Commentary.* Patristic Monograph Series 9. Cambridge: Philadelphia Patristic Foundation, 1981.

Staats, Reinhart. "Basilius als Lebendige Mönchsregel in Gregors von Nyssa 'De Virginitate.'" *Vigiliae Christianae* 39 (1985) 228–55.

————. "Messalianism and Antimessalianism in Gregory of Nyssa's *De Virginitate*." *Patristic and Byzantine Review* 2 (1983) 27–44.

Studer, Basil. "Der Theologiegeschichtliche Hintergrund der Epinoiai-Lehre Gregors von Nyssa." In *Gregory of Nyssa: Contra Eunomium II; An English Version with Supporting Studies,* edited by Lenka Karfíková et al., 21–49. Leiden: Brill, 2007.

Trudinger, L. Paul. "Stephen and the Life of the Primitive Church." *Biblical Theology Bulletin* 14 (1984) 18–22.

Ulrich, Jörg. "Wallfahrt und Wallfahrtkritik bei Gregor von Nyssa." *Zeitschrift für Antikes Christentum* 3 (1999) 87–96.

Vaggione, Robert Paul. *Eunomius of Cyzicus and the Nicene Revolution.* Oxford: Oxford University Press, 2000.

Van Dam, Raymond. *Becoming Christian: The Conversion of Roman Cappadocia.* Philadelphia: University of Pennsylvania Press, 2003.

van Eijk, A. H. C. "'Only That Can Rise Which Has Previously Fallen': The History of a Formula." *Journal of Theological Studies* 22 (1971) 517–29.

Völker, Walther. *Gregor von Nyssa als Mystiker.* Wiesbaden: Franz Steiner, 1955.

Wainwright, Geoffrey, and Karen B. Westerfield, eds. *The Oxford History of Christian Worship.* Oxford: Oxford University Press, 2006.

Wickham, Lionel R., and Caroline P. Bammel, eds. *Christian Faith and Greek Philosophy in Late Antiquity: Essays in Tribute to George Christopher Stead.* Leiden: Brill, 1993.

Wilken, Robert L. "Free Choice and the Divine Will in Greek Christian Commentaries." In *Paul and the Legacies of Paul,* edited by William S. Babcock, 122–40. Dallas: Southern Methodist University Press, 1990.

————. *The Land Called Holy: Palestine in Christian History and Thought.* New Haven: Yale University Press, 1992.

Wilkinson, John, trans. *Egeria's Travels to the Holy Land.* Rev. and enl. ed. London: SPCK, 1981.

Williams, Rowan. "Macrina's Deathbed Revisited: Gregory of Nyssa on Mind and Passion." In *Christian Faith and Greek Philosophy in Late Antiquity: Essays in Tribute to George Christopher Stead,* edited by Lionel R. Wickham and Caroline P. Bammel, 227–46. Leiden: Brill, 1993.

Young, Frances. "Adam and Anthropos: A Study of the Interaction of Science and the Bible in Two Anthropological Treatises of the Fourth Century." *Vigiliae Christianae* 37 (1983) 110–40.

Zachhuber, Johannes. *Human Nature in Gregory of Nyssa: Philosophical Background and Theological Significance.* Leiden: Brill, 2000.

————. "Once Again: Gregory of Nyssa on Universals." *Journal of Theological Studies* 56 (2005) 75–98.

Subject Index

Adam, 80, 109, 123, 125, 140, 152, 191, 193, 205, 211–14, 221, 224
Ambrose of Milan, 10–11
angels, 2, 47, 50–51, 53, 59, 61, 66, 74, 79–80, 88, 90, 100, 106, 135, 139–40, 155–57, 162, 165, 173, 177, 187, 193–94, 200, 203, 212, 219, 223–25
Annisa, 6, 91, 179, 181, 197, 199
Apollinaris, 164
apokatastasis, 5, 223, 225
Arians, 146
Aristotle, 223
asceticism. *See* monasticism
Athanasius of Alexandria, 8, 146, 183
Augustine of Hippo, 6, 170, 173

baptism, 3, 5, 12, 81, 135–43, 145–48, 151, 153–55, 160, 169, 172, 177, 185, 221, 227–28
Basil of Caesarea, 6–9, 73, 86, 171, 179–80, 182–84, 188, 199, 204
body, 1, 3–5, 11, 17, 25, 27, 33–34, 36–37, 40–41, 43, 46–48, 50, 56, 58–59, 62, 65, 68–69, 86–88, 94, 96, 99–103, 105–8, 110–14, 122, 125–27, 129, 135, 141, 145, 147–50, 157, 159–60, 164–69, 174–75, 177–80, 184, 188, 191–94, 196, 200–201, 206–10, 212–20, 222–23, 225

Christ, 2–5, 9, 11–12, 19–20, 22, 24–32, 34–49, 52, 54–57, 60–68, 70, 73, 78–81, 84–86, 88, 90, 93, 105, 114, 117–18, 123–31, 136–51, 153–57, 159–61, 163, 169, 175, 177–78, 185–90, 193–201, 210–12, 215–17, 220–25, 228
Church, 3–5, 7–11, 25, 36, 50–51, 54–55, 64–65, 68–70, 76, 79, 85, 89–90, 92, 100, 126–27, 136, 141, 145, 147–48, 156, 159–60, 173, 176, 178–80, 182–84, 188–90, 195, 198, 200, 215, 227–28
Cicero, 208
community. *See* Church
Council of Constantinople 381, 2, 4, 6, 10, 189
creation, 2–3, 5, 11, 22, 25, 29, 37–38, 43, 46, 73–74, 101, 117, 127, 129, 136, 140, 146–47, 150, 153, 160, 164, 175, 179, 191, 201, 203–7, 209–14, 216, 223, 225
cross, 3, 45, 65–68, 71, 84, 130, 151, 157, 160, 191, 195, 197, 223

Daley, Brian, 149, 215
Daniélou, Jean, 4, 36, 53, 147–48, 159, 184, 204, 215, 217, 228
David, 62–63, 79, 194, 225
death, 1, 6, 8–9, 28, 30–31, 39–42, 46–48, 53–54, 56–60, 65–66, 68, 78–80, 82, 86–87, 89, 99, 102–5, 107–8, 112–13, 117, 122, 124–25, 127, 130, 133, 135, 138–39, 141, 143, 145, 147–48, 155–56, 163–65, 169, 172–75, 179, 190–94, 197, 200–201, 203, 215–16, 218, 221–22, 224

239

Scripture Index

OLD TESTAMENT